A SHORT HISTORY OF JUDAISM

Three Meals, Three Epochs

Jacob Neusner

Fortress Press
Minneapolis

A SHORT HISTORY OF JUDAISM
Three Meals, Three Epochs

Scripture quotations from the New English Bible are copyright © the Delegates of the Oxford University Press and the Syndics of the Cambridge University Press, 1961, 1970; reprinted by permission. Scripture quotations from the Revised Standard Version of the Bible are copyright © 1946, 1952, and 1971 by the Division of Christian Education of the National Council of Churches in the United States of America.

Cover art: Matzah cover by Suzanne R. Neusner
Cover design: Patricia Boman
Interior design: Keith McCormick
Photos: The Bettmann Archive, 94, 195; the Jewish Historical Society of the Upper Midwest, 92; M. Johnson, 38; the Religious News Service, 23, 37, 53, 80, 86, 104, 116, 146, 174, 203.

Library of Congress Cataloging-in-Publication Data

Neusner, Jacob, 1932-
    A short history of Judaism : three meals, three epochs / Jacob Neusner.
        p.   cm.
    Includes bibliographical references and index.
    ISBN 0-8006-2552-8 :
    1. Judaism—History. 2. Jews—Intellectual life. 3. Judaism—Customs and practices. I. Title.
    BM155.2.N455 1992
    296'.09—dc20   92-7929
                                                                  CIP

The paper used in this publication meets the minimum requirements of American National Standard for Information Sciences—Permanence of Paper for Printed Library Materials, ANSI Z329.48–1984. ∞™

Manufactured in the U.S.A.   AF 1-2552

96   95   94   93   92   1   2   3   4   5   6   7   8   9   10

For
THE BOARD OF PUBLICATION
of
AUGSBURG FORTRESS

*A salute to
the excellence
behind long-term and consistent
success
in finding the right people to do the right work
decade after decade*

The Ancient Near East

BLACK SEA

CASPIAN SEA

PERSIAN GULF

■ Persepolis

■ Elam

Lake Urmia

Lake Van

ASSYRIA

■ Nineveh
■ Asshur

R. Tigris

■ Akkad
■ Sippar
■ Kish ■ Babylon
■ Nippur
■ Shuruppak
■ Erech
Ur ■ ■ Eridu

AKKAD

MESOPOTAMIA

■ Dura-Europus

■ Mari

R. Euphrates

■ Haran

■ Carchemish

KINGDOM OF
THE HITTITES

R. Halys
■ Hattush

■ Tarsus

■ Hamath

■ Palmyra

SYRIA

■ Damascus

PHOENICIA

■ Rabbah

■ Jerusalem

■ Ugarit

■ Arvad
■ Byblos
■ Sidon
■ Tyre

■ Ashkelon

ARABAH

SINAI

MIDIAN

RED SEA

■ Avaris

R. Nile

■ Memphis

EGYPT

■ Thebes

THE GREAT SEA

■ Troy

miles   0   100   200
kilometers 0   100   200

Contents

Preface

Three meals serve as the touchstone for the presentation of the three epochs of the history of Judaism: formative, normative, and contemporary. If we understand who eats the meals and where, how, and what they eat, we may gain a sound and clear picture of the main traits of each epoch in turn, from beginning to the present. These pages endeavor to solve a problem that all teachers face in the study of religion: how to relate the religion described in books with the same religion as it is lived in the world beyond. In my earlier textbooks I have concentrated on book-Judaism, setting forth what we find in the holy books, providing an account of the relationship between what is in those books and the world of the people who wrote those books. Here my starting point is Judaism in the streets, the rites of the faith leading to an examination of its holy writings and their principal ideas. If this textbook succeeds, it will provide a model of how we may study religion beginning with the faith as it is expressed in its holy actions and only then proceeding to the faith as it is explained in its holy books.

I have worked out the same theory of matters in a textbook anthology,[1] meant to serve on its own as the single reader for a complete course in the history of Judaism. That book is quite different from this, but the same basic teaching problem is addressed in both: how to begin with the religion we know today, and work outward, and backward, to its historical unfolding.

This textbook takes its place among my many efforts to think through approaches to teaching about Judaism. Each book makes its own point. Diverse colleagues in schools, colleges, and universities have formed their own preferences, responding to their particular interests and those of their students. Because my primary professional commitment is to teaching, I have devoted

1. *An Introduction to Judaism: Textbook and Anthology* (Louisville: Westminster/ John Knox Press, 1992).

myself to writing textbooks and editing anthologies so that students may gain access to my subject, as I think it is to be understood and set forth in the academy in particular.

My various textbooks serve diverse purposes, and each makes its own points, although all of them speak for me. In them I have made the effort to translate my scholarly theories into terms and language that make sense to college and university students. That is as it should be, because at stake in the study of religion, including Judaism, is our understanding of the social order at hand, and any theory about the nature of a religion, including Judaism, finds its test and its validation in its power to explain in a plausible way the everyday realities of the workaday world. I have taken pride in this commitment, extending into its fourth decade, to speak to the coming generations and to offer them my best effort to make sense of Judaism in the context of the religious life of humanity. I am grateful that the various textbooks have gone through many printings and many editions during these more than thirty years. The study of Judaism in universities will have come of age when a new generation takes over the work of forming useful instruments of instruction for a new century.

It is from my coauthor, teacher, and friend, Andrew M. Greeley of the University of Arizona and the University of Chicago, that I learned about the priority of the life of piety and religious expression for the study of religion. He has insisted, in his ground-breaking work on the sociology of religion and of ethnicity, and in his detailed studies of Roman Catholic life and thought, that the loyalty of the Catholic is to the sacraments, and that the faith lives in the Eucharist, in the celebration of the faith, in the response to its story, and in the reenactment of its imaginative life of sanctifying analogies. As I read his remarkable writings on the character of religion as exemplified by Roman Catholic Christianity, I realized that a different approach to the study of religion is also required for Judaism. I presented my ideas, in response to him in particular, in *The Enchantments of Judaism: Rites of Transformation from Birth through Death.*[2] Some paragraphs of that book serve in the present one as well. When asked to write a chapter on Judaism for a textbook on religions,

2. (New York: Basic Books, 1987; second printing, Atlanta: Scholars Press, 1991).

I was stimulated by the questions of my editor at that time, Robert Forman, of Hunter College, to try to state a comprehensive theory of Judaism ("an introduction") in response to precisely the same problem: how to link the Judaic faith as lived by people to the Judaic faith as described by books. While I chose to formulate matters as a freestanding book rather than in the book he was editing, I benefited from Forman's stimulating questions. He was a fine editor, and I am glad to acknowledge how much I learned in my conversations with him.

Two other of my textbooks bear comparison with this one. Each serves its own purpose, and neither competes with this one. As I said, my anthology, *Introduction to Judaism*, is meant to serve an entire semester's course on Judaism, more than a unit or two of reading, such as is provided in these pages. *The Way of Torah: An Introduction to Judaism*[3] continues to set Judaism forth in the more conventional way, that is, primarily through an account of the intellectual history of the faith. There are points of intersection between that book and this one, particularly in the presentation of some of the liturgies and rites. Nevertheless, each has its merits and teaches its lessons.

From comparable textbooks, let me turn to a subject of legitimate interest to students not treated here or in my other textbooks, namely (in blunt theological language), Why did the Jews reject Christ? or, in more neutral language, What is the relationship of Judaism to Christianity? I do not deal with that subject in these pages, because it is not important for the study of the history of Judaism, which proceeds along its own lines and not by definition of relationships with other religions. I have devoted four books to that problem, which have unfolded in a simple and logical way, each one setting the issue to be addressed in the next. These are *Jews and Christians: The Myth of a Common Tradition; The Bible and Us: A Priest and a Rabbi Read the Scriptures Together*,[4] with Andrew M. Greeley, and two titles forthcoming.

In *Jews and Christians* I argue that Judaism and Christianity are entirely autonomous of one another; Christianity is not "the

3. In *Living Religion of Man*, ed. Frederick Streng (Encino: Dickenson Publishing Co., 1970; third ed. revised, Belmont: Wadsworth, 1979; fifth ed. revised, 1992).
4. *Jews and Christians: The Myth of a Common Tradition* (New York: Trinity Press Int., 1990); *The Bible and Us: A Priest and a Rabbi Read the Scriptures Together* (New York: Warner Books, 1990).

daughter religion," and there is no shared and ongoing "Judeo-Christian tradition." The second, *The Bible and Us*, written with one of the truly great figures in the study of religion today, conducts a sustained argument to make the point—on my part—that Judaism and Christianity do not intersect, even when they read the Bible. The result is that even when the two religions read the same document, they bring different questions and reach different conclusions—no shared tradition there. My dear friend, Father Greeley, takes the opposite view. He thinks he won the argument; I think I did; and we are closer friends than ever before. The two forthcoming books were possible only because of Father Greeley's profound affection for the faith and his inspiration. Otherwise I think I would not have bothered to pursue the matter. I did not want to leave off engagement with a religion able to shape so remarkable a soul as Andrew Greeley.

The third book addresses the question, If there is no Judeo-Christian tradition, can there be a dialogue between these two religions? I explain why I think that not only has there never been a dialogue, but neither was there a desire on either side to have one. I illustrate how I think the very beginnings of religious conversation can be attempted. The fourth book presents one kind of a dialogue that I think a practicing Jew can propose to have with Christianity: a flatout argument with Jesus himself. It is not the first dialogue, and it is surely not the best, but I do take Christianity's founder seriously, without condescension ("a great prophet, but . . .") and without dissimulation (" a great rabbi, but . . ."). I argue in that book that the way forward is by telling stories to one another. Clearly, the relationships between, and the comparison of religions demand attention in their own context. I have devoted a fair amount of time and effort to elucidate them, but not here.

As always, in working with Fortress Press, I benefited from close collaboration with my editors. From my first encounter, with Norman Hjelm, through my close friends and coworkers in many projects, Harold Rast (now with Trinity Press International) and Davis Perkins (now with Westminster/John Knox Press), and the late, much missed John Hollar, onward to Marshall Johnson and his entire staff of colleagues, Fortress Press, now with Augsburg Fortress, has found for me ideal editors, all with their distinctive merits, but all of them sharing a certain excellence of editorial judgment, vigor of intellect, and professionalism. To judge from my own career at the University of South Florida, first-rate academic leadership is no accident but the work of an ongoing process of selection, consistently finding excellent people. Persistent excellence in leadership is no accident. In my dedication I pay my compliments to people I do not know, but who have never failed their authors in finding first-rate staff members, for many years in my own experience.

It remains to express my continuing thanks to my coworker in many projects and partner in conversation, William Scott Green, of the University of Rochester, for sharing his judgment and ideas with me; many of the most interesting initiatives in this book, as in others, began in conversations with him, and with his questions and ideas.

I express my genuine pleasure at the opportunity for a life of learning through both teaching and scholarly inquiry that is afforded to me by the University of South Florida. I express thanks for its generous support of my scholarly work. My colleagues in the Department of Religious Studies have restored my faith in the academy and shown me that when its rules govern, a genuinely humane and intellectually vigorous community takes shape, to the benefit of all those who ask, What if? and, Why not? and, Why?

JACOB NEUSNER

Prologue: The Three Meals of Judaism

Judaism explains how people sustain life. When we know the people who are to come to table to eat a meal, with whom they eat, the food they eat, the words they say when they eat, then we can tell the story of Judaism. Three meals form the chapters of the tale: (1) the meal with God in the Temple of Jerusalem; (2) the meal with other Jews, anywhere and at any time; and (3) the meal with the family, at home, and only on a special occasion. The first is a meal eaten in a holy place and shared with God. It is the meal of meat, bread, and wine produced in the land of Israel, eaten in the Temple in Jerusalem. Priests eat that meal every day, other Israelites on special occasions. The second is every meal, eaten in any place and at any time by anybody, with a menu of any food acceptable for Israel, the holy people, commemorating that meal eaten with God in the holy place. The third is a very special banquet celebrated only in a home, with a menu of food suitable only for that holy occasion, eaten by a family and people made part of the family for that one evening. It is a different meal from those of every day, celebrating what makes the family who eats that meal different from everybody else (except for other families who eat the same meal in the same way on the same day).

In all three meals, the people who assemble call themselves "Israel." The first meal represents the Jews when most of them lived in a single place, called the land of Israel, with their focus on the table of God in Jerusalem, a meal shared by the priests all the time, and by everybody some of the time, from the time of Solomon, who built the First Temple in Jerusalem in ca. 900 B.C.E., to the destruction of the Second Temple in Jerusalem in ca. 70 C.E.[1] The second meal represents the Jews from somewhat after 70 C.E. into the nineteenth century in Christian Europe and

---

1. I use the theologically neutral B.C.E., before the Common Era, and C.E., Common (= Christian) Era used in Judaic scholarly writing, although B.C. and A.D. are common.

1

North America, and to 1948 (marking the creation of the State of Israel) in the Muslim world, when most Jews lived outside of a single place, but in accord with a single pattern of life. The third meal represents the period from the nineteenth century in Europe and from 1948 for Jews deriving from Muslim countries. It points to Jews, wherever they live, who are purely Jewish only some of the time, and who are many other things much of the time. When we know the story of these three meals, we can tell the tale of Judaism.

Overview

A Preliminary Definition of Judaism

Let us start with a simple definition of what we are studying. Judaism is a religion that has three components: (1) It takes as its Scripture the Torah revealed by God to Moses at Mount Sinai, meaning, specifically, the Five Books of Moses (Genesis, Exodus, Leviticus, Numbers, and Deuteronomy, also called the Pentateuch) and certain other records of revelation in addition; (2) it believes that its adherents through all times and places form part of that extended family, or "Israel," the singular or holy people of whom the Pentateuch speaks; and (3) it requires "Israel" to live in accord with the teachings of the Torah. These three components define Judaism's worldview, social entity, and way of life. The worldview is defined by how the Torah is read; the social group of Judaism—its "church" in Christian terms—comprises Israel, the holy people; and the way of life is set forth in the Torah.

Therefore the definition of Judaism has three aspects: the components of the canon as displayed in Judaism's sacred writings, as they emerge at a particular time and place; the context of the social group that constituted Judaism; and the system of questions and answers that served that group of Jews. The Judaism that emerged as the normative religious system in a given period answered its particular problems. The problems persisted and, because the persistent and chronic problems were adequately answered by Judaism, the Judaism that solved that problem endured and enjoyed success among the Jewish people. We can define Judaism, in any of its several systems over time, when we can define the critical questions addressed by a given system and specify the valid answers to those questions.

Defining a religion demands two distinct exercises, analysis of the past and synthetic description of the present. First we take account of a long and varied history. That requires us to differentiate one Judaism from some other, because there have

been many Judaisms, and they did not stand in linear relationship, or harmonize, with one another, yet we must also explain
how all Judaisms form species of a single genus, Judaism. Second, in the living world believers identify not with the particular
Judaism that they practice, but with "Judaism"—no longer dif-
ferentiated into its species at all, because it is the single Judaic
system that believers affirm. Defining a religion requires clear
description of a particular religious world, a singular Judaism
seen as a whole by its own believers. In this context we wish to
see what it means to real people, living their everyday lives, to
practice that religion.

That demands not differentiations among Judaisms, but the
integration of a single Judaism into a cogent view of life. For
that purpose a single Judaism comes into view, and, in the setting
of this textbook, Americans who practice Judaism form the focus
of attention. Studying religion in its history therefore tells everything but what we want to know. While the history of a
religion tells us about Judaisms in culture, society, and politics,
only the contemporary reality of that same religion can tell us
how a version of that religion actually affects those who believe
in it—what it means to them. We therefore define Judaism both
in historical times and in the present, choosing Judaism as it
thrives in America and Canada as the integrated and unitary
Judaism to represent the faith as people live it.

What is the story that we shall hear? Why is it important to
listen? We want to know why Judaism thrives in a given form
at one time and in another form at some other time. The history
of Judaism can be divided into five periods: (1) ancient Israel
before Judaism, that is, from the beginnings to 586 B.C.E.; (2)
the age of the beginning of Judaism, the sixth and fifth centuries
B.C.E., after the destruction of the First Temple, in 586 B.C.E.; (3)
the age of the formation of rabbinic Judaism, after the destruction
of the Second Temple, in 70 C.E.; (4) the period of the domination
of rabbinic Judaism, from the rise of Christianity to political
power in the time of Constantine (312) to the end of the political
hegemony of Christianity in the eighteenth century; (5) the age
of diverse Judaisms, from the American and French revolutions,
1776 and 1789, to the present. What urgent questions found
valid answers in the initial formulation of Judaism? When,
where, and why were those answers reworked in time to come?

Why does a specific (form of) Judaism thrive when it does and fall from prominence when it does? Of special interest to us is why the Judaism just now called "rabbinic," a term described at some length in pages to come, lasted for such a long time but then, rather abruptly, lost its monopoly and faced the competition of other Judaisms.

Judaism Compared with Other Religions

Like Christianity, Islam, and Buddhism, Judaism is a world religion. For most of its history Judaism has flourished in many places, not only in the land of Israel but also all over Europe, in Africa, and in Asia, in Christendom and Islam. People who originated in diverse groups became "Israel" whenever and wherever they adopted the Torah, that is, the religion of Judaism. By practicing Judaism, they became members of "Israel," meaning, the holy family and people to whom the Torah was revealed. Judaism has not limited itself to a single ethnic group or geographical area, but has been and still is an international and multiracial religion, but with a difference that leads to confusion.

Unlike conversion to Islam or Christianity, when someone adopts Judaism, that person becomes not only a "Judaist," a practitioner of Judaism, but also enters an intensely ethnic community, the Jewish people. By contrast, if you adopt Islam, you do not become an Arab, and if you adopt Roman Catholic Christianity, you do not become Polish, Irish, Italian, Spanish, or Brazilian, even though those nations (among many) identify themselves as Roman Catholic. The overlap of religious belief into ethnic identity marks Judaism in such a way that the history of the Jews as an identifiable group, society, ethnic group, or nation (the category is not important) and the history of Judaism intersect. For most of recorded time, to be an ethnic Jew has meant to believe in the religion, Judaism, just as adopting the religion imposed an ethnic identification. That has meant, and still means, that Judaism flourishes wherever Jews are located, and it is at once international—utopian, located in no special place—and multicultural, but also ethnic and locative—focused on a single group, in a single place.

What makes Judaism interesting among religions is the interplay between the history of the people and the formation of the faith. What you will learn about religion from Judaism is how, through religious response, people can work out considerable political problems. Fundamental changes in the political order in which the people Israel lived raised urgent questions, to which the religion, Judaism, presented answers that proved relevant and self-evidently valid. When the questions lost their urgency, the answers were no longer obviously right, but merely interesting, and, as it happens, another formulation of matters took over: new questions, renewed responses.

Judaism is like Islam and Christianity in some ways but not in others.[1] Among differences not in detail but in basic character, the most striking is that there are a great many more Christians and Muslims than there are Jews, and differences in quantity are related to differences in character and quality as well. Judaism is a religion that looks backward upon a long past and takes as its principal focus of interest the affairs of a small and unimportant group and identifies what happened to that group as the principal problems of concern. The result is that the critical issues addressed by Judaism find their definition in the events of the history of a small and weak people—defeat, disappointment, and disillusion, rather than victory and worldly vindication. Judaism in most of its systems treated the given as a gift, something to be cherished. The life of the family and holy people endured because the family kept its promise—the covenant it had made, and makes day to day, with God. That explains—so diverse Judaic systems or Judaisms explain—the life of the people, vindicating the losers, the weak and the victim, because in the end they are survivors, by God's will. From the beginning, when Abraham complained to God that he had no heirs (Genesis 15), the family and people Israel has been the ever-dying people,

---

1. To Islam and Christianity, Judaism enjoys importance because the Hebrew Scriptures of ancient Israel derive from Judaism—so they maintain—only to be taken over and superseded by Christianity, or to be absorbed and restated in the seal of prophecy in Islam. Given credit for its past, Judaism never gained valid standing in its present from Islam or Christianity. But Judaism bears comparison to Islam and Christianity in its own terms, and not in theirs alone, because, exactly as they do, it addresses the whole of humanity in the name of the one and unique God revealed to Abraham and Sarah, Isaac and Rebeccah, Jacob, Rachel, and Leah, and the prophets of ancient Israel. But the peculiar circumstances under which Judaism flourished, within the life of a long-lived but weak people, dictated the issues that Judaism would be expected to address wherever and whenever it flourished.

asking generation after generation whether, truly, this might be the last. But so far it has never been the last, and it is the task of Judaism wherever and whenever the question is asked to give the reason for this.

Over and over again the history of Judaism is marked by the story of how that weak and unimportant group met defeat, either by overreaching the narrow limits of its own power, or by simply encountering a stronger nation. Yet if we were to conclude that Judaism is a religion that states in theological language the self-important message contained within the petty history of a minor principality—such as the story of Bolivia, Liechtenstein, Cambodia, or Rwanda retold in pretentious, indeed cosmic terms—we should make a grave error of description, analysis, interpretation, and judgment. Judaism's power to treat the particular as exemplary makes it a religion capable of transcending its origins, as it obviously has. Judaism tells its story in such a way as to transform a particular group's history into something of enduring consequence and interest: an account of the whole of humanity. Its story of origins starts not with the beginning of the family to which all Israelites are supposed to belong, with Abraham and Sarah, Isaac and Rebecca, and Jacob, Rachel, and Leah, but with the beginning of the creation of the world and of humankind, Adam and Eve. That perspective on the family and holy people Israel as the center of human history marked the first document of Judaism, the Five Books of Moses, as important long after the time of which it spoke, far beyond the limits formed by the circumstance of place and people to whom it was addressed.

Among the many important ways in which Judaism is like Christianity and Islam, the most striking is that there are many Judaisms, as there have been a variety of Christianities and Islams. Just as there are Roman Catholic, Orthodox, and various Protestant Christianities, and Sunni and Shiite Islams, so today there are Reform, Conservative, Reconstructionist, and various Orthodox Judaisms. It follows that while we speak of "Judaism," in fact, through history there have been diverse ways of reading the Torah and even of defining what belongs within the Torah; hence it would be more exact to speak of Judaisms. But just as we know a Christianity from a Judaism or an Islam, so we can define what marks a Judaism as a species of the genus, Judaism.

All Judaisms have always had in common the three traits given
as the definition above: (1) appeal to the same Torah, the Pentateuch, which all read as authoritative; (2) insistence upon forming "Israel," members of the extended family to whom the Torah
was given; and (3) providing a well-defined account of how
people should live their lives by the instruction of the Torah,
that is, in accord with the will of God. Judaism therefore begins
at the point at which the Pentateuch was completed. Because
scholarship on the Scriptures of ancient Israel ("Old Testament"
in Christianity, "the Torah" or "the written Torah" in Judaism)
maintains that the Pentateuch was completed at the time of Ezra
the Scribe, ca. 450 B.C.E., the first Judaism reached its written
expression in the fifth century B.C.E. All subsequent Judaisms
would appeal to that same Scripture, each for its own purpose
and in response to the questions it found urgent.

In the Christian West, there are two assumptions about Judaism, both misleading, if not wrong. The first is that Judaism
is the religion of the Old Testament. That is true but not true.
Judaism is the religion of the Torah, which begins with the Five
Books of Moses and encompasses the Old Testament. But Torah
stands for more than the Pentateuch or even the whole Old
Testament. The second is that Judaism is virtually synonymous
with the Jews' history and culture. That is an error based on the
fact that what happens to Israel, the Jewish people, defines the
critical questions to be addressed by Judaism. But the answers
that comprise Judaism are not represented as the result of public
opinion but of God's will and word. A religion that appeals to
revelation contained in authoritative and holy writings and presented by qualified teachers by its own word cannot be reduced
to whatever a group of people say and do at a given time or
place. The theology of Judaism—authoritative truth, set forth in
a systematic way—cannot be confused with the sociology or the
politics of the Jews.

When people identify Judaism as "the religion of the Old
Testament" in contradistinction to Christianity, which has both
the Old and the New Testaments, they do not realize that the
Old Testament, in particular the Pentateuch, forms only part of
the Torah of Judaism, and that other holy books take their place
within the canon, just as Christianity appeals to the Old Testament as well as to other holy books. They furthermore take

for granted that the religion that is portrayed within the Old Testament is the same religion to which we refer when we speak of Judaism. Like Christianity, Judaism draws upon the writings of the Old Testament, reading these writings within the framework of the worldview and way of life that came to expression only later, with the formation of the Pentateuch and in the centuries beyond. When people take for granted that Judaism is the same as the history and culture of the Jews as an ongoing group in history, Judaism as a religion is identified with the Jews' ethnicity and their history. But a religion that appeals to holy books cannot be defined merely by appeal to history and culture, and the Torah cannot be confused with whatever a given group of Jews happens to think at any given time or place.[2] It is important at the outset to recognize how, in general, what people assume that they know as fact about Judaism is wrong.

Ancient Israel before
Judaism, prior to 586 B.C.E.

Judaism traces its beginnings to the creation of the world. Following the biblical record, Judaism maintains that God created the world and for ten generations, from Adam to Noah, despaired of creation. Then for ten generations, from Noah to Abraham, God waited for humanity to acknowledge the sovereignty of the one God, creator of heaven and earth. Through their children Sarah and Abraham founded Israel, the people of the Lord, to whom, at Sinai, God later revealed the Torah, the complete record of God's will for humanity, beginning with Israel, the Jewish people. The biblical record goes on to speak of David, the king of Israel and founder of the ruling household, from which, at the end of time, the Messiah is destined to come forth. Judaism tells the story of the world from creation in Adam and Eve, through the revelation of the Torah at Sinai, to the redemption of humanity through the Messiah at the end of time—a picture of the world, beginning, middle, and end. That account of the history of humanity and of all creation derives

2. William Scott Green, "Old Habits Die Hard: Judaism in *The Encyclopedia of Religion*," in *Critical Review of Books in Religion* 1989, 24.

from a people that traces its origins to the beginnings of time and yet thrives in the world today.

The record of the Holy Scriptures of ancient Israel, called the Old Testament in Christianity and the written Torah in Judaism, came together after the end of the period of which they speak. Most of the writings in the Hebrew Scriptures describe events of the period before 586 B.C.E., but they were written afterward in their existing form. The importance of the events of that year also made people look backward for an explanation. The destruction of the Temple in Jerusalem was the crucial event. That temple, a place for sacrifice to God of the natural produce of the land—grain, wine, meat—on altar fires, had been built four centuries earlier. The writings from pre-586 B.C.E. Israel that were drawn together—the Pentateuch, as well as important writings of history and prophecy (Joshua, Judges, Samuel, Kings, Isaiah 1-39, Jeremiah, Ezekiel), and some shorter works—were all meant to explain what had happened.

The question was framed in two ways. First, the pentateuchal traditions, now drawn together into a single account, specified that Israel stood in a contractual relationship with God. God had revealed the Torah to Israel, and the Torah contained God's will for Israel. If Israel kept the Torah, God would bless the people, and, if not, as Leviticus 26 and Deuteronomy 28 clearly explained, God would exact punishment for violation of this covenant. Second, the prophetic writings emphasized that God shaped history—significant events—in a pattern that bore profound meaning. Not only so, but all events carried out God's will, which the prophets conveyed. Foretelling the destruction that would come, the prophetic writings therefore contained a message entirely harmonious with the Pentateuch. Judaism in all its forms begins with the formation of the Hebrew Scriptures. We may therefore say that while Israel, the Jewish people, traces its origins back to Abraham and Sarah, Isaac and Rebecca, and Jacob, Rachel, and Leah, and while historians tell the story of Israel from remote antiquity, that continuous and unfolding religious tradition we know as Judaism, in all its forms, begins with Scripture, and Scripture as we have it commences with the destruction of the First Temple.

The Beginning of Judaism (586 B.C.E.–70 C.E.)

The Pentateuch took shape during the first period in response to three events: (1) the destruction of the First Temple of Jerusalem; (2) the exile of Jews from the land of Israel to Babylonia by the conquering Babylonians; and (3) the restoration of some Jews from Babylonia to the land of Israel by the Persians, who had conquered the Babylonians. At that time there were various Judaisms, that is, diverse compositions of a worldview and a way of life that people believed represented God's will for Israel, the Jewish people. During that long period, nearly six hundred years, a number of different kinds of Judaism came into being. Also during that time Christianity and the Judaism of the dual Torah, written and oral, came into being and competed for Jews' loyalty; the latter prevailed among Jewry in the land of Israel and in Babylonia; the former made some progress among Jewry in the Greek-speaking world and among Gentiles.

The Formative Age of Rabbinic Judaism (70–640 C.E.)

During the period from the destruction of the Second Temple in 70 and addressing critical issues presented by that event, the canon—authoritative writings—of rabbinic Judaism, which became normative, took shape. The myth of rabbinic Judaism maintained that God revealed the Torah to Moses at Sinai in two media, written and oral. It follows that the canon of that Judaism, claiming to comprise "the one whole Torah of Moses," who was called "our rabbi," reached Israel in two forms, that is, through two media, encompassing not only the written Torah—the Hebrew Scriptures or the Old Testament—but other books, originally memorized, later written down as well. The first of the documents that preserved this memorized and orally transmitted Torah in writing was the Mishnah, the last was the Talmud of Babylonia. Between these two, writings of two kinds reached authoritative status: first, amplifications and commentaries on the Mishnah, second, the same sort of writing for Scripture.

Thus the formative age saw the composition of a single, cogent canon, that one whole Torah of Moses our rabbi, that constituted Judaism.

The Domination of Rabbinic Judaism (600–1800)

A single Judaism, one teaching the dual Torah of Sinai, came to full definition and predominated where Jews lived, in the Christian and the Muslim worlds of Europe, North Africa, and the Near East. Rabbinic Judaism addressed the paramount questions presented to the Jews by the majority status of Christianity in Europe and of Islam in part of Europe, North Africa, and the Middle East. During that time Jews worked out important ideas or issues within the categories of Judaism of the dual Torah. For example a variety of mystical ideas and practices entered the world of Judaism and attained naturalization within the Torah. A further example derives from a philosophical tradition that restated the truths of the Torah in terms of Greek modes of thought represented by Aristotle and Plato as the Muslim philosophical schools transmitted those modes of thought to the West. In the mystical tradition, the great work was the Zohar, written toward the end of the thirteenth century in Spain. In the philosophical tradition, the most important figure was Maimonides (1135-1204), who restated the whole of Judaic law and theology in a systematic and profoundly philosophical way. Both of these encompassing modes of thought, the mystical and the philosophical, transformed "the one whole Torah of Moses, our rabbi" from a mythic to an intensely felt and profound doctrine of the true nature of God's being, and, at the same time, an intellectually rich and rational statement of the Torah as truth. Both found an ample place well within the received canon, to which each made a massive contribution of new and authoritative writings. The power of the one whole Torah, oral and written, to encompass and make its own essentially fresh ways of thought and life testifies to the classical character of this Judaism, everywhere definitive. Mysticism and philosophy alike made their contribution to the Judaism of the dual Torah.

The Age of
Competing Judaisms (1800 to the Present)

In modern times, with the end of the definitive standing of Christianity in the politics and culture of the West, the diversity characteristic of the period of origins has once again come to prevail. Now the symbolic system and structure of the Judaism of the dual Torah competes for Jews' attention with other Judaic systems on the one side, and with a diverse range of symbols of non-Jewish origin and meaning on the other. What is the relationship of the Judaism of the dual Torah to the life of Israel, the Jewish people over time (not to be identified only with the contemporary State of Israel, which came into being in 1948)? That Judaism of the dual Torah endured and flourishes today as the religion of a small group of people.

Beginning at the start of the nineteenth century a number of other Judaic systems—worldviews, ways of life, addressed to an "Israel"—came into being. One of these was Reform Judaism, the first and most important of the Judaisms of modern times. The changes, deemed "reforms," involved at first matters of liturgy, then important issues of doctrine. But small reforms generated the conception of a major, historical reform, thus Reform Judaism was born. Why did it succeed, as it did? Reform took seriously the political changes that accorded to Jews the rights of citizens and demanded that they conform to the common practices of their countries of citizenship. Reform took shape in the first quarter of the nineteenth century. Some decades later, in the middle of the century, Orthodoxy stated the position that one may observe the law and may also enter into the civilization of the West. Affirming the divine origin of the Torah, Orthodoxy effected a selective piety, for example affirming secular education in addition to study of the Torah. A third movement, called the Historical School in Europe and, some decades later, Conservative Judaism in America, took a middle position, affirming the Orthodox position on keeping the rules of the Torah and the Reform view of the importance of critical scholarship. It follows that the Judaic systems of the nineteenth and twentieth centuries took shape within a span of not much more than one hundred years, from somewhat before 1800 to somewhat after 1900.

Having sketched the history of Judaism—formative, normative, and contemporary—now we ask, How does each Judaic system, in turn, hold together? What questions does each system as a whole address? and, Why do those questions find valid answers—for those who ask the questions and accept the answers—in the writings of the Judaism at hand? We move from a historical account of sequence to an analytical account of substance.

Part One

THE PRIEST'S MEAL WITH GOD IN THE TEMPLE OF JERUSALEM: THE JUDAISM OF SACRED PLACE AND HOLY TIME

CHAPTER ONE

The Temple and
Israel in Its Land

Covenant: The Torah, Israel, and the Land

Judaism, like Christianity, Islam, and Buddhism, originated in Asia. Nevertheless, unlike those religions, when explaining its origins, Judaism appealed to not a man, such as Jesus Christ, Muhammed, the seal of prophecy, or the blessed Buddha, but to God and God alone as its founder. The word, in Judaism, for "Judaism," means "the Torah," and the religion originated when God gave the Torah to Moses at Mount Sinai. God's message, expressed in the wording that God used to convey that message, concerned the story of humanity, created by God, in the language of the Torah, "in our image, after our likeness," and focused upon Israel, the children of Abraham, Isaac, and Jacob, Sarah, Rebecca, Leah, and Rachel, and their descendants, among whom members of the religions of Christianity and Islam count themselves. The message of Judaism addresses the world through the medium of the worldly life of Israel, the Jewish people, whom God first loved among humanity by reason of the trust in God of their ancestors, Abraham and Sarah, and to whom, therefore, God gave the Torah.

The Pentateuch traces the beginnings of Israel to the creation of the world. According to the Torah, God created the world but, for ten generations, from Adam to Noah, God despaired of creation. Then for ten generations, from Noah to Abraham, God waited for humanity to acknowledge sovereignty of the one God, creator of heaven and earth. Through their children Sarah and Abraham founded Israel, the people of the Lord. Ten generations after Sarah and Abraham, at Sinai, talking with Moses the prophet, God revealed the Torah to the descendants of Sarah and Abraham—Rebecca and Isaac, Leah, Rachel, and Jacob. This extended family, called Israel, was meant to inherit a special land, "the land of Israel." It was to be the place they would live as a nation in accord with the will of God revealed in the Torah. That is the message of the Torah set forth in the Five Books of Moses.

The paramount theme of the Torah concerns the relationships of the people Israel, the land, which they came to call "the land of Israel," and the Torah. This is conveyed in a concrete way in the story of Abraham and Sarah and Israel after them. God promised Abraham and Sarah that they would be the parents of many children, and that they would have a land to call their own. Abraham and Sarah were childless; they had left their birthplace and, when told by God to move onward, they wandered to a land that belonged to other people. But they believed that God would keep those promises. The covenant with God, which governed their children and their inheritance in the land, embodied their faith, a perfect trust in God. Their great-grandchildren left the land in time of famine and went to Egypt, where they were enslaved. God saved Israel from slavery in Egypt, took them to Sinai, and promised to bring them back to the same land that their ancestors had left. This was on the basis of the covenant, or agreement, that Israel would accept the Torah and keep its commandments, which concerned the life of an entire people living in its land.

The Meal:
Serving God in the Temple in Jerusalem, through Sacrifice by the Priests Every Day, and by Everybody Three Times a Year

The first meal that stands for Judaism is made up of the produce of the holy land; it is eaten by God in the holy Temple of Jerusalem, and shared by the priests every day, and by all Israel on special occasions. The story told by the Torah explains that one important way in which Israel was supposed to keep the covenant was to give back to God a part of what the holy land, given by God to Israel, produced. The land produced food that sustained life: herds of sheep, cattle, and goats supplying meat, fields of wheat and barley producing bread, and vineyards yielding wine. God gave it; Israel was to give back part. The pentateuchal record contained elaborate instructions on how these gifts were to be given, in Exodus 24-40, all of Leviticus, most of Numbers, and important parts of Deuteronomy. These rules were carried out in a particular place, Jerusalem, in a house, the Temple, and on a table, called an altar, which was set up for the purpose of presenting these gifts, where a fire was kept burning. Certain things were burned in the fire on the altar in the Temple in Jerusalem, wafted to heaven in the smoke with a pleasant odor. God on high received the gifts of the land, given to him by his people. From the beginning of humanity—so the story of Genesis goes—people had made such offerings. Cain and Abel, Noah, Abraham, Isaac, Jacob—all had done so.

What was the purpose of the gifts? It was to atone for sin, for not keeping the commandments of the covenant. God understood, so the Torah says, that humanity was not perfect, and therefore people would violate the commandments. God provided a means of setting matters right through "atonement for sin," and that involved the gift of the blood of an animal. The animal was to be killed by the cutting of the neck arteries; blood would gush forth, be received in a bowl, and be sprinkled on the altar by the priest in charge of the rite. Blood represents life. The life blood of the beast burned on the altar fires, then wafted upward, a sweet scent to God, atoning for the life of the sinner down below. The Temple formed the point at which God and Israel came together, marking the exchange of life. What nourished the life of Israel in the holy land, meat, bread, and wine, was sent upward on the altar fires to mark the sustaining life of the covenant with God. The priests ate some of the meat and bread from day to day. Ordinary Israelites presented certain types of offerings, for example, on pilgrim festivals when they came seasonally to Jerusalem. They ate part of the animal that they presented to the Lord and the altar fires sent upward another part of the same animal. Life was lived in shared communion with God, humanity and God sustained in the same way.

This atonement was made day by day, not once for all time. The premise of this Judaism was that Israel would endure forever in its land, and in its way of life would sin and require atonement. Thus we see here not an eschatological forgiveness of sins, once for all time, but a day to day forgiveness in the life of an ongoing and enduring holy people.

Israel, the Pilgrim People

The Torah set forth a religious life in which all of Israel, settled in the holy land, shared in the service of God through the blood rite of the Temple. Pilgrims came to share in the holy communion of the altar of Jerusalem at three holy seasons each year: Passover, the first full moon after the vernal equinox, hence in April; Pentecost, fifty days later, in May; and Tabernacles, the first full moon after the autumnal equinox, in October. These were important turning points in the agricultural calendar together with the end (in the spring) and the beginning (in the autumn) of the rainy season that sustained the land. Pilgrims brought their own sacrifices, in addition to those of the nation as a whole to the Temple, cooked the meat and ate it in the holy city. From near and far pilgrims climbed the paths to Jerusalem. Distant lands sent their annual tribute, taxes imposed by a spiritual rather than a worldly sovereignty. Everywhere Jews turned to the Temple mountain when they prayed.

For centuries Israel sang with the psalmist, "Our feet were standing within thy courts, O Jerusalem." They had exulted, "Pray for the peace of Jerusalem! May all prosper who seek your welfare!" People yearned to see the priests upon their platform, to hear the Levites in their great choir singing the psalms, to receive the blessing of the Lord in the Temple in Jerusalem. The activity was endless. Priests hurried to and fro, officiating at the sacrifices morning and evening, busying themselves through the day with the Temple's needs. They were always careful to keep the levitical rules of purity, which they believed God had decreed in Leviticus for just this place and hour. Levites assisting them and responsible for the public liturgies could be seen everywhere.

In the outer courts Jews from all parts of the world, speaking many languages, changed their foreign currency for the Temple coin. They brought up their shekel, together with the freewill offering, or peace offering, or sin offering, or other offerings they were obliged to give. Through the gift of the shekel, each person purchased a share in the offerings made on behalf of the community as a whole, so the entire people collectively, and individuals on their own, atoned for whatever sins or failings marked a break with the covenant of the Torah. Outside, in the city beyond, artisans created the necessary vessels or repaired broken ones. Incense makers mixed spices. Animal dealers selected the most perfect beasts. In the schools young priests were taught the ancient law, to which in time they would conform as had their ancestors before them, exactly as their fathers did that very day. All the population was engaged in some way in the work of the Temple either directly or indirectly. The city lived for it, by it, and on its revenues.

Temple sacrifice was the way to serve God. True, there were other ways believed to be more important, for the same Torah that described the correct way to kill animals and offer up blood, fat, and meat on the fires of the altar also spelled out what it meant to live as a kingdom of priests and a holy people. The lessons covered justice at home as much as sacrifice in the Temple. Morality, ethics, humility, good faith—these, too, the Torah required. But good faith meant loyalty to the covenant, which had specified, among other things, that the priests do just what they were doing. The animal sacrifices, the incense, the oil, wine, and bread were to be arrayed in the service of the Most High.

Explaining the Formation of the Judaism of Land and Temple Sacrifice

Animal sacrifice, according to the record of the Hebrew Scriptures, went on from the very beginning. That mode of relating to God through shared food formed a principal focus. Creation, for example, in Genesis 1, is represented as the story of the formation of the world, with emphasis on the orderly pattern leading, at the end, to the creation of food and then of man and woman. But serving God by shared meals finds its true meaning in the larger context of the biblical story of the creation of the world and the formation of Israel, the holy people. That story provides an extended account of how Israel attained the land God gave them, why Israel could keep that land or would lose it, and how the covenant between God and Israel governed all matters. In that context, the Temple of Jerusalem, with its mode of worship through animal sacrifice, brought to concrete expression the large questions with which the narrative of the Pentateuch dealt. Stated simply, when Israel kept the covenant, it flourished in the land, producing the offerings of the land, which the altar fires carried to heaven as a mark of its good relationship with God. When Israel violated that same agreement, it was punished, in the end losing the land and the mark of grace and favor represented by making those offerings and sharing that food.

The pentateuchal story made that point by narrating events of a long-ago past: the creation of the world; the making of man and woman; the fall of humanity through disobedience; the flood that wiped out nearly all of humanity except for Noah, progenitor of all humanity; the decline of humanity from Noah to Abraham; then the rise of humanity through Abraham, Isaac, Jacob (also called Israel); the twelve sons of Jacob; exile in Egypt; and, ultimately, Sinai. There, the scriptural narrative continues, God revealed the Torah (revelation) to Moses, and that revelation contained the terms of the covenant that God then made with Israel, the family of Abraham, Isaac, and Jacob.

The book of Genesis narrates the story of creation and then of the beginnings of the family that Israel would always constitute, the children of Abraham, Isaac, and Jacob. Exodus presents the story of the slavery of the children of Israel in Egypt and how they made their exodus from slavery. God redeemed them from Egyptian bondage, saving their lives when the Egyptians pursued them to the Sea of Reeds (Red Sea) by bringing them across on dry land and then calling the sea to form a wall to defend them from their pursuers, who drowned. After that miracle God brought them to Sinai, there to make a covenant, or contract, with them by which they would accept the Torah and carry out its rules. These rules covered all of the affairs of a nation: civil law and government, family affairs, and the like. They also set forth how the Israelites were to build a tabernacle in the wilderness, which (in the narrative of the Pentateuch) would become the model, later on, for the holy temple that would be built in Jerusalem.

An aerial view of Jerusalem, showing the western wall, the Temple Mount, and excavations of the City of David.

Leviticus portrays the founding of the priests' service of God through the sacrifice of the produce of the holy land to which God would bring Israel, specifying the rules and regulations to govern the kingdom of priests and the holy people. Numbers provides an account of the wandering in the wilderness. Deuteronomy then presents a reprise of the story, a long sermon by Moses looking back on the history of Israel from the beginnings through the point of entry into the promised land, followed by a restatement of the rules of the covenant, or contract, between Israel and God.

In subsequent books of the Hebrew Scriptures—Joshua, Judges, Samuel, and Kings—the story is told of how the tribes settled down in the land and lived there. The important point, made over and over again, was that when they obeyed God they prospered, and when they disobeyed they were punished. Of special interest is the formation of the monarchy, with the principal figure, David, represented as a magnificent figure, who both governed and also wrote psalms, who created a considerable kingdom in war, but dreamed of building a temple in a time of peace. He called his son and heir by a name that means "peace," Solomon, *Shelomo,* from the word *shalom.* It was Solomon who built that permanent building, the Temple, to which the pentateuchal books alluded both indirectly and, in Deuteronomy, directly. Other biblical books, Isaiah, Jeremiah, Ezekiel, and the twelve minor prophets, develop the pentateuchal theme that Israel's relationship with God is governed by a covenant, which means that when people do what is right and just, in accord with the Torah, God will give them peace, and when they do not, God will punish them.

In 586 B.C.E., Jerusalem was captured by the Babylonians and the Temple was destroyed. Many Jews were taken away as slaves to Babylonia (present-day Iraq). The enemy is described as the rod of God's punishment, carrying out his will. The captives are described as exiles. Three generations later, at the end of that same century, the Persians conquered Babylon, and their king, Cyrus, permitted those Jews in Babylonia who wished to return to Jerusalem to do so. Some time later they restored the Temple in that city and resumed the service of God that had been interrupted. In about 450 B.C.E., the Persians sent a Jewish governor Nehemiah, along with an administrator, Ezra, to Jerusalem, and they built a proper temple.

This brief explanation of the Judaism of land, Israel, and the Torah, is the story of the Hebrew Scriptures themselves. Those Scriptures, and in particular, the Pentateuch, were formulated only after two definitive events. The first was the destruction of the First Temple in 586 B.C.E. The second was the conclusion of the return and restoration under Ezra, by ca. 450 B.C.E. At that point people wanted to record what had happened, not only to explain the past but also to direct a question to the future: How can we avoid losing the land again? A substantial heritage of writings of the period before 586 were reworked into the Pentateuch as we now have it, and, in the formation of the Pentateuch, Judaism was born.

Ancient Israel before Judaism (prior to 586 B.C.E.)

Ancient Israel—tribes of various origins—had entered the land of Canaan, which became the land of Israel, some time before

1000 B.C.E. We have seen that these diverse groups are all described as having descended from a single man Abraham, and his wife, Sarah. We have also seen how the children of Jacob, Leah, and Rachel went down to Egypt due to a famine, multiplied there, became enslaved, and, led by Moses, under God's orders, escaped to the wilderness of Sinai, there to receive the Torah, or revelation of God for the founding of their nation and the ordering of their lives. We can dispense with a recounting the diverse and various processes of conquering the land and settling in it. This has no bearing on the history of Judaism, except as a statement in linear and incremental terms of a set of traditions, each with its own point of origin, each taken out of its original context and placed into that larger cogent, linear, and incremental setting in which we now receive them all.

If we were to describe the history of Judaism by a paraphrase of what the Hebrew Scriptures say, we would merely repeat, in our own words, what the theology of every form of Judaism says about the faith. True, it is common for people to begin with the narrative of the Pentateuch, reviewing the stories of Abraham, Isaac, Jacob, Israel in Egypt, Moses' receiving the Ten Commandments, or the Torah, at Sinai; then the tale of the conquest of the land of Israel (later called Palestine), the rule of David and Solomon and the building of the First Temple in Jerusalem, the account the faithless kings and inconstant people told in the historical and prophetic writings of Joshua, Judges, Samuel, Kings, Isaiah, Jeremiah, Ezekiel, and the twelve minor prophets; the destruction of the Jerusalem Temple in 586 B.C.E. by an enemy described as doing God's will as the rod of God's punishment. That approach to the description of Judaism retells the story that Judaism itself tells. But in recapitulating the Old Testament narrative, that description of Judaism does not tell anything about the religion that tells that story. In claiming that the religion begins with Abraham, we do not accomplish the work at hand, namely to say what this religion *is*, rather than what it says.

We may not simply ignore everything that happened before the formation of the Pentateuch in the time of Ezra. If we were to do so, we would lose all possibility of comparison and contrast. There were religious systems in ancient Israel prior to the time of Ezra, and, while different from the Judaic religious system that came to expression in the formation of the Pentateuch, these systems produced writings that were used in the Pentateuch and that were preserved in the Hebrew Scripture or Old Testament. If we were to ignore those pre-Judaic Israelite systems, we would be unable to place the Judaism of the Pentateuch into relationship with the religious systems set forth by those who developed their own systems and set them forth in materials now included in the Pentateuch. That would deprive us of perspective on the character of the Pentateuch whole and complete.

There is a second reason to consider the writings of Israel before Judaism. Not only is the Pentateuch, completed in Ezra's time as the Torah, composed of a variety of stories and writings that originated long before the fifth century B.C.E., but the remaining Hebrew Scriptures of ancient Israel revered by Judaism from the beginning include many other writings produced before the destruction of the Temple built by Solomon in 586 B.C.E. These ancient writings flowed into the Torah as it would be defined by Judaism, even though they did not make up all the books of the Torah, and Judaism richly re-presented the writings of ancient Israel within its larger canon. Therefore, while we cannot confuse Judaism with "the religion of the Old Testament," we must still consider the religious world of Israel of the earliest times, before 586.

Attributed to the authorship of Moses, the Pentateuch is a tapestry of materials, of which there are several strands that can be identified. Two of the documents that contributed to the making of the Pentateuch are clearly distinguishable. One is Deuteronomy, called D, which explicitly announces that it will recapitulate everything that has gone before, and then resolutely rewrites the whole—history, law, and theology alike. The other is the Priestly Code, recognized as "the Torah of the priests" even by the rabbis of the Talmud (although, of course, they understood it to be God's Torah for the priests, rather than the Torah in God's name written by the priests, as we now know it to be). The Priestly Code, referred to as P, covers parts of Genesis and Exodus, and the whole of Leviticus and Numbers.

What about the other components? In some passages we find one name for the deity, in others, another; when these passages handle the same materials, we can disengage the two distinct accounts of the same event by identifying the signs of the divine name. For example, Gen. 1:1—2:3 calls the divinity

Elohim, translated "God." The story of creation involves an orderly unfolding of how each component came into being in its right time and place. Gen. 2:3—3:24 has a different story of the creation of the world and humanity. Here the divinity is called Yahweh Elohim, translated the "Lord God." There are important differences in detail and overall viewpoint between the two accounts of the beginnings. The former is identified with the priestly strand of Scripture; the latter is called JE (Yahweh used to be represented in English, through an error, as Jehovah, thus the J, and E for Elohim), and it is an important component of Genesis and much of Exodus. The "deuteronomic" strand (D) stands at the head of a series of historical books, specifically, Joshua, Judges, Samuel, and Kings. JE, P, and D—the principal components of the Pentateuch—are themselves to be analyzed further, because each makes use of a variety of received materials for its own purposes. For our purposes it is sufficient to concentrate, within the sacred writings of ancient Israel, on how these strands, each on its own terms, presented a worldview and explained the way of life of an Israel—its Israel, the Israel to which the authorship of a given strand meant to speak. When we sort out the strands of the Torah, we see how each represents a whole system—a worldview, addressed to the way of life of an Israel of a particular order.

The Yahwist's Judaism for Imperial Israel

When we consider the systems set forth by two of the strands, J and D—or, really, fragmentary statements of systems, we see in a very brief way how each one addressed an "Israel" in its own context and circumstance. J addressed the world of an imperial Israel. It spoke to the Israel of David and Solomon, ca. 950 B.C.E., and answered the questions of success. D lets us listen to an authorship that spoke to Israel after a long period of foreign rule, ca. 620 B.C.E., and includes a later layer of work accomplished even after the destruction of the Temple in 586 B.C.E. Both of these systems were later absorbed into the final statement, the "The Torah of Moses," concluded after 586. Neither of these systems made those points that were important to the paramount system that imparts to the final Torah its flavor and message. That other, definitive, pentateuchal system was the one created after 586 by the priesthood, called P.

We turn in particular to J, the writing of an author who called God Yahweh, understood by theologians to mean, "who brings into being . . . ," and ordinarily translated "the LORD." The basis for identifying a strand of the Pentateuch as the writing of the Yahwist (Genesis 2-11, 12-16, 18-22, 24-34, 38, 49; Exodus 1-24, 32, 34; Numbers 11-12, 14, 20-25; Judges 1) is not only the use of the name Yahweh for God. It is also the association of the appearance of that name with other indications. For example, the Yahwist calls Moses' father-in-law Reuel; the mountain is Sinai; the Palestinians are Canaanites. In the Elohist strand, Moses' father-in-law is Jethro; the mountain, Horeb; the Palestinians, Amorites. For another example, the creation story of Genesis 1 has Elohim create the world, then Gen. 2:5-25 has Yahweh make the world, and the latter creation story differs in substance and style from the former. The biblical narrative covers the same ground two or more times. For example, a patriarch deceives a foreign king three times about his wife's status (Gen. 12:10-20; 20:1-18; 26:1-11), twice with Abraham and Abimelech.[1]

When we examine the Yahwist's account of Israel—Who and what is Israel? How should Israel see the world? What should Israel do?—we see a system, a Judaism, quite different from that of the Pentateuch as a whole, as the priests after 586 revised it. The Yahwist's account was written in the time of David and Solomon and asked questions that faced a mighty and successful empire: For what? How Long? Why us? As we shall see, these questions in no way intersect with the issues raised by the time of the final formulation of the Pentateuch. Later the question that would predominate would be, On what condition? By contrast, J is a firm and final statement. The enduring life of Israel was not subject to doubt; no conditions therefore were set for Israel's continuing its life in history. Only when matters were called into doubt would conditions and stipulations be introduced into what was taken for granted at the time of the author of J. In the time of King Solomon, people looked backward to account for the great day at hand. The Yahwist's account, produced at the height of the glory of the Davidic monarchy in the

1. W. Lee Humphreys, *Crisis and Story: Introduction to the Old Testament* (Palo Alto, Calif.: Mayfield Publishing Co. 1979), 65-69.

time of Solomon, around 950 B.C.E., wanted to tell the story of
the federation of tribes, now a single kingdom under Solomon,
with a focus on Zion and Jerusalem, the metropolis of the federation. He told the history, the theology of Israel from its origins.
He made the familiar point that the hand of Yahweh directed
events. He derived the message of grace from that fact. Out of
the past he wanted to know the present and future of the empire
and monarchy at hand.[2] The Yahwist told the story of the creation
of the world to the fulfillment of Israel in the conquest of the
land. His purpose was to affirm that what happened to Israel—
its move from a federation of tribes to an empire under David
and Solomon—was the doing of God, whom he called Yahweh.

Lee Humphreys summarizes the worldview of Yahwist's Judaism to explain an imperial Israel and the way of life of Israel
as empire: "The Israel of the empire was Yahweh's creation for
which Yahweh had a mission." The writer lays great emphasis
on how God chose a particular person to carry out the mission:
Abraham and Sarah, Isaac and Rebecca, Jacob, Leah, and Rachel
and others. All appeared unworthy and weak, but God chose
them. The message, as Lee Humphreys paraphrases it, is this:

> The Yahwist focused attention on just one man, then on twelve
> sons, then on a band of slaves in Egypt, then on fugitives in
> Sinai's wastes. Repeatedly endangered, seemingly about to
> vanish on many occasions, small, weak, and often unworthy,
> these ancestors of the Israelite empire of David and Solomon
> were sustained again and again, even in the land of the god-
> king pharaoh, because they were a chosen people, elected by
> a god who upheld and preserved them.[3]

That is the message. What is Moses' place as law-giver in this
picture? It is minor. The Yahwist's picture reduces the covenant
at Sinai to modest propositions; the legal stipulations are few,
focused in Exodus 34.

> The LORD said, Here and now I make a covenant . . .
> You shall not make yourselves gods of cast metal.
> You shall observe the pilgrim-feast of Unleavened Bread . . .

2. Humphreys, 65-78.
3. Humphreys, 76.

Every first birth of the womb belongs to me . . .
For six days you shall work, but on the seventh day you shall
cease work . . .
You shall observe the pilgrim-feast of Weeks . . .
You shall not offer the blood of my sacrifice at the same time
as anything leavened . . .
You shall bring the choicest first fruits of your soil to the house
of the LORD your God.
You shall not boil a kid in its mother's milk.

(Exod. 34:10-26, NEB)

The patriarchs take priority, the unconditional quality of the
promises of God to Abraham—and later to David—dominates
throughout.

At issue then are the promises to the patriarchs and their
children, not the contract between God and Israel. Israel is destined by divine grace for its present glory, in Solomon's time.
For the Yahwist, Moses is a minor figure relative to the patriarchs.
What is important about Moses is not the giving of law but some
of the narratives of his leadership (Exodus 1-24, 32, 34). These
reflect the mentality of the Davidic monarchy. So when we tell
the tale of the golden calf, the breaking of the tablets, and the
forgiveness of God as an act of grace, we listen to sublime narratives told in the age of Solomon and to the world of Solomon:
God's grace favoring Israel, in an age cognizant of grace, a powerful message to a self-confident empire—in all, an American
dream (to commit an anachronism). Humphreys provides a systematic statement of what we may call this Judaism:

Adam and Eve are driven from the garden and must thereafter
scratch out a living from the ground by hard labor. In time
they must die, for they no longer have access to the tree of
life. The disorder intensifies as brother turns against brother
. . . then man is set against man in a blood feud . . . The
boundary separating the divine and the human is trespassed
. . . Because of human perverseness, nature and the deity
destroy humankind in a flood. . . . Finally an attempt by humans to overreach themselves with their tower results in a
scattering of nations and confusion of tongues. . . . The human
family grows ever more alienated from the deity and from one

another until the harmonious order has in every way dissolved. The state of blessing found in the garden has become one of curse. . . . In the Yahwist's epic, death becomes the human fate because of an act of human disobedience, the flood is just punishment by a deity whose creation has turned against him. . . . The range of vision abruptly narrows [with the entry of Abraham]. An alien having only limited contact with the natives and setting but shallow roots, he lives with a promise that alone sustains him. . . . In time the deity's blessing and charge were transferred to his son Isaac, then to Jacob, and through Jacob to the Twelve Tribes. . . . By implication the blessing and charge passed from the Twelve Tribes to the Israel of David and Solomon.

Israel is given a mission, to serve as a blessing for all the families of the earth. Yahweh's promise to Abraham, Humphreys notes, "recalls the promise made through Nathan the court prophet to David in 2 Sam. 7:9: 'I will make for you a great name, like the name of the great ones of the earth.' " The promise to Abraham thus comes to fulfillment in the empire of David and Solomon. The monarchy fulfills Yahweh's promise, and God in his promise to Abraham in fact validates the empire building of David and Solomon. Why did God favor Israel? It was, again in Humphrey's summary, "to be the vehicle for life, peace, integrity, and harmony in the created order, to reverse the currents set in motion by the first human act of disobedience."

The narrator joins the themes of the formation of the tribes into a federation and those of the building of Jerusalem and the monarchy, using the stories to legitimize the empire. The importance of the Yahwist's picture is the unconditional character of the account. The promise to Abraham is not conditional, rests on no stipulations. The promise is tied to no strings: "The assurances found in Genesis 23:2 and 2 Samuel 7:9-16 carry the force of certainty, of actions already coming into effect."[4]

> I took you from the pastures. . . . I have been with you wherever you have gone. . . . I will make you a great name among the great ones of the earth. I will assign a place for my people

4. Humphreys, 76.

Israel; there I will plant them, and they shall dwell in their
own land. . . . The LORD has told you that he would build up
your royal house. When your life ends and you rest with your
forefathers, I will set up one of your family, one of your own
children, to succeed you and I will establish his kingdom.

(2 Sam. 7:8-13, NEB)

What we do not find is more interesting than what we do: the
absence of emphasis on a covenant or contract, the conditional
character of Israel's existence, the uncertain right to the land,
the unclear identification of the people. Those traits of a heightened reality, in which possession of the land depends on the
character of the society built upon it, in which the very existence
of the people constantly demands explanation and justification—
these recurrent characteristics of Judaisms beyond 586 play slight
role in the Yahwist's serene and confident Judaism, his view of
the world from the height of Jerusalem, his account of the way
of life of a normal people, living securely in its rightful place.
No later Judaism would conform.

The Deuteronomist's Judaism
for an Age of Uncertainty

The fact that the Yahwist's Moses speaks to the imperial age of
Solomon surely made his or her account of Israel's life implausible
to the two authorships of Deuteronomy, one ca. 620 B.C.E., at
the end of the long period of Assyrian hegemony in the southern
kingdom, Judea, the other at ca. 570, after the destruction of
Jerusalem but long before the return to Zion under Persian sponsorship. They give us a Moses different from the Yahwist's, for
instance. The Yahwist's Moses for an imperial age did not serve
the Deuteronomistic authorships because that set of writers gives
us another way of life and worldview for another Israel (as well
as a fresh Moses). If we turn to the book of Deuteronomy, we
find a different picture from that of the Yahwist. Now Moses
stands at the center, and he gives a magnificent sermon,
preached before his death, as a narrative of Israel's history. That
sermon, moreover, forms the setting for an enormous law code.
At the heart of matters is this claim: Here is God's law, which

you will keep as your side of the contract that God made with you in bringing you out of Egypt and into the promised land. Moses now serves to validate the laws of the book at hand, that is, of Deuteronomy.

Deuteronomy came into existence in a time of the political shaking of the foundations of the Near East and of Israel. The book of Deuteronomy in its earliest phase came to light toward the end of the seventh century, about 620 B.C.E., forty years prior to the destruction of the First Temple of Jerusalem. In the period of the writing of Deuteronomy Israel had spent a whole generation under Assyrian influence, and only now, with the waning of Assyrian rule over the Near East, emerged from that sphere of cultural influence. In fact, it was a time of transition in which the established political system of the Near East gave way. For nearly two thousand years prior to ca. 600 B.C.E., Egypt and Mesopotamia had formed the centers of international power. Syria and Palestine constituted a buffer. One final empire, Babylonia under Nebuchadnezzar, came to center stage at the end of the seventh century B.C.E. Having conquered Jerusalem and exiled the Jews to Babylonia in 586, it fell by the mid-sixth century B.C.E. That marked the end of the old order of the Near and Middle East.

Deuteronomy is a brilliant work of fictional autobiography, presenting a long speech by "Moses," as an account out of the past for the present. The book addresses a fully articulated national state and projects contemporary problems and matters of doubt into what at that time appeared to be a more secure past.[5] Humphreys provides our account of the message and purpose of Deuteronomy:

> Israel had prospered when it was loyal to the covenant and had suffered when it was disloyal. This pattern is revealed in the framework that was used to bind together the once separate stories about the federation's tribes and judges in the Book of Judges [as well]. . . . Loyalty to Yahweh and his stipulations brings life and security, gifts of the god who first called Israel into being from Egyptian slavery. Disloyalty will result only in death.[6]

5. Humphreys, 147.
6. Humphreys, 148-49.

The book is in two parts. One is Deut. 12–26, for 2 Kings 22 tells the story of the supernatural discovery of a book of the law, and many maintain that it corresponds to this part. A point of emphasis in these chapters is that in Jerusalem and only there may Yahweh be worshiped; only the priests of Jerusalem are valid. The book of Deuteronomy in its earliest layer makes two points: One can worship only Yahweh, and one can worship Yahweh only in Jerusalem. Moses then forms the authority for the story, but not the leading actor. That is the first part of the story. That message hardly served the needs of Israel after 586, when the people could not go to Jerusalem.

When Deuteronomy reached its final stage, it answered a critical question concerning disaster and destruction. The book took its part in a much more encompassing and massive history of Israel, with Joshua, Judges, Samuel, and Kings. That great work of historical narrative came into being, in its final composition, after 586 and was assembled in the light of the catastrophe in order to answer a question of life and death: Why have these things happened to us? The past must live again to explain the present and secure the future. This second phase in the unfolding of the tale of the Deuteronomistic historians took place after the destruction of the Temple in 586. Then Moses again provided the authority for an explanation of the entire history of ancient Israel, culminating, as it had, in the tragedy at hand. Now Moses is lawgiver, and the laws form the contract between Israel and God. Israel has violated that covenant or contract, and the result, destruction, is at hand. Again Humphreys summarizes:

> In Judah and Jerusalem some would turn back to Moses, attempting to redeem the crisis of 587 B.C. [when the Temple was destroyed] by placing it in the theological framework of the old federation story of Israel's origins, for only in this way could Israel's tragic end be understood as the harsh but just action of its god Yahweh. In Moses, who had led Israel from Egyptian slavery, who had mediated the covenant on Mount Sinai, and whose death before the promise of land had been fulfilled had given an effective symbol to Israel's tragically unfulfilled promise, they found a mirror in which to view their own experience. This group found their charter in the book of

Deuteronomy, which received its final form at their hands. From this base they reviewed Israel's history from the entrance into Canaan to the exile in Babylon after 587 . . . They produced an extended theological survey of Israel's history that now comprises the books of Joshua through 2 Kings. Their book is called the deuteronomistic history because the basis for judgment is found in Deuteronomy.[7]

The Moses of Deuteronomy is a great preacher and gives a sermon on the plains of Moab. He projects out of a secure past an account of the later issues and problems and doubts.[8] In Deuteronomy Moses says a great deal and does much less; in the Yahwist chapters of Exodus, Moses does much but gives few laws. The contrast is clear. The message is that Yahweh has worked through the Babylonians because Israel had followed the policies of its kings during the Assyrian hegemony.

The "Judaism" of Deuteronomy contains many of those motifs that predominate later, with its emphasis on covenantal nomism and on keeping the contract that God had made with Israel by carrying out the rules that constituted the conditions of the contract. Nevertheless, the later definitive traits scarcely break through. These marks of self-consciousness include emphasis on the conditional character of the life of Israel, the insecure hold on the land, the uncertain identification of the nation, and its need to constantly affirm its identity. The appeal to Israel's past accounts for the present. But the Deuteronomistic strand of the Torah of "Moses" contains little instruction on what is required for the future.

The Priests' Pentateuch and the Beginning of Judaism

That small number of Israelite families who remembered the exile survived in Babylonia, and then, toward the end of the sixth and fifth centuries B.C.E., returned to Zion. They knew things that Israel before 586 could never have imagined: the

7. Humphreys, 146.
8. Humphreys, 147.

experiences of exile and return. But the biblical narrative suggests
that these families were few in number. Many in Babylonia never
went back to the land of Israel. That fact shows us the true
character of the Judaism that would predominate: It began by
making a selection of facts to be deemed consequential, hence
historical, and ignoring, in making that selection, the experiences
of others who had a quite different perception of what had
happened—and, for all we know, a different appreciation of the
message. The fact that the ones who came back (and many who
were taken away) were priests made all the difference, as the
books of Ezra and Nehemiah indicate. To the priests what mattered in 586 was the destruction of the Temple, and what made
a difference "three generations later" was the restoration of Zion
and the rebuilding of the Temple. To them the cult was the key;
the Temple the nexus between heaven and earth.

The nation restored to its land may be compared to a person
healed from a life-threatening illness. Nothing can ever look the
same as it did before to such a person. Life cannot be taken for
granted. It becomes a gift, each day an unanticipated surprise.
Everything demands explanation, but uncertainty reigns. The
comparison fails, to be sure, when we realize that while the
consciousness of life as a gift of grace changes things for the
survivor alone, the return to Zion, cast as it was into the
encompassing language of the Five Books of Moses, imposed
upon the entire nation's imagination and inner consciousness
the unsettling encounter with annihilation avoided, extinction
postponed, life renewed—temple restored as portrayed in P's
Leviticus and Numbers. Identifying the experience of exile and
return as definitive in Scripture, we may conclude that the Judaic
system supplies a self-evidently valid answer to an urgent question. It thrives, therefore, so long as the answer remains obviously the truth, so long as the question is critical. The initial
Judaism, the one set forth in the Five Books of Moses, addressed
a crisis, and each subsequent Judaic system was precipitated by
a crisis as well. The initial Judaic system would impose its model
upon the later ones, by defining attitudes and expectations that
would shape the urgent questions people would find critical later
on. That initial system reached expression in the centuries between the destruction of the First Temple of Jerusalem, in 586
B.C.E., when the Hebrew Scriptures of ancient Israel reached the

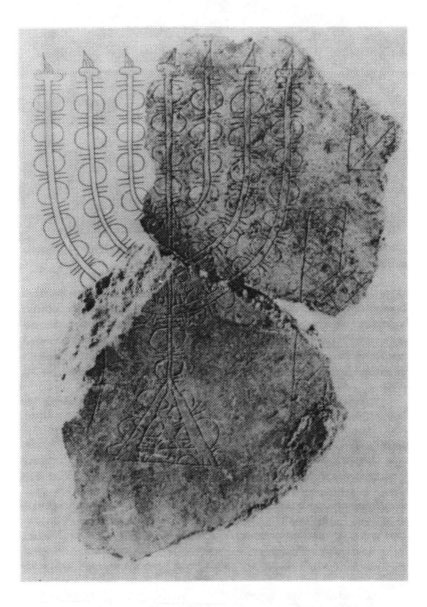

The earliest known depiction of the menorah of the Second Temple, found in excavations in Jerusalem's Old City.

Model of the Second Temple of Jerusalem reconstructed by Y. Aharoni and displayed at the Holyland Hotel in Jerusalem.

form in which we have them, and the destruction of the Second Temple in 70 C.E. Among many succeeding Judaisms, rabbinic Judaism, which became paramount, took shape in the period between the rise of Islam in the Middle East, North Africa, and southern Europe in the seventh century C.E. That Judaism flourished in Christian Europe and the Muslim Middle East and North Africa.

In sum, the Hebrew Scriptures—the Old Testament—came into existence in the aftermath of the exile of the Jews from their homeland to Babylonia in 586 B.C.E. and their return approximately seventy years later. In 539 Babylonia fell, and in 538 the new ruler of the Middle East, the Persian emperor Cyrus decreed that exiles might return to their homelands; this allowed the Jews to return to the land of Israel. Some years later a few did. The destruction of the Temple in 586 was followed by its reconstruction, completed in the time of Ezra and Nehemiah in ca. 450 B.C.E. Questions demanded attention: Who are we? and, Why have these things happened to us? The answers provided by the Pentateuch and the prophets appeared equally self-evident.

All Judaic systems took shape in the experience of defeat followed by restoration, loss of political standing, and exile from the land, then recovery of politics and renewed possession of the land. People saw in a fresh light what they had lost and then regained. Their group life and their location in the land could no longer be taken for granted. What others had earlier treated as givens a new generation found surprising. An intense sense of the land as something lost and then regained, and self-consciousness about themselves as a special group because they had lost, and then regained, their original situation demanded a cogent explanation. The original Judaism, expressed in the Five Books of Moses when assembled, supplied it. Judaism was born in that setting and it answered the question of the meaning of what had happened. That Judaic system comprised of Scripture explained the relationship of the people to the land, and of members of the people to one another, and of all, land and people alike, to God—a considerable story indeed. The setting is clear. The scriptures reached their initial definition, that is, the selection that formed the first Judaic canon, as a result of that sequence of calamitous events.

Not all of the materials joined in the Five Books of Moses derived from priestly authors, and a sizable proportion represented views held long before 586, but the priests put it all together, and their perspective comes to expression throughout. What is important about the version of Judaism in the Pentateuch in its final form? The answer is simple. While making ample use of ancient tales, the framers of the Pentateuch as we now have it flourished in Babylonia after 586. There they drew together the elements of the received picture and reshaped them into the fairly coherent set of rules and narratives we now know as the Pentateuch. The priests' setting of Judaism imparts ultimate meaning to the Scripture: response to historical disaster followed by unprecedented triumph (to the Jews' mind). Humphreys characterized their vision as follows:

> In the priests' narrative the chosen people are last seen as pilgrims moving through alien land toward a goal to be fulfilled in another time and place, and this is the vision, drawn from the ancient story of their past, that the priests now hold out to the scattered sons and daughters of old Israel. They too are exiles encamped for a time in an alien land, and they too must focus their hopes on the promise ahead. Like the Israelites in the Sinai wilderness, they must avoid setting roots in the land

through which they pass, for diaspora is not to become their
permanent condition, and regulations must be adopted to fa-
cilitate this. They must resist assimilation into the world into
which they are now dispersed, because hope and heart and
fundamental identity lay in the future.Thus, the priestly document not only affirms Yahweh's continuing authority and
action in the lives of his people but offers them a pattern for
life that will ensure them a distinct identity.[9]

The several segments of the earlier traditions of Israel were so
drawn together as to make the point peculiarly pertinent to Israel
in exile. The original Judaic system, the one set forth by the
Pentateuch, answered the urgent issue of exile with the self-
evident response of return. The question was not to be avoided,
the answer not to be doubted. The center of the system, then,
lay in the covenant, the contract containing the rules by which
Israel would be governed. At the heart of the covenant was the
call for Israel to form a kingdom of priests and a holy people.

The version of the covenant in Leviticus 19:1-18 expresses
the priests' Judaism:

> And the Lord said to Moses, "Say to all the congregation of
> the people of Israel, You shall be holy, for I the LORD your God
> am holy. Every one of you shall revere his mother and his
> father, and you shall keep my sabbaths: I am the LORD your
> God. Do not turn to idols or make for yourselves molten gods:
> I am the LORD your God.
>
> "When you offer a sacrifice of peace offerings to the LORD,
> you shall offer it so that you may be accepted. It shall be eaten
> the same day you offer it or on the morrow; and anything left
> over until the third day shall be burned with fire. If it is eaten
> at all on the third day, it is an abomination; it will not be
> accepted, and every one who eats it shall bear his iniquity,
> because he has profaned a holy thing of the LORD; and that
> person shall be cut off from his people.
>
> "When you reap the harvest of your land, you shall not
> reap your field to its very border, neither shall you gather the
> gleanings after your harvest. And you shall not strip your

9. Humphreys, 217.

vineyard bare, neither shall you gather the fallen grapes of your vineyard; you shall leave them for the poor and for the sojourner: I am the LORD your God.

"You shall not steal, nor deal falsely, nor lie to one another. And you shall not swear by my name falsely, and so profane the name of your God: I am the LORD.

"You shall not oppress your neighbor or rob him. The wages of a hired servant shall not remain with you all night until the morning. You shall not curse the deaf or put a stumbling block before the blind, but you shall fear your God: I am the LORD.

"You shall do no injustice in judgment; you shall not be partial to the poor or defer to the great, but in righteousness shall you judge your neighbor. You shall not go up and down as a slanderer among your people, and you shall not stand forth against the life of your neighbor: I am the LORD.

"You shall not hate your brother in your heart, but you shall reason with your neighbor, lest you bear sin because of him. You shall not take vengeance or bear any grudge against the sons of your own people, but you shall love your neighbor as yourself: I am the LORD."

(Lev. 19:1-18, RSV)

The children of Abraham, Isaac, and Jacob are to form a people of God, keeping the rules, the covenant, God sets forth. We should regard this mixture of rules as cultic regarding sacrifice, moral regarding support of the poor, ethical regarding right-dealing, and above all religious regarding "being holy for I the LORD your God am holy." The passage portrays a complete and whole society. Elsewhere Leviticus contains a clear statement of the consequence geared to the events of the recent past: "If you walk in my statutes and observe my commandments and do them, then I will give you your rains in their season" (Lev. 26:3-4, RSV), "But if you will not hearken to me, and will not do all these commandments . . . I will do this to you: I will appoint over you sudden terror . . . and you shall sow your seed in vain, for your enemies shall eat it. . . . Then the land shall enjoy its sabbaths as long as it lies desolate, while you are in your enemies' land" (Lev. 26:14-34, RSV). The Judaism of the priests therefore responded to the loss of the land and its restoration to the Jews' possession. It confronted the overwhelming question of the meaning of what had happened and supplied the answer: Israel must obey the rules of holiness, and, if it does, then by keeping its part of the agreement or covenant, it could make certain God would keep his part: "And I will give peace in the land, and you shall lie down and none shall make you afraid" (Lev. 26:6, RSV).

While the Old Testament contained many more writings than those of the priests, and the work of drawing together the entire heritage of Israel before 586 encompassed many more authors than the priestly, one strand in the larger fabric imparts its texture to the whole. The priests laid emphasis upon the Temple and its orderly and meticulous service to God through sacrifice. The way of life expressed the requirements of the covenant of God with Moses, (covenantal nomism,) and the worldview explained the meaning of the everyday life of the people and the historical existence of the nation in terms of the Five Books of Moses. It therefore defined Judaism.

There are two reasons that the normative Judaism of the land of Israel from the return to Zion after 586 to the destruction of the Second Temple should find definition in the priests' conception. First, the priests were the ones who organized and set forth the Torah revealed by God to Moses at Sinai as the Jews would receive and revere it. Consequently their perspective, emphasizing the Temple with its holiness, and the cult with its critical role in sustaining the life of the land and the nation, predominated. Because the Torah defined the faith, explained what had happened, and set forth the rules for God's continuing favor to Israel, the final shape and system of the Torah had an immense impact. The structure of the whole—as distinct from its parts—derived from the perspective and paramount influence of the priesthood of the Jerusalem Temple.

Second, the issue that formed the critical center of the Torah persisted, with the result that the urgent question answered by the Torah retained its original character and definition, and the Torah—read in the synagogue every Sabbath morning, as well as on Monday and on Thursday—retained its relevance. Generation after generation, the resentment, the product of a memory of loss and restoration, and of recognizing the danger of a further loss assured that the priests' authoritative answer would not lose its power to persist and to persuade. The second of the two reasons is more important: The question answered by the Five Books of Moses persisted at the center of the national life and remained urgent, if chronic. The answer provided by the Pentateuch therefore retained its importance. To those troubled by the question, the answer enjoyed the status of fact. The reason that the Five Books of Moses, with their paramount, priestly emphasis on sanctification (holiness), had their formative power is that the problems addressed and solved by the Judaism of the Five Books of Moses remained chronic long after the period of its beginning.

Pentateuchal Judaism: Urgent Question, Self-Evidently Valid Answer

The Priestly Code states a powerful answer to a pressing and urgent question. Because that question continued to trouble Israelites for a long time, it is not surprising that the priestly answer to it, so profound and fundamental in its character, continued to attract and impress people as well. Because the same tensions persisted—specifically, the question, What marks ancient Israel as distinctive? Israel's ongoing preoccupation with defining itself—the initial system imposed its pattern on all others. The urgent issue derived from the loss and recovery of the land. Because of Israel's amazing experience of going into exile, but also of returning to Jerusalem, Israel had attained a self-consciousness that continuous existence in a single place under a single government excluded others. Nothing was given, nothing taken for granted, in the life of a nation that had ceased to be a nation on its own land and then once more recovered that land.

The issue was, and would remain, Who is Israel? What are the rules that define Israel as a social and a political entity? In one way or another Israel, the Jewish people wherever they lived, sought means of declaring themselves distinct from their neighbors. The emphasis on exclusion of neighbors from the group, and of the group from neighbors, in fact runs contrary to the situation in ancient Israel, with unmarked frontiers of culture, the constant giving and receiving among diverse groups, generally characteristic in ancient times. The persistent emphasis on differentiation, yielding a preoccupation with self-definition, also contradicts the facts of the matter. In the time of the formation of the Pentateuch, the people Israel were deeply affected by the shifts and changes in social, cultural, and political life and institutions.

A century and a half after the formation of the Pentateuch under Ezra and Nehemiah, when the Greeks under Alexander the Great conquered the entire Middle East (ca. 320 B.C.E.) and incorporated the land of Israel into the international Hellenistic culture, the problem of self-definition came to renewed expression. The war of independence fought by the Jews under the leadership of the Maccabees (ca. 160 B.C.E.) produced an independent state for a brief period. That state found itself under the government of a court that accommodated itself to the international style of politics and culture. What was different? What made Israel separate and secure in its land and in its national identity? In that protracted moment of confusion and change, the heritage of the Five Books of Moses came to closure. That same situation persisted that had marked the age in which the Pentateuch had delivered its message, answering the urgent question of the nation's existence.

The result of the codification and closure of the Torah under Ezra and Nehemiah was the production of a law code that emphasized the sanctification of Israel, in secular terms the exclusivist character of the Israelite God and cult. "Judaism" gained the character of a cultically centered way of life and worldview. Both rite and myth aimed at the continuing self-definition of Israel by separation from and exclusion of the rest of the world. Order against chaos meant holiness over uncleanness, life over death. The purpose was to define Israel against the background of the other peoples of the Near and Middle East, with whom Israel had much in common, and, especially, to differentiate Israel from its neighbors, for example, Samaritans, in the same country. Acute differentiation was required in particular because the social and cultural facts were precisely to the contrary. Common traits hardly bespoke clear-cut points of difference, except of idiom. The mode of differentiation taken by the Torah literature in general, and the priestly sector of that literature in particular, was cultic. The meaning, however, was also social. The power of the Torah composed in this time lay in its control of the Temple. The Torah made that Temple the pivot and focus. The Torah literature, with its concerned God, who cares what people do about rather curious matters, and its Temple cult, which totally excluded the non-Israelite from participation, and from cultic commensalism, raised high those walls of separation and underlined such distinctiveness as already existed. The life of Israel flowed from the altar; what made Israel itself was the center, the altar.

Note the contrast to the life of Israel, the Jewish people, before 586, as reflected in the pictures of the Yahwist and the Deuteronomist, on which we briefly focused earlier. As long as Israel remained essentially within its own land and frame of social reference, that is, before the conflagration of the sixth century B.C.E., the issue of separation from neighbors could be treated casually. When the core and heart of what made Israel itself were penetrated by the doubly desolating and disorienting experiences of both losing the land and then coming back, the question, Who is Israel? came to the fore. Confusion in economic and social relationships, and the fact that the land to which Israelites returned in no way permitted contiguous and isolated Israelite settlement, made it certain that the issue of self-definition clearly would emerge. It would remain on the surface and chronic. It persisted for the remainder of Israelite history, from the return to Zion and the formation of the Torah literature down to the present. The reason for this persistence? The social forces that lent urgency to the question of who Israel is (later, who a Jew is) remained. This confusion about the distinctive and on-going identification to be assigned to Israel defined the framework of the social and imaginative ecology of the Jewish people. As long as memory remained, the conflicting claims of exclusivist Torah literature and universalist prophecy, of a people living in utopia, in no particular place, while framing its vision in the deeply locative symbols of cult and center, made the abiding issue of self-definition vivid.

Why Judaism Endured: Resentment and Remission

When we ask why the Temple with its cult proved enduringly central in the imagination of the Israelites in the country—as indeed it did—we need only repeat the statements that the priests of the Temple and their imitators in the sects were prepared to make. These explain the critical importance of cult and rite. If we reread the priestly viewpoint as it is contained in the books of Leviticus and Numbers, as well as in priestly passages of Genesis and Exodus, this is the picture we derive: The altar was the center of life, the conduit of life from heaven to earth and from earth to heaven. All things were to be arrayed in relationship to the altar. The movement of the heavens demarcated and celebrated at the cult marked out the divisions of time in relationship to the altar. The spatial dimension of the land was likewise demarcated and celebrated in relationship to the altar. The natural life of Israel's fields and corrals, the social life of its hierarchical caste-system, the political life (this was not only in theory) centered on the Temple as the locus of ongoing government—all things in order and in place expressed the single message. The natural order of the world corresponded to, reinforced, and was reinforced by the social order of Israel. Both were fully realized in the cult, the nexus between those opposite and corresponding forces, the heavens and the earth.

The lines of structure emanated from the altar. It was these lines of structure that constituted high and impenetrable frontiers to separate Israel from the Gentiles (non-Israelites). Israel, which was holy, ate holy food, reproduced itself in accord with the laws of holiness, and conducted all of its affairs in accord with the demands of holiness. The cult defined holiness. Holiness meant separateness. Separateness meant life. Why? Because outside the land, the realm of the holy, lay the domain of death. The land is holy. Other lands are unclean. For the scriptural vocabulary, one antonym for "holy" is "unclean," and one antonym of "unclean" is "holy." The synonym of "holy" is "life." The principal force and symbol of uncleanness and its highest expression are death. The Torah stood for life, the covenant with the Lord guaranteed life, and the way of life required sanctification in the natural world. It follows that, since the life of the group is uncertain, subject to conditions and stipulations, nothing is set in stone; all things are a gift: land and life itself. What actually did happen in that uncertain world—exile but then restoration—marked the group as special, different, select.

Recast in the pentateuchal narratives, the experience of the uncertainty of the life of the group formed the paradigm. With the promulgation of the "Torah of Moses" under the sponsorship of Ezra, the Persians' viceroy ca. 450 B.C.E., all future Israels would refer back to that formative experience as it had been set down and preserved as the norm for Israel in the mythic terms of that "original" Israel, the Israel not of Genesis and Sinai and the entry into the promised land, but the "Israel" of the families that recorded as the rule and the norm the story of both the exile and the return. In that story of exile and return, alienation and remission—imposed on the received stories of preexilic Israel, adumbrated time and again in the Five Books of Moses, and addressed by the framers of that document in their work over all—we find that paradigmatic statement in which every Judaism, from then to now, has found its meaning, syntax of social existence, and the vocabulary of its intelligible message.

Not only so, but that same paradigm created expectations that could not be met, so it renewed the resentment captured by the myth of exile, while at the same time setting the conditions for remission of resentment, thus resolving the crisis of exile with the promise of return. There was nothing given, nothing to be merely celebrated (as the Yahwist thought) or taken for granted (as the Deuteronomist thought) in the life of a nation that had ceased to be a nation on its own land and then once more had regained that (once normal, now unexpected) condition. Judaism took shape as the system that accounted for the death and resurrection of Israel, the Jewish people, and pointed, for the source of renewed life, toward sanctification now, and salvation at the end of time.

Part Two:

ALL ISRAEL'S MEAL WITH GOD, NO PLACE IN PARTICULAR: THE JUDAISM OF ANY PLACE AND ALL THE TIME

CHAPTER TWO

The Formation of the Judaism for Everywhere All the Time

The Components of Rabbinic Judaism: Pharisees, Scribes, and the Torah as Taught by Sages to Disciples

Rabbinic Judaism presented answers to the urgent questions posed by the political catastrophes of the destruction of the Temple in 70 C.E., the Bar Kokhba Revolt in 132, and the Christianization of the Roman Empire in the fourth century, beginning with Constantine's legitimation of Christianity in 312. But that Judaic system did not begin in 70. It drew in part upon teachings and traditions of the Pharisees, who had formed a sect within the larger Judaic world of the land of Israel. After 70, the Pharisees formed the single most influential group. They were led by a sage, Yohanan ben Zakkai, and represented by elements of the pre-70 aristocracy such as Gamaliel, grandson of the Gamaliel mentioned in Acts 5:34, as well as by the Jewish general, Josephus, who had gone over to the Romans during the war. Once the Romans determined to reestablish their system of governing through native allies, they selected the Pharisees as the

party most likely to succeed in keeping the peace. The Jewish
government recognized by Roman authority, therefore, came
under the influence of the descendants of the Pharisees of the
period before 70. The Pharisees contributed more than political
representatives to the renewed Jewish government. They also
contributed a method and a viewpoint. The viewpoint addressed
"all Israel," and the method focused upon the sanctification of
all Israel. The Pharisees contributed to the nascent system aborning after 70 a fundamental attitude that everyone mattered and
a basic emphasis on the holiness of everyday life. But the rabbinic
Judaism that was aborning took within itself a second group,
the heirs and continuators of the scribes from the period before
70.

These scribes had formed a profession, not a sect, and the
mark of their profession was knowledge of the Scriptures and
traditions of Israel and capacity to bring those Scriptures to bear
on the everyday life of the people. Teachers of Scripture, clerks
in the preparation of those documents required for the conduct
of an orderly society, some of the scribes who survived came to
the place in which the Jewish government was reorganizing and
joined with the Pharisees' successors and continuators (and some
Pharisees were scribes, as some scribes were Pharisees). The
scribes contributed to the nascent system the emphasis on the
Torah and study of the Torah as critical to the holy way of life.
They did not invent the Torah, nor did they uniquely espouse
its definitive importance. These were commonplace in the normative religion of Israel before 70. The scribes in the new Judaism
did contribute their special learning, their detailed knowledge,
and, above all, their traditions on the correct procedures and
conduct of the common affairs of state.

The Judaism that emerged after 70 succeeded the Judaic
system of Temple and priesthood. It was a Judaism formed upon
essentially political lines and its task was to govern a Jewish state
and people in its land. The sect of the Pharisees and the profession of the scribes—together with surviving priests who
joined them—framed a Judaism to take the place of the Judaism
of Temple and cult. It emerged as a Judaism in which each of
the elements of the Judaism of Temple and cult would find a
counterpart: (1) in place of the Temple, the holy people,

A relief sculpture from the Arch of Titus in Rome depicting a triumphal parade of Roman soldiers carrying spoils from the Temple of Jerusalem in 70 C.E.

in whom holiness endured even outside of the cult, as the Pharisees had taught; (2) in place of the priesthood, the sage, the holy man qualified by learning, as the scribes had taught; (3) in place of the sacrifices of the altar, the holy way of life expressed through the carrying out of religious duties (*mitzvot*, "commandments"), and acts of kindness and grace beyond those commanded (*maasim tovim*, "good deeds"), and, above all, through studying the Torah.

This third element shows us the union of the pharisaic sectarian perspective that all Israel must become holy, the kingdom of priests and holy people, and the scribal professional ideal that study of the Torah was the central task. In joining the social ideal of the Pharisees that everyone, not just the priests, undertake to live the holy life, with the professional goal of the scribes that laid emphasis on the study of the Torah, Judaism presented an amalgam. It involved the obligation of everyone to be holy through studying the Torah. All Israel must study the Torah in the model of the sage, the new priest, who was given the honorific title, rabbi, (meaning simply, "my lord," formerly assigned to diverse holy men, and used in Syriac Christianity as *rabban*, for many centuries to come).

Precisely what comprised this "Torah" that people were to study? The answer is in two parts: First, the Torah comprised precisely what it had always been, the Hebrew Scriptures ("Old Testament"); but, second, in addition to the Torah—now, "the written Torah"—certain writings came into being which, in centuries to come, attained the status of divine revelation, hence of Torah, and so became part of the Torah. The first of these writings was the Mishnah, which was completed in about 200. A generation later, in about 250, a tractate, Avot, the Fathers, joined the Mishnah and explained the authority of the Mishnah in an interesting way. That document begins with a list of authorities in the Torah, beginning with Moses at Sinai, and ending with names of important authorities cited in the Mishnah itself! The implicit proposition was that the teachings of the Mishnah authorities teachings form part of the Torah that Moses received from God at Mount Sinai. In the fifth-century documents such as the Talmud of the land of Israel, ca. 400 C.E., began to refer to these other writings, including the Mishnah, as "the oral Torah," in the theory that when God revealed the Torah to Moses at Sinai, God gave the Torah in two media, one in writing, the other orally, that is, in memory, hence, *Torah shebikhtav*, "Torah in writing," and *Torah shebeal peh*, "Torah in memory," or oral.

It follows that once the pharisaic ideal that all Israel should become holy joined the scribal professional doctrine that the Torah must define the holy life of all Israel, the next step lay in the development of a fresh ideal of sanctification, one that would use the Torah to explain how—for the moment without a Temple, without a cult, and without a governing priesthood—Israel might carry out the tasks of living a holy way of life. The Mishnah's authors, from after the Bar Kokhba War to the year 200, framed a full and encompassing statement of the sanctification of the life of Israel, covering both the Temple (then in ruins) and also the enduring life of the people in their villages and homes, fields and families. Drawing upon traditions contributed by both the Pharisees from before 70 and the scribes from earlier times as well, dealing also with topics important to the priesthood (and perhaps accommodating rules preserved by the surviving priests), the authors of the Mishnah presented a document to the living Israel of the households and the farms and drew together the traditions of Pharisees, scribes, and priests into a single, remarkably cogent statement. The Mishnah represents the movement of the Pharisees from the status of sect to church, and of the scribes from the status of profession to state, addressing both the program of the priesthood of the period before 70 and the everyday life of all Israel afterward. It is an amazing document, specifying in full and rich detail what the holy life of Israel in the age without the Temple, as well as in the coming age of the restoration of the Temple, must mean.

The Mishnah outlines the many areas of sanctification that endure: land and priesthood, in agriculture, in everyday time, in appointed times, not to mention the record of the Temple, studied and restudied in the mind's reenactment of the cult. But, as we see, the Mishnah emphasized sanctification, to the near omission of the other critical dimension of Israel's existence, salvation. Only later—in the aftermath of the third and final crisis in the formation of Judaism—would Scripture exegetes complete the structure of Judaism, a system resting on the twin foundations of sanctification in this world and salvation in time to come.

The Sages and Their System

Rabbinic Judaism is the creation of a group of holy men called "sages," in Hebrew, hakhamim. It was a Judaism set forth through the teaching of sages to disciples, just as Moses, viewed as a sage or rabbi, taught Joshua, and so on since Sinai. Let us begin with a definition of the sage, and then examine what sages created, beginning with their first and most important document, the Mishnah. The sage in the setting of the Mishnah is a kind of wise man. The Mishnah represents the sage as a man of learning and also of holiness, learning in this world, holiness in the supernatural world. A sage taught disciples and so became the students' supernatural father while the disciples became his supernatural sons. In later writings, the sage as a holy man could do wonders and work miracles, and it was through his learning that the sage became a supernatural man and could do wonders.

The sage later became the model for the Messiah, so that the Messiah at the end of time would be in all respects a master of the Torah and the model sage. Thus King David, prototype and progenitor of the Messiah, was represented in the unfolding writings of Judaism as the ideal rabbi, that is, the sage par excellence. The sage's learning therefore represented knowledge of the rules of creation as God had laid them down in the Torah, knowledge of the rules of the holy way of life as God had revealed them at Sinai, and knowledge of the rules that would make Israel worthy of salvation through the coming of *Rabbi* David's son, the Messiah, in time to come. The sage bears much in common with the wise men of ancient times in general, clerks and teachers, but the Judaic sage also exhibits traits that mark him as distinctive and particularly representative of the Judaic system that he embodied.

Attention to the sages' system brings us to their first and principal work, the Mishnah, completed at ca. 200 C.E., and later recognized as the original document of the oral Torah. The Mishnah is a kind of law code, covering six principal topics: sanctification of the economy and support of the priesthood, the holy caste; sanctification of time, with reference to special occasions, appointed times, and the Sabbath; sanctification of the family and the individual; the proper conduct of points of social conflict, the political life of the people; the sanctification of the Temple and its offerings, with special emphasis on the everyday and the routine occasions; and, finally, the protection of the Temple from uncleanness and the preservation of cultic cleanness. These six principal subjects form the center of the Mishnah's six divisions and, all together, cover the everyday life of the holy people in the here and now. The rules are phrased in the present tense—people do this, people do not do that—and, overall, they provide an account of an ideal world. At issue was not merely the everyday, but the sacred, and holiness persisted even though the everyday did not yield such evidence as it had before. The message is clear: The established sanctification of Israel endured; events changed nothing.

The Mishnah's Judaism of Sanctification

The topical program of the Mishnah, as distinct from the issues worked out through discussion of the topics, focuses upon the sanctification of the life of Israel, the Jewish people. The questions taken up by the Mishnah, in the aftermath of the destruction of the Temple, are whether and how Israel is still holy. The self-evidently valid answer is that Israel is indeed holy, and so far as the media of sanctification persist beyond the destruction of the holy place—and they do endure—the task of holy Israel is to continue to conduct that life of sanctification that had centered upon the Temple. Where does holiness reside now? It is above all in the life of the people, Israel. The Mishnah may speak of the holiness of the Temple, but the premise is that the people—that kingdom of priests and holy people of Leviticus—constitute the center and focus of the sacred. The land retains its holiness too, and in raising the crops, the farmer is expected to adhere to the rules of order and structure laid down in Leviticus, keeping each thing in its proper classification, observing the laws of the sabbatical year, for instance. The priesthood retains its holiness, even without the task of carrying out the sacrificial cult. Priests must continue to observe the caste rules governing marriage, as specified in Leviticus.

The relationship of husband and wife forms a focus of sanctification, and that retains its validity even now. The passage of time—day to day, with the climax at the Sabbath; week to week, with the climax at the sanctification of the new month; and season to season, with the climax at the holy seasons—continues to indicate the fundamental state and condition of Israel the people. The day to day has its climax at the Sabbath; the week to week has its climax at the sanctification of the new month; the season to season has its climax at the holy seasons, in particular the first new moon after the autumnal equinox, marked by Tabernacles, and the first new moon after the vernal equinox, marked by Passover. All these modes of sanctification endure, surviving the destruction of the holy Temple. In these and other foci of interest, the Mishnah lays forth a Judaic system of sanctification, joining discourse on the foci of sanctification that no longer survived with discussion on those that flourished even beyond the disaster. If we had to specify the single urgent and critical question and the single self-evident answer, it would be this colloquy: The compelling question, Is Israel yet holy? has the self-evident answer, Sanctification inheres in the life of the people.

Four of the six principal parts of the Mishnah deal with the cult and its officers: (1) Holy Things addresses the everyday conduct of the sacrificial cult; (2) Purities takes up the protection of the cult from sources of uncleanness specified in Leviticus (particularly Lev. 12-15); (3) Agriculture centers on the designation of portions of the crop for the use of the priesthood (and others in the same classification of a holy caste, such as the poor), and thus provides for the support of the Temple staff; and (4) Appointed Times, the larger part of which concerns the conduct of the cult on such special occasions as the Day of Atonement, Passover, Tabernacles, and the like (and the rest of which concerns the conduct in the village on those same days, with the basic conception that what you do in the cult forms the mirror image of what you do in the village). Two further divisions of the document deal with everyday affairs: (1) Damages concerns civil law and government; (2) women takes up issues of family, home, and personal status. That is the program of the Mishnah, sum and substance.

Clearly, much of the Mishnah attends to topics of a utopian character. That is to say, many of its rules pertained to an institution that lay in ruins: the laws on the Temple and its conduct on an everyday basis, in the fifth division; on special occasions, in the second division; on the support of the priesthood, in the first division; on the matter of cultic cleanness, in the sixth division. Clearly, the framers hoped and expected that, at some time in the future, the Temple would be rebuilt and its cult restored. They prayed for that eventuality, but when they produced the Mishnah, there was no Temple. No offerings went up in smoke to God in heaven; no priests presided at the altar; no Levites sang on the platform; no Israelites brought their offerings of the produce of the holy land to send up to the holy God in heaven.

The Mishnah's Contribution to the Formation of Judaism

Why did the Mishnah matter to generations to come? The Mishnah mattered, on the near term, because of its importance to the Jewish states of the day, one in the land of Israel, governed by the Roman Empire, the other in Babylonia, a western province of the Persian Empire. The Romans reestablished Jewish self-government after the Bar Kokhba War, and by the middle of the second century a Jewish government conducted the politics of the Jewish community of the land of Israel. When the Mishnah was published in ca. 200, it immediately became the foundation document of that Jewish government. The clerks of the Jewish government mastered the document and applied it, appealing to their knowledge of the Mishnah's laws as validation for their authority. On the near term, the code exercised immediate and practical authority in those matters to which it was relevant.

The Mishnah mattered on the long term because of its centrality in the intellectual life of the Jews' sages. These sages, many of them employed by the Jewish governments of the land of Israel and of Babylonia, believed—and persuaded many—that the Mishnah formed part of the Torah, God's will for Israel revealed to Moses at Sinai. So the Mishnah, originally not a work of religion in a narrow sense, attained the status of revelation. How did this happen? The first great apologetic for the Mishnah, the Sayings of the Founders (*Pirqé Avot*), issued in ca. 250, approximately a generation after the Mishnah itself, tells us the answer. The text begins, "Moses received Torah on Sinai and handed it on to Joshua . . ." and, the chain of tradition goes on, the latest in the list turn out to be authorities named in the Mishnah itself. What these authorities teach they have received in the chain of tradition since Sinai. What they teach is Torah. The Mishnah, which is their teaching, enjoys its standing and authority because it comes from sages, and, it follows, the sages' standing and authority come from God.

Such a claim imparted to the Mishnah and its teachers a position in the heart and mind of Israel, the Jewish people, that would ensure the long-term influence of the document. What happened beyond 200 and before 400 were two processes, one of which generated the other. The first was that the Mishnah was extensively studied, line by line, word by word. The modes of study were mainly three: First, the sages asked about the meanings of words and phrases. Then they worked on the comparison of one set of laws with another, finding the underlying principles of each, comparing and harmonizing those principles. They formed of the rather episodic rules a tight and large fabric.

Third, they moved beyond the narrow limits of the Mishnah into still broader and more speculative areas of thought. In all, the sages responsible to administer the law also expounded and expanded the law willy nilly. Ultimately, in both countries the work (of Mishnah commentary) developed into two large-scale documents, each called a Talmud. We have them as the Talmud of the Land of Israel (which I have translated into English) completed by about 400, and the Talmud of Babylonia, completed by about 600.

The second process—besides the work of Mishnah commentary—drew attention back to Scripture. Once the work of reading the new code got under way, an important problem demanded attention. What is the relationship between the Mishnah and the established Scripture of Israel, the written Torah? The Mishnah only occasionally adduces texts of the Scriptures in support of its rules. Its framers worked out their own topical program, only part of which intersects with that of the laws of the Pentateuch. They followed their own principles of organization and development. They wrote in their own kind of Hebrew, quite different from Biblical Hebrew. The question naturally arose, Can we through sheer logic discover the law? Must we tease laws out of Scripture through commentary, through legal exegesis? The Mishnah represented an extreme in this debate because many of its topics do not derive from Scripture, and further, a large part of its laws ignores Scripture's pertinent texts in that these texts are simply not cited. When, moreover, the framers of the Sayings of the Founders placed sages named in the Mishnah on the list of those who stand within the chain of tradition beginning at Sinai, they did not assign to those sages verses of Scripture, the written Torah (except in one or two instances). Rather, the Torah saying assigned to each of the named sages is not scriptural at all. Thus the sages enjoy an independent standing and authority on their own; they are not subordinate to Scripture, and their sayings enjoy equal standing with sentences of Scripture.

The work of exegesis of the Mishnah also drew attention to the relationship of the Mishnah to Scripture. Consequently, important works of biblical commentary emerged in the third and fourth centuries. These works focus on such books as Leviticus (Sifra), Numbers (Sifré to Numbers), and Deuteronomy (Sifre to

Deuteronomy). A paramount issue is whether law emerges solely on the basis of processes of reasoning, or whether only through looking in verses of Scripture are we able to uncover solid basis for the rules of the Mishnah. In that discourse we find the citation of a verse of Scripture followed by a verbatim citation of a passage of the Mishnah. Because this mode of reading Scripture is apt to be unfamiliar to many readers, let me give a concrete example of how the process of Mishnah exegesis in relationship to Scripture exegesis was carried forward in the third and fourth centuries. The following example is from Sifré to Numbers, but equivalent passages for Leviticus can be found in Sifra, and for Deuteronomy, in Sifré to Deuteronomy, among other places in the writings of the rabbis:

Pisqa **VI:II.1**
A.   ". . . Every man's holy thing shall be his; whatever any man gives to the priest shall be his" (Num. 5:10).
B.   On the basis of this statement you draw the following rule:
C.   **If a priest on his own account makes a sacrificial offering, even though it falls into the week [during which] another priestly watch than his own [is in charge of the actual cult, making the offerings and receiving the dues], lo, that priest owns the priestly portions of the offering, and the right of offering it up belongs to him [and not to the priest ordinarily on duty at that time, who otherwise would retain the rights**

We have here a citation of the verse plus a law in a prior writing (in this case not the Mishnah, but the Tosefta, a compilation of supplements to the Mishnah's laws), which the verse is supposed to sustain. The formal traits require citation of a verse, with or without comment, followed by a verbatim citation of a passage from the Mishnah or the Tosefta. We have a formal construction in which we simply juxtapose a verse, with or without intervening words of explanation, with a passage of the Mishnah or the Tosefta. When sages proposed to provide a counterpart to what they were even then creating for the Mishnah, a commentary for Scripture, they sought to build bridges from the Mishnah to Scripture.

In doing so the sages articulated the theme of the Mishnah, the sanctification of Israel. But what of salvation? Where, when, and how did sages then shaping Judaism address that other complementary category of Israel's existence? We ask further, Is the work of linking the Mishnah to Scripture the only kind of scriptural commentary sages produced between the first and the fourth century? Not at all. Sages turned to Scripture to seek the laws of Israel's history, to ask the questions of salvation, of Israel's relationship to God, that they tended to neglect in the Mishnah and in the works of amplification of the Mishnah. In chapter 4 we shall see when, where, how, and why they did so. First let us consider the Mishnah and see for ourselves some of its salient traits. (For this purpose, a sample chapter of the Mishnah is given in the Appendix.)

The Mishnah's Social Vision: Women

The Mishnah says the same thing about everything. Accordingly, knowing the urgent questions and the self-evidently valid answer of the system, we can predict what the system has to say about any topic it chooses to treat. A sample chapter of the Mishnah is representative of the rhetoric of the document, which is uniform throughout, and the way the document frames the issue of any given topic typifies the way it will treat every other topic. For the purpose of providing a direct encounter with the Mishnah (the fundamental document of Judaism after Scripture), we turn to a subject critical in the Judaism of the dual Torah, the formation of the social order. Because women form half of that order, and because the sanctification of the family through marriage forms the building block of the society of Judaism, we ask how the document addresses that critical subject.

The social vision of the Mishnah's Judaism encompasses issues of gender, social structure and construction, wealth and property transactions, and the organization of the castes of society. In all these matters the system seeks the principles of order and proper classification, identifying as problems the occasions for disorder and improper disposition of persons or resources. Our document says one thing about many topics. This tells us that it stands for a well-considered view of the whole, and, when we come to the theological and philosophical program of the same writing, that consistent viewpoint will guide us to what matters and what is to be said about what matters.

The principal focus of a social vision framed by men, such as that of the Mishnah, not only encompasses, but focuses upon, woman, who is perceived as the indicative abnormality in a world where man is the norm. But to place into perspective the Mishnah's vision of woman, we have to locate woman within the larger structure defined by the household. That is for two reasons: First, as a matter of definition, woman forms the other half of the whole that is the householder; second, because, as we have already seen, the household forms the building block of the social construction envisioned by the Mishnah's framers, it is in that setting that all other components of the social world of the system situate themselves.

In the conception at hand, which sees Israel as made up of households and villages, the economic unit also framed the social one, and the two together composed, in conglomerates, the political one, hence a political economy (from the Greek *polis, oikos*), initiated within an economic definition formed out of the elements of production. Women cannot be addressed outside of the framework of the economic unit of production defined by the household, because throughout, the Mishnah makes a single cogent statement that the organizing unit of society and politics finds its definition in the irreducible unit of economic production. The Mishnah conceives no other economic unit of production than the household, although it recognizes that such existed; its authorship perceived no other social unit of organization than the household and the conglomeration of households, although that limited vision omitted all reference to substantial parts of the population perceived to be present, for example, craftsmen, the unemployed, the landless, and the like. But what about woman in particular?

The framers of the Mishnah, for example, do not imagine a household headed by a woman; a divorced woman is assumed to return to her father's household. The framers make no provision for the economic activity of isolated individuals out of synchronic relationship with a household or a village made up of householders. Accordingly, craftsmen, day laborers, or other workers, skilled and otherwise, enter the world of social and economic transactions only in relationship to the householder. The result is that the social world is made up of households, and, because households may be made up of many families (for

example, husbands, wives, children, all of them dependents
upon the householder), households in no way are to be confused
with the family. The indicator of the family is kinship, that of
the household, "propinquity or residence." And yet, even residence is not always a criterion for membership in the household
unit since the craftsmen and day laborers are not assumed to
live in the household compound at all. Accordingly, the household forms an economic unit, with secondary criteria deriving
from that primary fact.

The mishnaic law of women defines the position of women
in the social economy of Israel's supernatural and natural reality.
That position acquires definition in relationship to men, who
give form to the Israelite social economy. It is effected through
both supernatural and natural action. What men and women do
on earth provokes a response in heaven, and the correspondences are perfect. The position of women is defined and secured
in heaven and here on earth, and that position, always and
invariably relative to men, is what comes into consideration. The
principal point of interest on Mishnah's part is the time at which
a woman changes hands. She becomes or ceases to be holy to
a particular man, enters or leaves the marital bond. These are
the dangerous and disorderly points in the relationship of wom-
en to men, therefore, as I said, in the relationship of women to
society.

Five of the seven tractates that pertain to women and family
are devoted to the transfer of women, the formation and dissolution of the marital bond. Of these, three treat what is done
by man here on earth—formation of a marital bond through
betrothal and marriage contract and dissolution through divorce
and its consequences: Qiddushin, Ketubot, and Gittin. One of
them is devoted to what is done by woman here on earth: Sotah.
Yebamot, the greatest of the seven in size and informal and
substantive brilliance, deals with the corresponding heavenly
intervention into the formation and dissolution of marriage—
the effect of death upon the marital bond, and the dissolution,
through death, of that bond. The other two tractates, Nedarim
and Nazir, draw into one the two realms of reality, heaven and
earth, as they work out the effects of vows—generally taken by
married women and subject to the confirmation or abrogation
of the husband—from earth to Heaven. These vows have a deep

impact upon the marital relationship of the woman who has taken them. We consider the natural and supernatural character of the woman's relationship to the social economy framed by man—the beginning, middle, and end of that relationship.

For our sample of the Mishnah's treatment of women, we consider the disposition of matters of doubt in marital ties. In M. Yeb. 10:1-5, we consider the results of an erroneous union. Let us consider the composition of the sustained passage. M. Yeb. 10:1 is the keystone of the first unit. There we discover that a woman's husband has gone abroad and has been reported dead. The woman remarries. Then it is discovered that the husband has not died after all. At first glance, the consequences are unambiguous. The woman is put away by both men and receives financial compensation from neither. These penalties treat the woman like an adulterer. But there are some complications: First, several second-century authorities protest that, in certain property matters, the woman does have a valid claim; second, M. Yeb. 10:1S makes explicit that these rules are invoked if the woman marries with a court's permission. In this case she has deliberately violated the sanctity of her first marriage. If she does not have permission to remarry, she may return to her first husband, and the second marriage is null. M. Yeb. 10:2 contradicts this view, saying that if the woman remarried with a court's permission, she is nonetheless put away; but she owes no sin offering. If she did not have a court's permission, she also is put away, but now she does owe an offering. The harmonization of these rules at M. Yeb. 10:1S and M. Yeb. 10:2A need not detain us.

At M. Yeb. 10:3-4 we have a series of cases in which a man or a woman enters into a marriage and finds out it was not valid. For instance, if a man goes abroad with his son, and his wife is told that the man has died, and then the son also died, she is exempt from levirate marriage. If she finds out that she was not exempt—the son having died first—she must be divorced from the second husband. Children by that husband are *mamzers*. That is to say, these children may never legitimately marry another Israelite and are permanently excluded from the community, an awful fate. There are several other cases in which marriage has taken place because of incorrect information, with the result that the woman must go forth and the children are *mamzers*. In M.

Yeb. 10:4 we have the case of a man who marries his wife's sister, falsely assuming his wife has died. Such a marriage is null and of no effect. If a man is told that his wife has died and he marries her sister and discovers that at the time of the remarriage the wife had not died, but she subsequently did die, then children born before the actual death are deemed *mamzers*, those afterward, not.

A. The woman whose husband went overseas,

B. and whom they came and told, "Your husband has died,"

C. and who remarried,

D. and whose husband afterward returned,

E. (1) goes forth from this one [the second husband] and from that one [the first].

F. And (2) she requires a writ of divorce from this one and from that.

G. And she has no claim of (3) [payment of her] marriage-contract, (4) of usufruct, (5) of alimony, or (6) of indemnification, either on this one or on that.

H. (7) If she had collected anything [of G] from this one or from that, she must return it.

I. (8) And the offspring is deemed a *mamzer*, whether born of the one marriage or the other.

J. And (9) neither one of them [if he is a priest] becomes unclean for her [if she should die and require burial].

K. And neither one of them has the right either (10) to what she finds or (11) to the fruit of her labor, or (12) to annul her vows.

L. [If] (13) she was an Israelite girl, she is rendered invalid for marriage into the priesthood; a Levite, from eating tithe; and a priest-girl, from eating heave-offering.

M. And the heirs of either one of the husbands do not inherit the property and funds provided in her marriage settlement [*ketubah*].

N. And if they died, a brother of this one and a brother of that perform the rite of removing the shoe that severs the relationship with the childless deceased's husband's surviving brother [called the rite of *halisah*] but they do not enter into levirate marriage with the childless deceased's husband's surviving brother.

O. R. Yosé says, "Her marriage-contract is [a lien] on the property of her first husband."

P. R. Eleazar says, "The first husband has a right to what she finds and to the fruit of her labor and to annul her vows."

Q. R. Simeon says, "Having sexual relations with her or performing a rite of *halisah* with her on the part of the brother of the first husband exempts her co-wife [from levirate connection].

R. "And offspring from him is not a *mamzer*."

S. But if she should remarry without permission, [since the remarriage was an inadvertent transgression and null], she is permitted to return to him.

(M. Yeb. 10:1)

We have here a clear-cut case of deliberate remarriage in error. The husband has not died; the second marriage is null. There are, as I count them, thirteen specific consequences of that fact, all of them based on the conception that the deliberate remarriage was valid and the woman is penalized on its account. The woman is prohibited from remaining wed to either man (E). She must be properly divorced by each (F). She has no material claim on either man (G, H); she loses her payment of a marriage contract. The husband does not have to support her. He does not have to compensate her for the wear and tear on property belonging to her. If she has collected any of the items listed in G, she must restore the goods. If she produced offspring with the second husband, the child is a *mamzer*; if she went back to the first man and produced offspring with him, that child would be a *mamzer* also (I). Neither one is deemed her husband as regards burial (J) or any other aspect of marriage (K). L is clear as stated. The marriage contract is not inherited by the heirs (M). The reference is to male heirs of the woman, who ordinarily would have a claim on the payment of the marriage contract. If the woman and the two men die, the male children do not inherit the payment. N is consistent with F. Just as the second man must give a writ of divorce, so his surviving brother must perform the rite of *halisah*. Yose, as we saw, differs from G3. The first husband does owe the marriage contract. Eleazar concurs with Yosé's general conception, but at K Simeon turns to N and regards the brother of the first husband as levir in all regards; therefore the second man's brother need not perform the rite of *halisah*. R differs from I (8). Offspring from the first husband are valid. It follows that, in the specified details, authorities for O–R will not concur that the first husband's relationship has been totally severed by the unfortunate mistake of his wife.

S is a separate conception. It interprets the most fundamental supposition of the whole. It holds that we invoke these thirteen penalties specifically when the woman went to court and got permission to remarry. They believe she has done so deliberately. But if she did not go to court and simply assumed the husband was dead, her action was in error. The second marriage was never valid, as it would have been had she enjoyed a court's protection. It follows that, in the conception of S, we invoke none of the penalties and the woman simply reverts to her original status.

A. [If] she was remarried at the instruction of a court,

B. She is to go forth,

C. but she is exempt from the requirement of bringing an offering.

D. [If] she did not remarry at the instruction of a court, she goes forth,

E. and she is liable to the requirement of bringing an offering.

F. The authority of the court is strong enough to exempt.

G. [If] the court instructed her to remarry, and she went and entered an unsuitable union,

H. she is liable for the requirement of bringing an offering.

I. For the court permitted her only to marry [properly].

(M. Yeb. 10:2)

M. Yeb. 10:2 augments M. Yeb. 10:1A–D, on which the pericope depends for context and meaning. A–C are balanced against D–E, then F comments on the whole. G–I form an integral, additional gloss. The point is that if the court approved her remarriage, she does not owe a sin offering, but otherwise she does. G–I then clarify the obvious: If she married as a widow to a high priest or as a divorcee to an ordinary priest, the court's instruction has not been carried out and its leniency no longer pertains. The real question is whether M. Yeb. 10:1S and M. Yeb. 10:2A–B are in accord with one another. We understand that M. Yeb. 10:1S allows the woman to return to the first husband, and M. Yeb. 10:2B has her leave both men.

I. A. The woman whose husband and son went overseas,

    B. and whom they came and told, "Your husband died, and then your son died,"

    C. and who remarried,

    D. and whom they afterward told, "Matters were reversed"—

    E. goes forth [from the second marriage].

    F. And earlier and later offspring are in the status of *mamzer.*

II. G. [If] they told her, "Your son died and afterward your husband died," and she entered in levirate marriage, and afterward they told her, "Matters were reversed,"

    H. she goes forth [from the levirate marriage].

    I. And the earlier and later offspring are in the status of a *mamzer.*

III. J. [If] they told her, "Your husband died," and she married, and afterward they told her, "He was alive, but then he died,"

    K. she goes forth [from the second marriage].

    L. And the earlier offspring is a *mamzer,* but the later is not a *mamzer.*

IV. M. [If] they told her, "Your husband died," and she became betrothed, and afterward her husband came home,

    N. she is permitted to return to him.

    O. Even though the second man gave her a writ of divorce, he has not rendered her invalid from marrying into the priesthood.

    P. This did R. Eleazar b. Matya expound, "*And a woman divorced from her husband* (Lev. 21:7)—and not from a man who is not her husband."

(M. Yeb. 10:3)

V. A. He whose wife went overseas, and whom they came and told, "Your wife has died,"

    B. and who married her sister,

    C. and whose wife thereafter came back—

    D. she is permitted to come back to him.

    E. He is permitted to marry the kinswomen of the second, and the second woman is permitted to marry his kinsmen.

    F. And if the first died, he is permitted to marry the second woman.

VI. G. [If] they said to him, "She was alive, but then she died"—

    H. the former offspring is a *mamzer* [born before the wife died], and the latter is not a *mamzer.*

    I. R. Yosé says, "Anyone who invalidates [his wife] for [marriage] with others invalidates her for marriage for himself, and whoever does not invalidate his wife for marriage with others does not invalidate her for himself.

(M. Yeb. 10:4)

At M. Yeb. 10:3 we have three parallel cases (A-L). The opening unit is in the expected apocopation, and the remainder in declarative sentences, as indicated. The important point throughout is the status of the offspring. The woman has one child before she hears that matters are not as she had supposed, then she has one after she received the report. In the first case, the woman assumes that since her husband did not die childless (A-C), she may remarry without levirate rites. If matters are reversed (D), then her remarriage is null. The second marriage now is invalid. All offspring produced in the second marriage are in the status of a *mamzer* (in Aqiba's view [M. Yeb. 4:13]), because the woman has remarried without the rite of *halisah*. The same rule applies in the contrary situation (G-I), in which the woman discovers that she has married her brother-in-law, but not in a levirate connection, which is prohibited. In the third case, the earlier offspring are produced before the husband died, the later ones, after his death. There is no reason for the latter to be deemed *mamzer*. The application of "earlier . . . later . . ." at F and I is meaningless, but at L is not (compare B. Yeb. 92a). M-P are distinct from the foregoing, although the basic problem is parallel. The betrothal is null and produces no effect, even though a writ of divorce is given.

M. Yeb. 10:4 gives us two cases parallel to M. Yeb. 10:3 G-I, J-L. In the former case, we have marriage to the woman's sister, which turns out to be illegal. It is treated as entirely null (E) I assume, along the lines of M. Yeb. 101 A. In the final case, we have a problem of offspring, flowing from the foregoing situation. The rule is the same as at M. Yeb. 10:3 J-L. An offspring produced while the wife was alive is a *mamzer*, but one produced after her death is not.

From the document's treatment of women, what have we learned about the social vision of the Mishnah? The answer to that question requires us to see the document in broad perspective, then return to what we have learned here. In everyday transactions, the framers of the document proposed to effect the vision of a steady state economy, engaged in equal exchanges of fixed wealth and intrinsic value. Essentially, the Mishnah's authorship aimed at the fair adjudication of conflict, worked out in such a way that no party gained or lost in any transaction. The task of Israelite society, as they saw it, was to maintain perfect stasis, to preserve the prevailing situation, to secure the stability of not only relationships but status and standing. To this end, in the interchanges of buying and selling, giving and taking, borrowing and lending, transactions of the market and exchanges with artisans and craftsmen and laborers, it is important to preserve the essential equality, not merely equity, of exchange. Fairness alone does not suffice. *Status quo ante* forms the criterion of the true market, reflecting as it does the exchange of value for value, in perfect balance. That is the way that, in reference to the market, the systemic point of urgency, the steady state of the polity, therefore also of the economy, is stated. The result of their economics is simple. No party in the end may have more than what he had at the outset, and none may emerge as the victim of a sizable shift in fortune and circumstance. All parties' rights in the stable and unchanging political economy are preserved. When, therefore, the condition of a person is violated, the law will secure the restoration of the antecedent status.

The Social Order
Proposed by the Mishnah

Critical to the social system of the Mishnah is its principal social entity, the village, imagined as a society that never changes in any important way, comprising households. The model, from household, to village, to "all Israel," comprehensively describes whatever part of "Israel" the authorship at hand has chosen to describe. We must therefore identify as systemically indicative the centrality of political economy—"community, self-sufficiency, and justice"—within the system of the Mishnah. It is no surprise, either, that the point of originality of the political economy of the Mishnah's system is its focus upon the society organized in relationship to the control of the means of production—the farm, for the household is always the agricultural unit. In line with what I just said, I cannot point to any other systemic statement among the Judaisms of antiquity, to any other Judaism, that, in the pattern of the Mishnah, takes as its point of departure the definition of an "Israel" as a political economy, that is, as an aggregation of villages made up of households. We realize, in the context of social thought of ancient times, that this systemic focus upon political economy also identifies the Mishnah's authorship with the prevailing conventions of a long-ago age and a faraway land, namely, Greece in the time of Aristotle. Thinkers represented by Aristotle took for granted that society was formed of self-sufficient villages, made up of self-sufficient farms—households run by householders. But, we know, in general, nothing can have been further from the facts of the world of "Israel," that is, the Jews in the land of Israel, made up not only of villages but of cities, not only of small but of larger holders, and, most of all, of people who held no land at all and never would.

In the context of a world of pervasive diversity, the Mishnah's authorship set forth a fantastic conception of a simple world of little blocks formed into big ones—households into villages, no empty spaces, but also, no vast cities. In the conception of the authorship of the Mishnah, community, or village (polis) is made up of households, and the household (*bayit/oikos*) constituted the building block of both society or community and also economy. It follows that the household forms the fundamental, irreducible, and of course, representative unit of the economy, the means of production, the locus and the unit of production. We should not confuse the household with class status, thinking of the householder as identical with the wealthy. The opposite is suggested on every page of the Mishnah, in which householders vie with craftsmen for ownership of the leavings of the loom and the chips left behind by the adze. The household, rather, forms an economic and a social classification, defined by function, specifically, economic function. A poor household was a household, and (in theory, the Mishnah's authorship knows none such in practice) a rich landholding that did not function as a center for a social and economic unit, such as a rural industrial farm, was not a household. The household constituted the center of the productive economic activities we now handle through the market. Within the household all local, (as distinct from cultic) economic, and therefore social activities and functions were held together. The unit of production also comprised the unit of social organization, and, of greater import still, the building block of all larger social (now also political) units, with special reference to the village.

In its identification of the householder as the building block of society, to the neglect of the vast panoply of "others"—"non-householders," including, after all, that half of the whole of the Israelite society comprising women—the Mishnah's authorship reduced the dimensions of society to only a single component in it: the male landowner engaged in agriculture. That is the sole option for a system that, for reasons of its own, wished to identify productivity with agriculture, individuality in God's image with ownership of land, and social standing and status, consequently, with ownership and control of the land, which constituted the sole systemically consequential means of production. If we were to list all of the persons and professions who enjoyed no role in the system, or who were treated as ancillary to the system, we must encompass not only workers—the entire landless working class!—but also craftsmen, artisans, teachers, physicians, clerks, officials, traders, merchants, and the whole of the commercial establishment, not to mention women as a caste. Such an economics, disengaged from so large a sector of the economy of which it claimed to speak, even if only in theory, can hardly be called an economics at all. Yet, as we have seen and shall realize still more keenly in the coming chapters, that economics bore an enormous burden of the systemic message and statement of the Judaism set forth by the authorship of the Mishnah.

Fair and just to all parties, the authorship of the Mishnah nonetheless speaks in particular for the Israelite landholding, proprietary person. The Mishnah's problems are the problems of the householder, its perspectives his. Its sense of what is just and fair expresses his sense of the givenness and cosmic rightness of the present condition of society. These are men of substance and of means, however modest, aching for a stable and predictable world in which to tend their crops and herds, feed their families and dependents, keep to the natural rhythms of the seasons and lunar cycles, and, in all, live out their lives within strong and secure boundaries on earth and in heaven. The sense of landed place and its limits, the sharp line drawn between village and world, on the one side, Israelite and Gentile, on the second, temple and world, on the third, evoke metaphysical correspondences. Householder, which is Israel in the village and temple beyond, form a correspondence. Only when we understand the systemic principle concerning God in relationship to Israel in its land shall we come to the fundamental and generative conception that reaches concrete expression in the here and now of the householder as the centerpiece of society.

In this regard, therefore, the Mishnah's social vision finds its definition of the realm to which "economics" applies within its conception of who forms the polis and who merely occupies space within the polis. In the Mishnah's social vision the householder is systemically the active force, and all other components of the actual economy (as distinct from the economics) prove systemically inert. Of course the Mishnah's social vision ignores most of the actuality of the Jewish people in the land of Israel in the first and second centuries. What of the economically active members of the polis who had capital and knew how to use it? If they wished to enter that elevated "Israel," which formed the social center and substance of the Mishnah's Israel, they had to purchase land. The Mishnah's social vision thus describes a steady state society. Within that vision, the disposition of a woman, always in relationship with a man, never ultimately on her own, forms a plank in a platform of a social order in which all things are at rest.

No wonder that the framers of the Mishnah conceived of the economy as one of self-sufficiency, made up as it was (in their minds, at least) of mostly self-sufficient households joined in essentially self-sufficient villages. They further carry forward the odd conception of the priestly authorship of Leviticus that the ownership of the land is supposed to be stable, indeed inalienable from the family, if not from the individual, as in Leviticus 27, so that, if a family alienates inherited property, it reverts to that family's ownership after a span of time. The conception of steady state economy therefore dominated, so that, as a matter of fact, in utter stasis, no one would rise above his natural or inherent standing, and no one would fall either. That is the economy they portray and claim to regulate through their legislation. In such an economy, the market did not form the medium of rationing but in fact had no role to play, except one: to ensure equal exchange in all transactions, so that the market formed an arena for transactions of equal value and worth among households, each possessed of a steady state worth. In the market as much as in the holding of land, no one emerged richer or poorer than when he came to market, but all remained precisely as rich or as poor as they were at the commencement of a transaction.

To place the social vision of the Mishnah's authorship into context, we must now ask a final question. For whom and to whom does the Mishnah speak? The answer allows us access to the social vision of the document.

The priesthood: In so far as the Mishnah is a document about the holiness of Israel in its land, it expresses that concept of sanctification and theory of its modes that has been shaped among those to whom the Temple and its technology of joining heaven and holy land through the sacred place defined their core of being. I mean the caste of the priests.

The scribe: In so far as the Mishnah takes up the way in which transactions are conducted among ordinary folk and takes the position that it is through documents with a supernatural consequence that transactions are embodied and expressed (surely the position of the relevant tractates on both women and damages), the Mishnah expresses what is self-evident to scribes.

Just as, to the priest, there is a correspondence between the table of the Lord in the Temple and the locus of the divinity in the heavens, so, to the scribe, there is a correspondence between the documentary expression of the human will on earth, in writs of all sorts, in the orderly provision of courts for the predictable and just disposition of exchanges of persons and property, and heaven's judgment of these same matters. When a woman becomes sanctified to a particular man on earth, through the appropriate document governing the transfer of her person and property, in heaven as well, the woman is deemed truly sanctified to that man. A violation of the writ therefore is not merely a crime. It is a sin. That is why the temple rite involving the wife accused of adultery is integral to the system of the division of women.

There are two social groups, the priestly caste and the scribal profession, not categorically symmetrical with one another, for whom in its topical program the Mishnah makes self-evident statements. We know, moreover, that in time to come, the scribal profession would become a focus of sanctification too. The scribe would be transformed into the rabbi, locus of the holy through what he knew, just as the priest had been, and would remain, locus of the holy through what he could claim for genealogy. The tractates of special interest to scribes-become-rabbis and to their governance of Israelite society, those of Women and Damages, together with certain others particularly relevant to utopian

Israel beyond the system of the land, would grow. Others would remain essentially as they were with the closure of the Mishnah. So we must notice that the Mishnah, for its part, speaks for the program of topics important to the priests. It takes up the persona of the scribes, speaking through their voice and in their manner.

The metaphor of the theater for the economy of Israel, the household of holy land and people, space and time, cult and home, leads to yet another perspective. When we look out upon the vast drama portrayed by the Mishnah, lacking an account of the one who wrote the book, and the one about whom the book was written, we notice yet one more missing component. In the fundamental and generative structure of the Mishnah, at the foundations of Judaism, we find no account of that other necessary constituent—the audience. The document never specifies to whom it speaks. The group ("class") that generates the Mishnah's problems is not at issue. True, it is taken for granted that the world of the Mishnah expresses the sanctified being of Israel in general. The Mishnah speaks about the generality of Israel, the people. But to whom the Mishnah addresses itself within Israel, and which groups are expected to want to know what the Mishnah has to say, are matters which never come to full expression.

Yet there can be no doubt of the answer to the question. The building block of mishnaic discourse, the circumstance addressed whenever the issues of concrete society and material transactions are taken up, is the householder and his context. The Mishnah knows about all sorts of economic activities, but for the Mishnah the center and focus of interest lie in the village. The village is made up of households, each a unit of production in farming. The households are constructed by, and around, the householder, father of an extended family, including his sons and their wives and children, his servants, his slaves (bondsmen), the craftsmen to whom he entrusts tasks he does not choose to do. The concerns of householders are in transactions in land. Their measurement of value is expressed in acreage of top, middle, and bottom grade. Through real estate critical transactions are worked out. The marriage settlement depends upon real property. Civil penalties are exacted through payment of real property. The principal transactions to be taken up are those of the householder who owns beasts which do damage or suffer it; who harvests his crops and sets some aside, and so by his own word and deed sanctifies them for use by the castes scheduled from on high; who uses or sells his crops and feeds his family; and who, if he is fortunate, will acquire still more land. It is to householders that the Mishnah is addressed: the pivot of society and its bulwark, the units of which the village is composed, the corporate component of the society of Israel in the limits of the village and the land. The householder, as I said, is the building block of the house of Israel, of its economy in the classic sense of the Greek word *oikos*, household, which yields our word, economics. So we see that how women are situated within the social order provides us with a key to the very structure and system that that vision of the social order is meant to convey.

To revert to the metaphor just now introduced, the great proscenium constructed by the Mishnah now looms before us. Its arch is the canopy of heaven. Its stage is the whole land of Israel. Its actors are the holy people of Israel. Its events are the drama of unfolding time and common transactions, appointed times and holy events. Yet in this grand design we look in vain for the three principal participants: the audience, the actors, and the playwright. Why? The reason is not difficult to discover when we recall that, after all, what the Mishnah really wants is for nothing to happen.The Mishnah presents a tableau, a wax museum, a diorama. It portrays a world fully perfected, and so fully at rest. The Mishnah does not want to tell us about change, how things come to be what they are. That is why there can be no sustained attention to the priesthood and its rules, the scribal profession and its constitution, and the class of householders and its interests. The Mishnah's pretense is that all of these have come to rest. They compose a world in stasis, perfect and complete, made holy because it is complete and perfect. It is an economy—again in the classic sense of the word—awaiting the divine act of sanctification, which, as at the creation of the world, would set the seal of holy rest upon an again complete creation, just as in the beginning. There is no place for the actors when what is besought is no action whatsoever, but only perfection, which is unchanging. There is room only for a description of how things are—the present tense, the sequence of completed statements and static problems. All the action lies within, in how these statements are made. Once they come to full expression, with nothing left to say, there is also nothing left to do, no need for actors, whether scribes, priests, or householders.

The components of the system at the very basis of things are the social groups to whom the system refers. These groups obviously are not comparable to one another. They are not three species of the same social genus; one is a caste, the second a profession, the third a class. What they have in common is, first, that they do form groups, and second, that the groups are social in foundation and collective in expression. That is not a sizable claim. The priesthood is a social group; it coalesces. Priests see one another as part of a single caste, with whom, for example, they will want to intermarry. The scribes are a social group because they practice a single profession, following a uniform set of rules. They coalesce in the methods by which they do their work. The householders are a social group, the basic productive unit of society around which other economic activity is perceived to function. In an essentially agricultural economy, it is quite reasonable to regard the householder, the head of a basic unit of production, as part of a single class.

This brings us back to the point at which we began—the social vision of the Mishnah, part of the encompassing worldview that the Mishnah's authorship sets forth, in the excruciating detail of the way of life that that same authorship prescribes for the social entity, holy Israel, that the authorship addresses. The Mishnah through its six divisions sets forth a coherent worldview and comprehensive way of living for holy Israel. It is a worldview that speaks of transcendent things, a way of life in response to the supernatural meaning of what is done, a heightened and deepened perception of the sanctification of Israel in deed and in deliberation. Sanctification means two things: first, distinguishing Israel in all its dimensions from the world in all its ways; second, establishing the stability, order, regularity, predictability, and reliability of Israel at moments and in contexts of danger. Danger means instability, disorder, irregularity, uncertainty, and betrayal. Each topic of the system as a whole takes up a critical and indispensable moment or context of social being. Each orders what is disorderly and dangerous. Through what is said in regard to each of the Mishnah's principal topics, what the system as a whole wishes to declare is fully expressed. These writers are obsessed with order and compelled by a vision of a world in which all things are in their right place, each bearing its own name, awaiting the benediction that comes when, everything in order, God pronounces the benediction and brings about the sanctification of the whole.

Judaism without Christianity

People commonly wonder why at the time of the formation of Christianity, in roughly the same period and under the same circumstances as the development of the Judaism of the dual Torah, the bulk of the Jews in the land of Israel and in Babylonia identified with the Judaism of the dual Torah and consequently did not adopt the new religion that had been born in their midst out of their own Scriptures. In fact Christianity, in all its varieties, and Judaism engaged in no dialogue. The issues important to one group did not pose urgent questions to the other, so they were different people talking about altogether different things. Christians and Jews in the first century and for the next two hundred years, to the fourth century, did not argue with one another. Each group went its way, emphasizing matters of concern to its own group in particular. One stressed the matter of salvation, the other of sanctification. When Christianity came into being in the first century, one important strand of the Christian movement emphasized issues of salvation, the Gospels maintaining that Jesus was, and is, the Christ, come to save the world and impose a radical change on history. At that same time, as we have seen, the Pharisees and, in their tradition, the rabbis afterward emphasized issues of sanctification, maintaining that the task of Israel is to attain that holiness of which the Temple was a singular embodiment. When, in the Gospels, we find the record of the church placing Jesus into opposition with the Pharisees, we witness the confrontation of different people talking about different things to different people.

If a principal motif of nascent Christianity was the Messiah, then Christianity raised a question that only some Jews were asking. That is clear because the Judaism without Christianity portrayed in the Mishnah did not present a richly developed doctrine of salvation and therefore did not assign to the Messiah seen as Savior an important place in its larger system. "Messiah"

Hadrian's gate, a Roman entryway into Jerusalem, built in the second century C.E. *and recently unearthed.*

in the Mishnah applied to a variety of priest, a priest anointed for battle, for example, and issues of history and the end of time occupy only a peripheral position in the Mishnah. The Mishnah's framers were answering other questions altogether, questions having to do with the two enduring pillars of the covenant: Torah and Israel. They worked out issues of sanctification rather than those of salvation. The reason is that the Mishnah emphasized the destruction of the Temple and the subsequent defeat in the failed war for the restoration. These issues, the framers of the Mishnah, maintained, raised the question of Israel's sanctity: Is Israel still a holy people, even without the holy Temple? and if so, What are the enduring instrumentalities of sanctification?

When sages developed a Judaism without a Temple and a cult, they produced in the Mishnah a system of sanctification focused on the holiness of the priesthood, the cultic festivals, the Temple and its sacrifices, as well as on the rules for protecting that holiness from levitical uncleanness—the theme of four of the six divisions of the Mishnah. In the aftermath of the conversion of the Roman Empire to Christianity and the triumph of Christianity in the generation beyond Julian "the apostate" (the fourth century), sages worked out in the pages of the Talmud of the land of Israel (the "Palestinian Talmud" or "Jerusalem Talmud") and in the exegetical compilations of the age a Judaism intersecting with the Mishnah's but essentially asymmetrical with it. That Talmud presented a system of salvation, but one focused on the salvific power of the sanctification of the holy people. The first of the two Talmuds, closed at the end of the fourth century, set the compass and locked it into place. The Judaism that was portrayed by the final document of late antiquity, the Talmud of Babylonia, laid equal emphasis on sanctification in the here and now and salvation at the end of time.

If Christianity presented an urgent problem to the sages behind the Mishnah, we cannot point to a single line of the document that says so. The figure of the Messiah in no way provided the sages of the Mishnah with an appropriate way of explaining the purpose and goal of their system, its teleology. That teleology appealing to the end of history with the coming of the Messiah came to predominate only in the Talmud of the land of Israel and in sages' documents beyond. What issues then proved paramount in a Judaism utterly divorced from Christianity in any form? We turn back to the Mishnah to find out.

The Mishnah presents a Judaism that answered a single encompassing question concerning the enduring sanctification of Israel, the people, the land, the way of life. What remained in the aftermath of the destruction of the holy place and holy cult, of the sanctity of the holy caste, the priesthood, the holy land, and, above all, the holy people and its holy way of life? The answer: sanctity persists, indelibly, in Israel, *the people*, in its way of life, in its land, in its priesthood, in its food, in its mode of sustaining life, in its manner of procreating and thus of sustaining the nation. That holiness would endure. The Mishnah then laid out the structures of sanctification: What does it mean to live a holy life? But that answer found itself absorbed, in time to come, within a successor system, with its own points of emphasis. That successor system, both continuous and asymmetrical with the Mishnah, would take over the Mishnah and turn it into "the one whole Torah of Moses, our rabbi," that became Judaism. The indicative marks are: (1) the central symbol of Torah as sages' teaching; (2) the figure of Messiah as sage; and (3) the doctrine that the people of Israel today are the family of Abraham, Isaac, and Jacob, heirs to the legacy and heritage of merit that, in the beginning, they earned and handed on to their children.

The system portrayed in the Mishnah emerged in a world in which as a political power there was no Christianity. What points do we *not* find? First, we find in the Mishnah no explicit and systematic theory of scriptural authority. We now know how much emphasis Judaism laid on Scripture in confrontation with Christianity, with important commentaries produced in the age of Constantine (fourth century). The framers of the Mishnah did not find necessary a doctrine of the authority of Scripture. Nor did they undertake a systematic exegetical effort at the linking of the principal document, the Mishnah, to Scripture. The authors saw no need. Christianity pressed the question of the standing and status of the Mishnah in relationship to Scripture, claiming that the Mishnah was compiled by humans and a forgery of God's will, which was contained only in Scripture. As a result, the doctrine of the dual Torah, explaining the origin and authority of the Mishnah, came to full expression. Sages therefore produced a document, the Mishnah, so independent of Scripture that, when the authors wished to say what Scripture said, they chose to do so in their own words and in their own way. Whatever the intent of the Mishnah's authors, therefore, it clearly did not encompass explaining to a competing Israel, heirs of the same Scriptures of Sinai, just what authority validated the document, and how the document related to Scripture.

Second, we look in vain for a teleology focused on the coming of the Messiah as the end and purpose of the system as a whole. The Mishnah's teleology in no way invokes an eschatological dimension at all. This Judaism for a world in which Christianity played no considerable role took slight interest in the Messiah and presented a teleology lacking all eschatological, therefore messianic focus.

Third, the same Judaism laid no considerable emphasis on the symbol of the Torah, although, of course, the Torah as a scroll, as a matter of status, and as revelation of God's will at Sinai, enjoyed prominence. It follows that the issues presented to Jews by the triumph of Christianity—which, informed the documents shaped in the land of Israel in the period of that triumph—did not play an important role in prior components of the unfolding canon of Judaism, in particular, the Mishnah and closely allied documents that reached closure before the fourth century. These present a Judaism, not despite Christianity, but a Judaism defined in utter indifference to Christianity. The contrast that we shall shortly draw between the Mishnah and the Judaic system emerging in the fourth century documents tells the tale.

The Mishnah shows us a Judaic system completely unaffected by the challenge of Christianity. The great motifs important to Christianity and therefore later on critical to Judaism as well play scarcely any role. To give four important examples: (1) The Mishnah presents no doctrine of the Messiah—when he will come, what Israel must do to warrant his coming; (2) The Mishnah contains no picture of the meaning of history and the place of Israel in the unfolding universal history of humanity; (3) The Mishnah provides no systematic account of the Torah and its contents—what books produced by the sages are part of the Torah of Sinai, for example—and its meaning and relationship to the Mishnah's own documents; (4) The Mishnah in no way asks the question, Who is Israel? or, Who is the true Israel? and provides no theory of what it means to be Israel.

Later, by the end of the fourth century, after Christianity had become not only legal but the state religion of the Roman Empire and therefore, in its triumph, its claims could no longer be ignored, Judaism addressed all these issues. Then the defining doctrines of Judaism emerged. At that time we find a fully articulated doctrine of the Messiah, a theory of who Israel is, a picture of the entirety of human history, and an account of what is in the Torah. All these matters, so critical as indicators of Judaism from the fourth century to the present, emerged in response to the challenge of the political triumph of Christianity, as we shall now see.

CHAPTER THREE

The Torah and Israel on Its Own

Covenant: Torah and Israel after the Temple: Israel outside of the Land

The covenant rested on three pillars: Torah, Israel, and land. When the Temple was destroyed in 70, the end of the sacrifice at the altar left only two. Israel endured in its land, but ceased to govern itself as it had before. As time passed, moreover, ever larger numbers of Jews settled in other parts of the world, so in a manner less dramatic than the destruction of the Torah, the land also faded into memory. The Judaism that focused upon life in the land, a meal shared with God made of the fruits of the land, all under the guidance of the priesthood, no longer answered the urgent questions facing the people Israel. The answers concerned the enduring components: the Torah and Israel, and the questions were, How is Israel holy? and, What does it now mean to be Israel without the Temple and the land that the Temple celebrated, as the priests had long ago taught? Of the three components of the initial Judaism, the Torah, Israel, and the land, joined through the worship of God in the Temple, Torah and Israel now formed the center of matters. While the land would remain a formidable presence, mainly in imagination, the Torah would now form the center of the Judaism that took shape around the life of the enduring people.

What now changed? Judaism had been a locative religion, centered on one place. It now became utopian, lived everywhere. Judaism had identified a hierarchy within Israel, with the priests at the apex. Now all Israelites shared equally in the labor of sanctification of everyday life and study of the Torah. To be holy now meant to live not in the holy land but in any place, yet to remain Israel, the people God first loved, and to live in accord with the Torah, the revelation of God's will, in God's own wording, which marked that love. Israel, wherever it lived, would keep the covenant by living the life made holy by the rules of the Torah and by studying the Torah, shaping everyday life within the patterns of sanctification that continued to pertain. The priests no longer mediated life from heaven to earth and earth to heaven, and the holy meal could no longer take place where it had. Now all the people would eat, in their homes, in such a way as to serve God as the priests had in the Temple, and the means of service would be obedience to and study of the Torah. We should expect that the second of the three meals of Judaism would involve everybody, all at once, at home, wherever home may be, eating all meals, under all circumstances. That is how things worked out, but once the home, not the Temple, and anywhere, not Jerusalem in particular, forms the place in which the faith takes place, then a variety of other modes of celebration and sanctification would come to the fore.

It follows that the covenant endured, but it was the Torah that was to be celebrated, the Torah, which set forth the record of the life of Israel in the land, serving God at the altar. The Torah came to the fore, therefore, as an account of what had been and what would come about once more. It was read as the story of how Israel was to live its life wherever it was located, that same holy way of life that had been embodied by the sanctity of the Temple. Moreover, the Torah also explained the conditions that had governed the possession of the land and the building of the Temple, with the promise that, when those conditions were met once again, when the Messiah would come, Israel would regain the land and rebuild the Temple. Meanwhile, Jews living wherever they were found, not only in the holy land, but

An elder patriarch kneeling in prayer in front of a Torah scroll.

among many other peoples, would study and carry out the Torah. Located throughout the world ("scattered among the
nations"), holy Israel would live by the Torah.

The Meal:
Everywhere, Any (Appropriate) Food, Everybody, All the Time

The Temple service in Jerusalem had set God's meals on the altar.
Holy Israel at the table at home would celebrate the land, the
Torah, the people, the covenant. This would come about through

words of thanksgiving of the grace recited after a meal. These would be recited not only by priests, but by ordinary folk; not only by men (for all priests were men) but also with women and children joining in; not only in one place or even in one land, but in every place sanctified by the presence of Israel and the Torah. Life now was with people. Meals of a family, at home, now were transformed into a remarkable event by words rather than by gestures, such as killing a lamb and sprinkling its blood on the altar. What is thought routine marks the measure of the extraordinary dimension of existence. That liturgy, like many others that characterized the life of Judaism in the new age, identified what was remarkable in the ordinary, changing the routine into the extraordinary.

What changes three times through the three daily meals is the notion of where one is eating, what one is eating, and the meaning of eating at all. These mere facts of hunger and satisfaction of hunger are made to represent exile and return, sin and remission of sin, this world and the world to come—all of those complementary opposites that bring to expression that life lived *as if*, that existence as metaphor and simile which have their origin in the startling notion that humanity is "in our image, after our likeness." To be a Jew now meant to live *as if*, to work out the meaning of a metaphor, and—among other occasions— three meals a day precipitate the enchantment that transforms through words the here and now into something other. That explains the enchantment of the Grace after Meals (in Hebrew, *Birkat Hammazon*) and how it transforms routine experience of hunger and satisfaction into a metaphor for Israel's life of anguished reality but ultimate redemption. Judaism is marked by all of the principal components of the faith appearing, all together, and all at once in the principal moments of transformation and enchantment.

As in Temple times, therefore, now a meal was turned into a moment of communion with the meaning of life as a part of Israel, God's people. But it was a meal that differed in every detail from the one eaten by the priests at the Lord's table in Jerusalem. The Grace after Meals tells the story, beginning with one of two psalms that is recited prior to the actual prayer. On weekdays one psalm prefaces the grace, and on Sabbaths and festivals, a second psalm is sung. The two—quite naturally—

form a complement. Let us consider them in sequence, first for the everyday:

> By the rivers of Babylon we sat down and wept
> when we remembered Zion . . .
> If I forget you, O Jerusalem,
> let my right hand wither away;
> let my tongue cling to the roof of my mouth
> if I do not remember you,
> if I do not set Jerusalem
> above my highest joy.
>
> (Ps. 137:1, 5-6 NEB)

For the Sabbath or festival:

> When the Lord brought back those that returned to Zion,
> we were like dreamers.
> Our mouth was filled with laughter,
> our tongue with singing. . . .
> Restore our fortunes, O LORD,
> as the streams in the dry land.
> They that sow in tears
> shall reap in joy.
>
> (Ps. 126:1-5)

The contrast tells the story. On weekdays we are in the here and now of exile, while on the Sabbath or festival we refer to the then and there of Zion as the world of redemption and salvation.

Judaism once more comes to expression in the eating of a meal. The act of eating entails engagement with Israel's history and destiny; and it invokes the specific moments, time past on weekdays, time future on holy days, that make the group distinctive, with a destiny all its own. The setting of the meal identifies the hunger with one historical moment, the satisfaction with another. "I was hungry and I ate and had enough." "We hungered but were fed and will have enough." From the *I* and the here and now, the occasion of the meal has moved *me* to the *we* of time and eternity. From the individual's experience of hunger and satisfaction I draw inferences about the encounter with calamity and renewal, today and the Sabbath, this life and the coming age. The psalms chosen as prelude to the Grace after Meals set the scene. Now to the action.

To understand the occasion and the setting, we must keep in mind that in the Judaism that took shape after the destruction of the Temple, the table at which meals were eaten was regarded as the equivalent of the sacred altar in the Temple. Before eating, each Jew had to attain the same state of ritual purity as the priest in the sacred act of making a sacrifice. So in the classic tradition the Grace after Meals is recited in a sacerdotal circumstance. The Grace is in four principal paragraphs, moving from the here and now to the time to come, from the meal just eaten to the banquet at the end of history. We start with the ordinary and say what is required, thanks for a real meal in today's world:

> Blessed art Thou, Lord our God, King of the Universe, who nourishes all the world by His goodness, in grace, in mercy, and in compassion: He gives bread to all flesh, for His mercy is everlasting. And because of His great goodness we have never lacked, and so may we never lack, sustenance—for the sake of His great Name. For He nourishes and feeds everyone, is good to all, and provides food for each one of the creatures He created.
> Blessed art Thou, O Lord, who feeds everyone.[1]

The first of the four principal paragraphs leaves us where we were—at the table at which we ate our meal. It effects no transformation, for it does not claim that we are someone other than whom we knew we were when we began the meal, and it does not say that we are located somewhere else. More to the point, the statement does not claim that we have eaten other than ordinary food, grown anywhere. It does say that God has given

---

1. The liturgy of Judaism is uniform in its texts, with minor variations. Where prayers are cited in these and later chapters, the translations are those in the *Weekday Prayer Book*, ed. Rabbinical Assembly of America Prayerbook Committee (New York: Rabbinical Assembly, 1962); the *Mahzor for Rosh Hashanah and Yom Kippur: A Prayer Book for the Days of Awe*, ed. Rabbi Harlow (New York: The Rabbinical Assembly, 1972); and *A Rabbi's Manual*, ed. Rabbi Harlow (New York: The Rabbinical Assembly, 1965). I cite Rabbi Harlow's translations (sometimes with minor variations) or those he has edited in these volumes. There are only minor variations between the Rabbinical Assembly's Hebrew texts and those that appear in prayerbooks published under Orthodox auspices, none that would affect anything I present here.

food, which any religious person may affirm. The food is not
transformed any more than we are. Now comes the first unanticipated statement:

> We thank Thee, Lord our God, for having given our fathers
> as a heritage a pleasant, a good and spacious land; for having
> taken us out of the land of Egypt, for having redeemed us
> from the house of bondage; for Thy covenant, which Thou
> hast set as a seal in our flesh, for Thy Torah which Thou has
> taught us, for Thy statutes which Thou hast made known to
> us, for the life of grace and mercy Thou hast graciously be-
> stowed upon us, and for the nourishment with which Thou
> dost nourish us and feed us always, every day, in every season,
> and every hour.
>
> For all these things, Lord our God, we thank and praise
> Thee; may Thy praises continually be in the mouth of every
> living thing, as it is written, *And thou shalt eat and be satisfied,*
> *and bless the Lord thy God for the good land which He hath given*
> *thee.*
>
> Blessed art Thou, O Lord, for the land and its food.

We have moved from what we have eaten to where we have
eaten, but that introduces a dissonant note. Where are we? and,
Who are we? We are no longer merely people who have eaten
a meal. Our thanks go for more than the food. Now we refer to
a "good and spacious land," meaning only what Judaism knows
as the land of Israel; to "our fathers;" to having been taken "out
of the land of Egypt," having been redeemed from slavery.

A considerable realm of being has taken over everyday reality. Now on the occasion of a cheese sandwich Judaism invokes
the entire sacred history of Israel, the Jewish people, from the
Exodus from Egypt to the circumcision of the penis. All are
invoked for a single occasion, a meal that has changed my condition from one of hunger to one of satisfaction. That is the very
meaning of the transformation, through the enchantment of the
statements at hand, of every meal—or, for the generality of Jews,
many public and communal meals—into the reenactment of the
former and present condition of Israel, the holy people. Not only
so, but the occasion points toward the end as well:

> O Lord our God, have pity on Thy people Israel, on Thy city
> Jerusalem, on Zion the place of Thy glory, on the royal house

of David Thy Messiah, and on the great and holy house which is called by Thy Name. Our God, our Father, feed us and speed us, nourish us and make us flourish, unstintingly, O Lord our God, speedily free us from all distress.

And let us not, O Lord our God, find ourselves in need of gifts from flesh and blood, or of a loan from anyone save from Thy full, generous, abundant, wide-open hand; so we may never be humiliated, or put to shame.

O rebuild Jerusalem, the holy city, speedily in our day. Blessed art Thou, Lord, who in mercy will rebuild Jerusalem. Amen.

The climax refers to Jerusalem, Zion, David, the Messiah, the Temple—where God was sustained in times past; then dependence on God alone, not on mortals; and the rebuilding of Jerusalem. All of these closely related symbols invoke the single consideration of time at its end: the coming of the Messiah and the conclusion of history as we now know it. The opening psalms have prepared us for this appeal to the end time: exile on weekdays, return to Zion on Sabbaths and holy days.

Blessed art Thou, Lord our God, King of the Universe, Thou God, who art our Father, our powerful king, our creator and redeemer, who made us, our holy one, the holy one of Jacob, our shepherd, shepherd of Israel, the good king, who visits His goodness upon all; for every single day He has brought good, He does bring good, He will bring good upon us; He has rewarded us, does regard, and will always reward us, with grace, mercy and compassion, amplitude, deliverance and prosperity, blessing and salvation, comfort, and a living, sustenance, pity and peace, and all good—let us not want any manner of good whatever.

The fourth and concluding paragraph of the Grace after Meals returns us to the point at which we began: thanks for lunch. What follows is tacked on for special occasions. Of the four paragraphs, the first and the fourth begin and end in the here and now. The fourth multiplies prayers for future grace alongside thanks for goodness now received. The two in the middle invoke a different being altogether. What has happened at the meal is

A bride and groom stand beside the ketubah, the legal wedding document.

simple. The diners were hungry and ate, a commonplace, entirely secular action, but through the medium of words the experience of hunger and of eating is turned into an encounter with another world of meaning altogether. The rite, an act of thought and imagination, transforms time and space, moving us from no where in particular to a particular place, changing all of us from the here and now into the social entity of the past and future then. The words we say change the world of the "I" by telling "me" that I am in more than the here and now, and live in more than the perceived present, because I am more than a mere I, part of a larger "we."

A Special Meal and Its Rite:
The Wedding Feast

If we asked for a definition of the Judaism that took shape in the aftermath of the end of Temple and cult, leaving Torah and people, the Grace after Meals provides a compendious and proportionate account. Nevertheless, we grasp the shape and structure of the faith as a whole—its worldview and the mythic representation of that worldview—in a variety of rites. In a well-integrated religious system such as this one, any rite serves to tell us everything all at once. We should not be surprised that just as the Grace after Meals turns a natural and common experience into the enactment and celebration of another place and time and world altogether, so does the rite of the *Huppah*—the marriage canopy—turn one thing into something else.

It is another meal, of course, for the marriage rite always involves a wedding feast. The seven blessings over wine said under the marriage canopy are repeated in the grace that follows the feast. When we examine the words recited both at the *Huppah* and at the wedding meal, we see how the prayer transforms the space, time, action, and community of the groom and the bride. It is now in the beginning, and we speak of Adam and Eve in Eden. The action then invokes creation, the making of a new Eden. Stripped down to essentials, the union of woman and man becomes the beginning of a new creation, so that the woman becomes Eve, the man, Adam. At the marriage rite a new world begins—a family, a social entity, humanity at the beginning of new creation of life.

These seven blessings (*sheva berakhot*) over a cup of wine begin with creation, that is, the world of Eden:

> Praised are You, O Lord our God, King of the universe, who created all things for Your glory.
>
> Praised are You, O Lord our God, King of the universe, Creator of Adam.
>
> Praised are You, O Lord our God, King of the Universe, who created man and woman in his image, fashioning woman from man as his mate, that together they might perpetuate life. Praised are You, O Lord, Creator of man.

A Jewish wedding with the marriage canopy.

The sequence of three is perfectly realized: first, creation of all things; then, creation of Man; finally, creation of man and woman in his image. These words invoke a world for which the occasion at hand serves as metaphor. "We now are like them then"—that is what is at stake.

Israel's history begins with creation—first, the creation of the vine, symbol of the natural world. Creation is for God's glory. All things speak to nature, to the physical as much as the spiritual, for all things were made by God. In Hebrew, the blessings end, "who formed the *Adam* (humankind)." All things glorify God; above all creation is Adam. The theme of ancient paradise is introduced by the simple choice of the word *Adam*, so heavy with meaning. The myth of man's creation is rehearsed: Man and woman are in God's image, together complete and whole, creators of life, "life God." Woman was fashioned from man together with him to perpetuate life. And again, "blessed is the creator of Adam." We have moved, therefore, from the natural world to the archetypical realm of paradise. Before us we see not merely a man and a woman, but Adam and Eve.

The enchantment works its wonder by identifying the moment at hand, by telling us what we are like, that is, what is really happening. Under the circumstances formed by that mode of metaphorical thought, the reality that generates meaning is "man and woman in his image," Eden, creation. The bride and groom become that reality. They wonder whether this is really true. The world is truly a stage, the men and women, really players. But here one actor takes two roles at once:

> May Zion rejoice as her children are restored to her in joy.
> Praised are You, O Lord, who causes Zion to rejoice at her children's return.

A jarring intrusion, Zion comes uninvited. No one mentioned her. But as we saw in the Grace after Meals, *if I forget you, O Jerusalem,* . . . and, given the standing of Zion as a metaphor for the resolution of Israel's exile and the human condition of suffering, simultaneously, who can find surprising the entry of this new character, this persona?

This Adam and this Eve are also Israel, children of Zion the mother, as expressed in the fifth blessing. Zion lies in ruins, her children scattered. Adam and Eve cannot celebrate together without thought to the condition of the mother, Jerusalem. The children will one day come home. The mood is hopeful yet sad, as it was meant to be, for archaic Israel mourns as it rejoices and rejoices as it mourns. Quickly then, back to the happy occasion, for we do not let mourning lead to melancholy: "Grant perfect joy to the loving companions," for they are creators of a new line in humankind—the new Adam, the new Eve. May their home be the Garden of Eden, and if joy is there, then "praised are you for the joy of bride and groom."

The joy of the moment gives a foretaste of the coming joy of restoration, redemption, and return. Now the two roles become one in that same joy, first Adam and Eve, groom and bride, Eden then, the marriage canopy now:

> Grant perfect joy to these loving companions, as You did to the first man and woman in the Garden of Eden. Praised are You, O Lord, who grants the joy of bride and groom.

That same joy comes again in the metaphors of Zion the bride and Israel the groom. This is made very specific, for the words in italics allude to Jeremiah's vision, when all seemed lost, that Jerusalem, about to fall and lose its people, would one day ring with the shouts of the returned and redeemed, the slaughtered and the enslaved. For this reason the concluding blessing returns to the theme of Jerusalem. This time it evokes the tragic hour of Jerusalem's first destruction. When everyone had given up hope, supposing that with the end of Jerusalem had come the end of time, only Jeremiah counseled renewed hope. With the enemy at the gate, he sang of coming gladness:

> Thus says the LORD: In this place of which you say, "It is a waste, without man or beast," in the cities of Judah and the streets of Jerusalem that are desolate, without man or inhabitant or beast, there shall be heard again the voice of mirth and the voice of gladness, the voice of the bridegroom and the voice of the bride, the voices of those who sing, as they bring thank offerings to the house of the LORD . . .
> For I will restore the fortunes of the land as at first, says the LORD.
>
> (Jer. 33:10-11, RSV)

The joy is not in two but in three masks: Eden then, marriage party now, and Zion in the coming age:

> Praised are You, O Lord our God, King of the universe, who created joy and gladness, bride and groom, mirth, song, delight and rejoicing, love and harmony, peace and companionship. O Lord our God, may there ever *be heard in the cities of Judah and in the streets of Jerusalem voices of joy and gladness, voices of bride and groom, the jubilant voices of those joined in marriage under the bridal canopy, the voices of young people feasting and singing.*

The closing blessing is not merely a literary artifice or a learned allusion to the ancient prophet. It defines the exultant, jubilant climax of this myth acted out: Just as here and now there stand before us Adam and Eve, so here and now in this wedding, the olden sorrow having been rehearsed, we listen to the voice of gladness that is coming. The joy of this new creation prefigures the joy of the Messiah's coming, hope for which is very present in this hour. When he comes, the joy then will echo the joy of bride and groom before us. Zion the bride, Israel the groom, united now as they will be reunited by the compassionate God—these stand under the marriage canopy.

As with the ordinary Grace after Meals, so here, the moment is transformed and transcends what is merely personal. These seven blessings say nothing of private people and of their anonymously falling in love, nor do they speak of the community of Israel, as one might expect on a public occasion. Lover and beloved rather are transformed from natural to mythical figures. The blessings speak of archetypical Israel, represented here and now by the bride and groom. All becomes credible not by what is said but by what is felt: that joy, that sense of witness to what we ourselves experience. These are the two ingredients that transform. The natural events of human life—here, the marriage of ordinary folk—are by myth heightened into a reenactment of Israel's life as a people. In marriage, individuals stand in the place of mythic figures, yet remain, after all, a man and a woman. What gives their love its true meaning is their performing the myth of creation, revelation, and redemption, here and now embodied in that love.

Everywhere, Everybody, All the Time: Daily Worship in Place of Sacrifice, The Shema.

SHEMA YISRAEL, ADONAI ELOHENU, ADONAI EHAD
HEAR, O ISRAEL, THE LORD OUR GOD, THE LORD IS ONE

The Judaism that developed in the aftermath of the destruction of the Temple makes the same statement in every setting, not only at meals. In times past, and in Orthodox Judaism today, public prayers are recited three times a day, at morning, dusk, and night, by individual women and men, and in the synagogue, going over the same themes that we have observed in the Grace after Meals. The emphasis throughout is on the holy life that is to be lived everywhere, not only in Jerusalem; by everybody, not only by the priests; all the time, daily and on holy days, and not only on pilgrim festivals or other special occasions on which people would find their way to the Temple. When the Temple was destroyed, Israel became the sanctuary, and prayer took the place of sacrifice.

The recitation of public prayers, obligatory to the community (as well as to the individual) encompasses three important matters: recitation of the creed, petition for the needs and welfare of the community and the individual, and the situation or identification of the community in its larger setting. Accordingly, we find ourselves on a tour through the world that Judaism composes for Israel: worldview, way of life, larger theory of who is Israel. I cannot imagine a more systematic or orderly exposition of that enchanted world precipitated by the recitation of the right words in the right way at the right time. The Shema, "Hear O Israel, the Lord, our God, the Lord is one" (*Shema Yisrael, Adonai Elohenu, Adonai ehad*) presents the creed, hence the view of the world in its entirety. The Prayer or Eighteen Benedictions (Hebrew: *Shemoneh esré*) covers the everyday needs of the community viewed in its own terms. The concluding prayer, *Alenu* ("It is our duty . . .") then states the theory of Israel to which the worldview of the Shema and the way of life outlined in the Eighteen Benedictions refer.

Evening and morning, Israel individually and communally proclaims the unity and uniqueness of God. The proclamation is preceded and followed by blessings. The whole constitutes the credo of the Judaic tradition. It is "what the Jews believe." Components recur everywhere. The three elements of the creed cover creation, revelation, and redemption, that is to say, God as Creator of the world, God as Revealer of the Torah, God as Redeemer of Israel. The recital of the Shema is introduced by a celebration of God as Creator of the world. In the morning, the individual, in community or not, recites these preliminary benedictions:

1. Creation of the world, attested by sunrise, sunset

Praised are You, O Lord our God, King of the universe.
You fix the cycles of light and darkness;
You ordain the order of all creation

You cause light to shine over the earth;
Your radiant mercy is upon its inhabitants.
In Your goodness the work of creation
Is continually renewed day by day. . . .
O cause a new light to shine on Zion;
May we all soon be worthy to behold its radiance.
Praised are You, O Lord, Creator of the heavenly bodies.[2]

The corresponding prayer in the evening refers to the setting of the sun:

Praised are You. . . .
Your command brings on the dusk of evening.
Your wisdom opens the gates of heaven to a new day.
With understanding You order the cycles of time;
Your will determines the succession of seasons;
You order the stars in their heavenly courses.
You create day, and You create night,
Rolling away light before darkness. . . .
Praised are You, O Lord, for the evening dusk.

Morning and evening, Israel responds to the natural order of the world with thanks and praise of God who created the world and who actively guides the daily events of nature. Whatever happens in nature gives testimony to the sovereignty of the Creator. That testimony is not in unnatural disasters, but in the most ordinary events: sunrise and sunset. These, especially, evoke the religious response to set the stage for what follows.

For Israel, God is not merely Creator, but purposeful Creator. The works of creation serve to justify and to testify to Torah, the revelation of Sinai. Torah is the mark not merely of divine sovereignty, but of divine grace and love, the source of life here and now and in eternity. Second blessing follows:

2. Revelation of the Torah as the expression of God's love for Israel

Deep is Your love for us, O Lord our God;
Bounteous is Your compassion and tenderness.

2. The Prayer, or Eighteen Benedictions, follows Rabbi Harlow's translation in *Mahzor for Rosh Hashanah and Yom Kippur*. The same is true for the remaining extracts in this chapter and the ones that follow, concerning the liturgy of Judaism.

You taught our fathers the laws of life,
And they trusted in You, Father and king,
For their sake be gracious to us, and teach us,
That we may learn Your laws and trust in You.
Father, merciful Father, have compassion upon us:
Endow us with discernment and understanding.
Grant us the will to study Your Torah,
To heed its words and to teach its precepts. . . .
Enlighten our eyes in Your Torah,
Open our hearts to Your commandments. . . .
Unite our thoughts with singleness of purpose
To hold You in reverence and in love. . . .
You have drawn us close to You;
We praise You and thank You in truth.
With love do we thankfully proclaim Your unity.
And praise You who chose Your people Israel in love.

Here is the way in which revelation takes concrete and specific form in the Judaic tradition: God, the Creator, revealed his will for creation through the Torah, given to Israel his people. That Torah contains the "laws of life."

Moved to worship by the daily miracle of sunrise and sunset, corporate Israel under all conditions, all together, responds with the prayer that Israel, like nature, may enjoy divine compassion. But what does that compassion consist of? The ability to understand and the will to study Torah! This is the mark of the relationship between God and the human being—the Jewish person in particular—that a person's eyes are open to Torah and that a person's heart is open to the commandments. These are the means of divine service and of reverence and love for God. Israel sees itself as "chosen"—close to God—because of Torah, and it finds in its devotion to Torah the marks of its chosenness. The covenant made at Sinai—a contract on Israel's side, to hear and do the Torah; on God's side, to be the God of Israel—is recalled by natural events and then confirmed by the deeds and devotion of corporate Israel. The corporate framework of the public prayers is implicit everywhere and explicit in the recurrent *we*. We look in vain for the private person. We see instead the community affirming its obligation, carrying out its duty. In this context, those rites of passage upon which, nowadays, people focus with such intent appear somewhat trivial and personal, forming a stunning contrast to the majestic and public concern for the entirety of the cosmos and all of life.

In the Shema, Torah (revelation) leads Israel to enunciate the chief teaching of revelation:

> Hear, O Israel, the Lord our God, the Lord is One.

This proclamation of the Shema is followed by three scriptural passages. The first is from Deuteronomy:

> You shall love the LORD your God with all your heart, and with all your soul, with all your might.
>
> (Deut. 6:5-9, RSV)

And further, one must diligently teach one's children these words and talk of them everywhere and always, and place them on one's forehead, doorposts, and gates. The second Scripture is Deut. 11:13-21, which emphasizes that if Jews keep the commandments, they will enjoy worldly blessings; but that if they do not, they will be punished and disappear from the good land God gives them. The third passage is Num. 15:37-41, the commandment to wear fringes on the corners of one's garments. The fringes today are attached to the prayer shawl worn at morning services by Conservative and Reform Jews, and worn on a separate undergarment for that purpose by Orthodox Jews. They remind the Jew of *all* the commandments of the Lord.

The proclamation is completed and yet remains open, for having created humanity and revealed his will, God is not unaware of events since Sinai. Humanity is frail, and in the contest between the Word of God and the will of humanity, Torah is not always the victor. We inevitably fall short of what is asked of us, and Jews know that their own history consists of divine punishment for human failure time and again. The theme of redemption, therefore, is introduced. Redemption—the third element in the tripartite worldview, in addition to creation and revelation—resolves the tension between what we are told to do and what we are actually able to accomplish. In the end it is the theme of God as Redeemer, rather than Creator or Revealer, that concludes the twice-daily drama:

3. Redemption of Israel then and in the future

You are our King and our father's King,
Our redeemer and our father's redeemer.
You are our creator. . . .
You have ever been our redeemer and deliverer
There can be no God but You. . . .
You, O Lord our God, rescued us from Egypt;
You redeemed us from the house of bondage. . . .
You split apart the waters of the Red Sea,
The faithful you rescued, the wicked drowned. . . .
Then Your beloved sang hymns of thanksgiving. . . .
They acclaimed the King, God on high,
Great and awesome source of all blessings,
The everliving God, exalted in his majesty.
He humbles the proud and raises the lowly;
He helps the needy and answers His people's call. . . .
Then Moses and all the children of Israel
Sang with great joy this song to the Lord:
Who is like You O Lord among the mighty?
Who is like You, so glorious in holiness?
So wondrous your deeds, so worthy of praise!
The redeemed sang a new song to You;
They sang in chorus at the shore of the sea,
Acclaiming Your sovereignty with thanksgiving:
The Lord shall reign for ever and ever.
Rock of Israel, arise to Israel's defense!
Fulfill Your promise to deliver Judah and Israel.
Our redeemer is the Holy One of Israel,
The Lord of Hosts is His name.
Praised are You, O Lord, redeemer of Israel.

Redemption is both in the past and in the future. That God not only creates but also redeems is attested by the redemption from Egyptian bondage. The congregation repeats the exultant song of Moses and the people at the Red Sea, not as scholars making a learned allusion, but as participants in the salvation of old and of time to come.

Then the people turn to the future and ask that Israel once more be redeemed. But redemption is not only past and future. In commonplace, daily events redemption is already present, when the needy are helped, when the proud are humbled, and the lowly are raised. Just as creation is not only in the beginning, but happens every day, morning and night, so redemption is not only at the Red Sea, but every day, in humble events. Just as revelation was not at Sinai alone, but takes place whenever people study Torah, whenever God opens their hearts to the commandments, so redemption and creation are daily events. We note once more that while the individual may recite these prayers, the affirmation concerns the entire social entity, holy Israel. The great cosmic events of creation in the beginning, redemption at the Red Sea, and revelation at Sinai are everywhere, everyday near at hand. Israel views secular reality under the aspect of eternal, ever-recurring events. What happens to Israel and to the world, whether good or evil, falls into the pattern revealed of old and made manifest each day. Historical events produce a framework in which future events will find a place and by which they will be understood. Everything that happens can be subsumed by the paradigm of creation, revelation, and redemption.

Everywhere, Everybody, All the Time: Daily Worship in Place of Sacrifice, The Prayer.

The creed of Judaism is contained in the Shema, the first of the three required components of obligatory public worship; the second component is prayers of petition. This is called "the Prayer," or "the Eighteen Benedictions." (The third of the three elements, a prayer of departing for the world to come, then follows.) The Prayer, made up of praise and petitions, directly addresses God with requests. What the community asks for—always in the plural—concerns the public welfare and matters we would today assign to the category of public policy as much as personal need. In the morning, noon, and evening these weekday prayers of petition comprise the Eighteen Benedictions. Some of these, in particular those at the beginning and the end, recur in Sabbath and festival prayers. The prayer of petition is said silently. Each individual prays by and for himself or herself,

A nineteenth-century menorah from North Africa.

but together with other silent, praying individuals. The Eighteen
Benedictions are then repeated aloud by the prayer leader, for
the prayer is both private and public, individual and collective.
To contemplate the power of these prayers imagine a room full
of people, all standing by themselves yet in close proximity, some
swaying this way and that, all addressing themselves directly
and intimately to God in a whisper or in a low tone. They do
not move their feet, for they are now standing before the King

of kings, and it is not mete to shift and shuffle. If spoken to, they will not answer. Their attention is fixed upon the words of supplication, praise, and gratitude. When they begin, they bend their knees—so too toward the end—and at the conclusion they step back and withdraw from the Presence. In the following text of the three opening benedictions, the introductory three paragraphs define the one to whom petition is addressed, the God of the founders, who is omnipotent and holy.

The founders:
Praised are you, Lord our God and God of our fathers, God of Abraham, God of Isaac, and God of Jacob, great, mighty, revered God, exalted, who bestows lovingkindness and is master of all things, who remembers the acts of loyalty of the founders and who in love will bring a redeemer to their descendants for his great name's sake. King, helper, savior and shield, praised are you, Lord, shield of Abraham.

God's power:
You are powerful forever, Lord, giving life to the dead. You are great in acts of salvation. You sustain the living in loyalty and bring the dead to life in great mercy, holding up the falling, healing the sick, freeing the prisoners, and keeping faith with those who sleep in the dirt. Who is like you, Almighty, and who is compared to you, King who kills and gives life and brings salvation to spring up. And you are reliable to give life to the dead. Praised are you, Lord, who gives life to the dead.

God's sanctity:
We shall sanctify your name in the world just as they sanctify it in the heights of heaven. . . . Holy, holy, holy is the Lord of hosts, the whole earth is full of his glory . . .

On weekdays petitionary prayer follows, covering these matters (the topic is followed by the prayer). The concluding phrase, "Praised are you," then marks the conclusion of the blessing at hand:

Wisdom-repentance
You graciously endow man with intelligence;
You teach him knowledge and understanding.
Grant us knowledge, discernment, and wisdom.

Praised are You, O Lord, for the gift of knowledge.
Our Father, bring us back to Your Torah.
Our King, draw us near to Your service;
Lead us back to You truly repentant.
Praised are You, O Lord who welcomes repentance.
Forgiveness-redemption
Our Father, forgive us, for we have sinned;
Our King, pardon us, for we have transgressed;
You forgive sin and pardon transgression.
Praised are You, gracious and forgiving Lord.
Behold our affliction and deliver us.
Redeem us soon for the sake of Your name,
For You are the mighty Redeemer.
Praised are You, O Lord, Redeemer of Israel.
Heal us—bless our years.
Heal us, O Lord, and we shall be healed;
Help us and save us, for You are our glory.
Grant perfect healing for all our afflictions,
O faithful and merciful God of healing.
Praised are You, O Lord, Healer of His people.
O Lord our God! Make this a blessed year;
May its varied produce bring us happiness.
Bring blessing upon the whole earth.
Bless the year with Your abounding goodness.
Praised are You, O Lord, who blesses our years.
Gather our exiles—reign over us.
Sound the great horn (shofar) to herald [our] freedom;
Raise high the banner to gather all exiles;
Gather the dispersed from the corners of the earth.
Praised are You, O Lord, who gathers our exiles.
Restore our judges as in days of old;
Restore our counsellors as in former times;
Remove from us sorrow and anguish.
Reign over us alone with loving kindness;
With justice and mercy sustain our cause.
Praised are You, O Lord, King who loves justice.
Humble the arrogant—sustain the righteous.
Frustrate the hopes of those who malign us;
Let all evil very soon disappear;
Let all Your enemies be speedily destroyed.

May You quickly uproot and crush the arrogant;
May You subdue and humble them in our time.
Praised are You, O Lord, who humbles the arrogant.
Let Your tender mercies, O Lord God, be stirred.
For the righteous, the pious, the leaders of Israel,
Toward devoted scholars and faithful proselytes.
Be merciful to us of the house of Israel;
Reward all who trust in You;
Cast our lot with those who are faithful to You.
May we never come to despair, for our trust is in You.
Praised are You, O Lord, who sustains the righteous.
Favor Your city and Your people.
Have mercy, O Lord, and return to Jerusalem, Your city;
May Your Presence dwell there as You promised.
Rebuild it now, in our days and for all time;
Re-establish there the majesty of David, Your servant.
Praised are You, O Lord, who rebuilds Jerusalem.
Bring to flower the shoot of Your servant David.
Hasten the advent of the messianic redemption;
Each and every day we hope for Your deliverance.
Praised are You, O Lord, who assures our deliverance.
O Lord, our God, hear our cry!
Have compassion upon us and pity us;
Accept our prayer with loving favor.
You, O God, listen to entreaty and prayer.
O King, do not turn us away unanswered,
For You mercifully heed Your people's supplication.
Praised are You, O Lord, who is attentive to prayer.
O Lord, our God, favor Your people Israel.
Accept with love Israel's offering of prayer;
May our worship be ever acceptable to You.
May our eyes witness Your return in mercy to Zion.
Praised are You, O Lord, whose Presence returns to Zion.
Our thankfulness
We thank You, O Lord our God and God of our fathers,
Defender of our lives, Shield of our safety;
Through all generations we thank You and praise You.
Our lives are in Your hands, our souls in Your charge.
We thank You for the miracles which daily attend us,
For Your wonders and favor morning, noon, and night.

You are beneficent with boundless mercy and love.
From of old we have always placed our hope in You.
For all these blessings, O our King,
We shall ever praise and exalt You.
Every living creature thanks You, and praises You in truth.
O God, You are our deliverance and our help. Selah!
Praised are You, O Lord, for Your goodness and Your glory.
Peace and well-being
Grant peace and well-being to the whole house of Israel;
Give us of Your grace, Your love, and Your mercy.
Bless us all, O our Father, with the light of Your Presence.
It is Your light that revealed to us Your life-giving Torah,
And taught us love and tenderness, justice, mercy, and peace.
May it please You to bless Your people in every season,
To bless them at all times with Your fight of peace.
Praised are You, O Lord, who blesses Israel with peace.

The first two petitions pertain to intelligence. Israel thanks
God for the mind—knowledge, wisdom, and discernment. But
knowledge is for a purpose, which is knowledge of Torah. Discernment leads to the service of God and produces a spirit of
repentance. We cannot pray without setting ourselves right with
God, and that means repenting for what has separated us from
God. Torah is the way to repentance and to return, so knowledge
leads to Torah, Torah to repentance, and repentance to God. The
logical next step is the prayer for forgiveness. That is the sign
of return. God forgives sin; God is gracious and forgiving. Once
we discern what we have done wrong through the guidance of
Torah, we seek to be forgiven. Sin leads to affliction. Affliction
stands at the beginning of the way to God; once we have taken
that way, we ask for our suffering to end; we beg redemption.
This is then specified. We ask for healing, salvation, a blessed
year. Healing without prosperity means we may suffer in good
health or starve in a robust body. So along with the prayer for
healing goes the supplication for worldly comfort.
    The individual's task is done. But what of the community?
Health and comfort are not enough. The world is unredeemed.
Jews are enslaved, in exile, and alien. At the end of days a great
shofar, or ram's horn, will sound to herald the Messiah's coming.
This is now besought. Israel at prayer asks first for the proclamation of freedom, then for the ingathering of the exiles to the

promised land. Establishing the messianic kingdom, God also needs to restore a wise and benevolent government, good judges, good counselors, and loving justice. Meanwhile Israel finds itself maligned. As the prayer sees things, arrogant men who hate Israel hate God as well; they should be humbled. The pious and righteous—the scholars, the faithful proselytes, the whole house of Israel that trusts in God—should be rewarded and sustained. Above all, remember Jerusalem. Rebuild the city and dwell there. Set up Jerusalem's messianic king, David, and make him to prosper. These are the themes of the daily prayer: personal atonement, good health, and good fortunes; collective redemption, freedom, the end of alienation, good government, and true justice; the final and complete salvation of the land and of Jerusalem by the Messiah. At the end comes a prayer that prayer may be heard and found acceptable, then an expression of thanksgiving for the miracles and mercies already enjoyed morning, noon, and night. At the end is the prayer for peace, a peace that consists of wholeness for the sacred community.

The third of the three components of the communal worship draws the community outward into the world. When Jews complete any of their worship services, they mark the conclusion by making a statement concerning themselves in the world—the corporate community looking outward. Every synagogue service concludes with a prayer prior to going forth, called *Alenu* (from its first word in Hebrew). Like the Exodus, the moment of the congregation's departure becomes a celebration of Israel's God, a self-conscious, articulated rehearsal of Israel's peoplehood, but now it is the end, rather than the beginning, of time that is important. When Jews go forth, they look forward:

> Let us praise Him, Lord over all the world;
> Let us acclaim Him, Author of all creation.
> He made our lot unlike that of other peoples;
> He assigned to us a unique destiny.
> We bend the knee, worship, and acknowledge
> The King of kings, the Holy One, praised is He.
> He unrolled the heavens and established the earth;
> His throne of glory is in the heavens above;
> His majestic Presence is in the loftiest heights.
> He and no other is God and faithful King,

Even as we are told in His Torah:
Remember now and always, that the Lord is God;
Remember, no other is Lord of heaven and earth.
We, therefore, hope in You, O Lord our God,
That we shall soon see the triumph of Your might,
That idolatry shall be removed from the earth,
And false gods shall be utterly destroyed.
Then will the world be a true kingdom of God,
When all mankind will invoke Your name,
And all the earth's wicked will return to You.
Then all the inhabitants of the world will surely know
That to You every knee must bend,
Every tongue must pledge loyalty.
Before You, O Lord, let them bow in worship,
Let them give honor to Your glory.
May they all accept the rule of Your kingdom.
May You reign over them soon through all time.
Sovereignty is Yours in glory, now and forever.
So it is written in Your Torah:
The Lord shall reign for ever and ever.

Difference—in secular terms people forming a separate, distinct group—becomes destiny here. Israel thanks God that it enjoys a unique destiny, but the community asks that he who made their lot unlike that of all others will soon rule as sovereign over all people. The secular difference, which stands for the unique destiny, is for the time being only. When the destiny is fulfilled, there will be no further difference. The natural eye beholds a social group with some particular cultural characteristics defining that group. The myth of peoplehood transforms difference into destiny.

Everywhere, Everybody, All the Time: The Sabbath, Festivals, and Days of Awe

THE SABBATH

Observed from most ancient times, the Sabbath came to prominence after the destruction of the Temple because it survived—

a regular, perennial holy occasion, one that everywhere everybody could keep, and that most people kept as the centerpiece
of their holy life. As with the Grace after Meals, the Shema, and
the Prayer, sanctifying the Sabbath formed the special occasion,
on which the entirety of the whole life would come to expression:
everything joined in one thing. Like the Grace after Meals and
the Shema, the Sabbath, a day of rest, relaxation, and study of
the Torah, joins together the paramount themes of creation,
revelation, and redemption.

The Sabbath celebrates the completion and perfection of creation, that is, of nature:

> When the heaven and earth were done, and all their array,
> when God had finished the work that he had been doing, then
> he rested on the seventh day from all the work that he had
> done. Then God blessed the seventh day and made it holy,
> because on it God desisted from all of the work of creating in
> which he had been engaged.
>
> (Gen. 2:1-3)

That account of the first Sabbath stands in judgment on those
who, like God, create, but, unlike God, never rest. How did
people then and how do people now keep the Sabbath? All week
long they look forward to it, and the anticipation enhances the
ordinary days. By Friday afternoon in general those who keep
the Sabbath will have bathed, put on their Sabbath garments,
and set aside the affairs of the week. At home, the family—
husband, wife, children, or whoever stands for family—will have
cleaned, cooked, and arranged the finest table. It is common to
invite guests for the Sabbath meals. The Sabbath begins at sunset
on Friday and ends when three stars appear Saturday night.
After a brief service the family comes together to enjoy its best
meal of the week, a meal at which particular Sabbath foods are
served.

In the morning comes the Sabbath service—including a public reading from the Torah and the prophetic writings—and an
additional service in memory of the Temple sacrifices on Sabbaths
of old. Then home for lunch and commonly a Sabbath nap, the
sweetest part of the day. As the day wanes, the synagogue calls
for a late afternoon service, followed by Torah study and a third

meal. Then comes a ceremony, *havdalah,* "separation," effected
with spices, wine, and candlelight, between the holy time of the
Sabbath and the ordinary time of weekday. I do not mean to
suggest that this idyllic picture characterizes all Jews' Sabbath
observance, nor do I believe that the only way to sanctify the
Sabbath is in the received way I have described (though many
do). Reform Judaism has displayed the wisdom to honor a variety
of abstinences and actions as acts of sanctification of the time of
the Sabbath. But, in the main, the Sabbath works its wonder
when people retreat into family—however they understand their
family—and take leave of work and the workaday world.

This simple, regular observance has elicited endless praise.
To the Sabbath-observing Jew, the Sabbath is the chief sign of
God's grace as is stated in the sanctification of the Sabbath wine.

> For thou hast chosen us and sanctified us above all nations,
> in love and favor hast given us thy holy Sabbath as an inher-
> itance.

Likewise in the Sabbath morning liturgy the Sabbath is seen as
a gift to Israel:

> You did not give it [the Sabbath] to the nations of the earth,
> nor did you make it the heritage of idolaters, nor in its rest
> will unrighteous men find a place.
> But to Israel your people you have given it in love, to the
> seed of Jacob whom you have chosen, to that people who
> sanctify the Sabbath day. All of them find fulfillment and joy
> from your bounty.
> For the seventh day did you choose and sanctify as the most
> pleasant of days and you called it a memorial to the works of
> creation.

Here again we find a profusion of themes, this time centered
upon the Sabbath. The Sabbath is a sign of the covenant. It is a
gift of grace, which neither idolaters nor evil people may enjoy.
It is the testimony of the chosenness of Israel, and it is the most
pleasant of days. Keeping the Sabbath is living in God's kingdom:

> Those who keep the Sabbath and call it a delight will rejoice
> in your kingdom.

So states the additional Sabbath prayer. Keeping the Sabbath now is a foretaste of the redemption: "This day is for Israel light and rejoicing." The rest of the Sabbath is, as the afternoon prayer affirms, "a rest granted in generous love, a true and faithful rest."

> Let your children realize that their rest is from you, and by their rest may they sanctify your name.

That people need respite from the routine of work is no discovery of the Judaic tradition. That the way in which they accomplish such a routine change of pace may become the very heart and soul of their spiritual existence is the single absolutely unique element in Judaic tradition. The word "Sabbath" simply renders the Hebrew *Shabbat;* it does not translate it, for there is no translation. In no other tradition or culture can an equivalent word be found. Certainly those who compare the Sabbath of Judaism to the somber, supposedly joyless Sunday of the Calvinists know nothing of what the Sabbath has meant and continues to mean to Jews.

The festivals mark the passage of time: not of the week but of the seasons. Those seasons of sanctification and celebration are three: *Sukkot,* the week following the first full moon after the autumnal equinox (called in the classical sources The Festival par excellence); *Pessah,* or Passover, we recall, the week following the first full moon after the vernal equinox; and *Shavuot,* or Weeks, seven weeks later. Each festival celebrates an event in nature, and commemorates an event in Israel's sacred history.

SUKKOT/TABERNACLES

The feast of tabernacles, *Sukkot,* marks the end of agricultural toil. The fall crops by then have been gathered in from the fields, orchards, and vineyards. The rainy season in the holy land of Israel, and the winter in North America is about to begin. It is time both to give thanks for what had been granted and to pray for abundant rains in the coming months. Called the festival of the ingathering, it was the celebration of nature, but the mode of celebration, after the fact, commemorates a moment in Israel's history, specifically, the wandering in the wilderness. At that time the Israelites lived not in permanent houses but in huts or booths. At a time of bounty it is good to be reminded of humanity's travail and dependence upon heavenly succor, which underlines the message of the Sabbath. The principal observance of the festival is still the construction of a frail hut, or booth, for temporary use during the festival. In warmer climates Jews eat their meals in it, outdoors. The huts are covered over with branches, leaves, fruit, and flowers, but light shows through by day, and the stars at night.

PESSAH/PASSOVER

Passover, *Pessah*, is the Jewish spring festival, and the symbols of the Passover seder—hard-boiled eggs and vegetable greens lying on a plate on the seder table but curiously neglected in the Passover narrative—are not unfamiliar in other spring rites. Here the spring rite has been transformed into a historical commemoration. The natural course of the year, while important, is subordinated to the historical events remembered and relived on the festival. Called the feast of unleavened bread and the season of our freedom, the Passover festival preserves ancient rites in a new framework.

For example, it is absolutely prohibited to make use of leaven, fermented dough, and the like. The agricultural calendar of ancient Canaan was marked by the grain harvest, beginning with the cutting of barley in the spring and ending with the reaping of the wheat approximately seven weeks later. The farmers would dispose of all of their sour dough, which they used as yeast, and old bread as well as any leaven from the previous year's crop. The origins of the practice are not clear, but it is beyond doubt that the Passover taboo against leaven was connected with the agricultural calendar. Just as the agricultural festivals were made into commemorations of historical events, rather than those of nature, likewise much of the detailed observance connected with them was supplied with historical "reasons" or explanations. In the case of the taboo against leaven, widely observed today even among otherwise unobservant Jews, the "reason" was that the Israelites had to leave Egypt in haste and therefore had to take with them unleavened bread, because they had no time to permit the bread to rise properly and be baked. Therefore we eat the *matzoh*, unleavened bread.

SHAVUOT/PENTECOST

The Feast of Weeks, *Shavuot* or Pentecost, comes seven weeks (fifty days) after Passover. In the ancient Palestinian agricultural calendar, it marked the end of the grain harvest and was called the feast of harvest. In Temple times, two loaves of bread were baked from the wheat of the new crop and offered as a sacrifice, the firstfruits of the wheat harvest, so *Shavuot* came to be called the day of the firstfruits. Judaism added a historical explanation to the natural ones derived from the land and its life. The rabbis held that the Torah was revealed on Mount Sinai on that day and celebrated it as "the time of the giving of our Torah," as the liturgy for the holy day says. Confirmation or graduation ceremonies of religious schools take place on *Shavuot* in Reform and Conservative synagogues today.

NEW YEAR AND THE DAY OF ATONEMENT

The Days of Awe, the ten momentous days beginning on Rosh Hashanah, the New Year, and reaching their climax on Yom Kippur, the Day of Atonement, take place in September or early October. What questions do people find answered on those days? The answer presented by the Days of Awe concerns the question of life and death. The New Year, Rosh Hashanah, celebrates the creation of the world: *Today the world was born.* The time of new beginnings also marks endings: *On the New Year the decree is issued: Who will live and who will die?* At the New Year—so the words state—humanity is inscribed for life or death in the heavenly books for the coming year, and on the Day of Atonement the books are sealed. The world comes out to hear these words. On the birthday of the world God made, God asserts his sovereignty, as in the New Year prayer:

Our God and God of our Fathers, rule over the whole world in Your honor . . . and appear in Your glorious might to all those who dwell in the civilization of Your world, so that everything made will know that You made it, and every creature discern that You have created him, so that all in whose nostrils is breath may say, "The Lord, the God of Israel is king, and His kingdom extends over all."[3]

3. Translation of Rabbi Harlow in the *Mahzor for Rosh Hashanah and Yom Kippur.*

A rabbi blowing the shofar at the western wall of Jerusalem.

Liturgical words concerning divine sovereignty, divine memory, and divine disclosure correspond to creation, revelation, and redemption. Sovereignty is established by creation of the world. Judgment depends upon law: "From the beginning You made this, Your purpose known . . ." Therefore, because people have been told what God requires of them, they are judged:

> On this day sentence is passed upon countries, which to the sword and which to peace, which to famine and which to plenty, and each creature is judged today for life or death. Who is not judged on this day? For the remembrance of every creature comes before You, each man's deeds and destiny, words and way. . . .

These are strong words for people to hear. As life unfolds and people grow reflective, the Days of Awe seize the imagination: I live, I die, sooner or later it comes to all. The call for inner contemplation implicit in the mythic words elicits deep response.

The theme of revelation is further combined with redemption; the ram's horn, or shofar, which is sounded in the synagogue during daily worship for a month before the Rosh Hashanah festival, serves to unite the two:

> You did reveal yourself in a cloud of glory. . . . Out of heaven
> you made them [Israel] hear Your voice. . . . Amid thunder
> and lightning You revealed yourself to them, and while the
> shofar sounded You shined forth upon them. . . . Our God
> and God of our fathers, sound the great shofar for our freedom.
> Lift up the ensign to gather our exiles. . . . Lead us happily
> to Zion Your city, Jerusalem the place of Your sanctuary.

The complex themes of the New Year, the most "theological" of Jewish holy occasions, thus weave together the tapestry of a highly charged moment in a world subject to the personal scrutiny of a most active God.

What of the Day of Atonement? Here too we hear the same answers, see the unfolding of a transformation of secular into sacred time.

The most personal, solemn, and moving of the Days of Awe is the Day of Atonement, *Yom Kippur*, the Sabbath of Sabbaths. It is marked by fasting and continuous prayer. On it, the Jew makes confession:

> Our God and God of our fathers, may our prayer come before
> You. Do not hide yourself from our supplication, for we are
> not so arrogant or stiff-necked as to say before You. . . .
> We are righteous and have not sinned. But we have sinned.
> We are guilt laden, we have been faithless, we have
> robbed. . . .
> We have committed iniquity, caused unrighteousness, have
> been presumptuous. . . .
> We have counseled evil, scoffed, revolted, blasphemed. . . .[4]

The Hebrew confession is built upon an alphabetical acrostic, as if by making certain every letter is represented, God, who knows

4. Translation of Rabbi Harlow in the *Mahzor for Rosh Hashanah and Yom Kippur.*

human secrets, will combine them into appropriate words. The very alphabet bears witness against us before God. Then:

> What shall we say before You who dwell on high? What shall we tell You who live in heaven? Do You not know all things, both the hidden and the revealed? You know the secrets of eternity, the most hidden mysteries of life. You search the innermost recesses, testing men's feelings and heart. Nothing is concealed from You or hidden from Your eyes. May it therefore be Your will to forgive us our sins, to pardon us for our iniquities, to grant remission for our transgressions.

A further list of sins follows, built on alphabetical lines. Prayers to be spoken by the congregation are all in the plural: "For the sin which we have sinned against You with the utterance of the lips. . . . For the sin which we have sinned before You openly and secretly. . . ." The community takes upon itself responsibility for what is done within it. All Israel is part of one community, one body, and all are responsible for the acts of each. The sins confessed are mostly against society, against one's fellow humans; few pertain to ritual laws. At the end comes a final word:

> O my God, before I was formed, I was nothing. Now that I have been formed, it is as though I had not been formed, for I am dust in my life, more so after death. Behold I am before You like a vessel filled with shame and confusion. May it be Your will . . . that I may no more sin, and forgive the sins I have already committed in Your abundant compassion.

While much of the liturgy speaks of "we," the individual focus dominates throughout. The Days of Awe speak to the heart of the individual, telling a story of judgment and atonement. The individual Jew stands before God—possessing no merits, yet hopeful of God's love and compassion. If that is the answer, can there be any doubt about the question? The power of the Days of Awe derives from the sentiments and emotions aroused by the theme of those days: What is happening to me? Where am I going?

Moments of introspection and reflection serve as guideposts in people's lives. That is why people treasure such moments and respond to the opportunities that define them. The themes of the Days of Awe stated in mythic terms address the human condition, and the message penetrates to the core of human concerns about life and death, the year past, the year beyond, the wrongs, the sins, the remissions, and atonement.

A review of the range of public and communal celebration has shown us how the Judaism that took shape after 70 integrated the individual and the community, the private and the public, the life of the people, Israel, wherever it was lived, blending the whole into a single pattern of this-worldly sanctification aimed at salvation at the end of time. How did this Judaism come into being?

Explaining the Formation of the Judaism of the Torah and Israel on its Own

The Pentateuch came into being in response to the destruction of the First Temple and answered the urgent question, in light of the exile, On what conditions does Israel hold the land and remain in covenant in relationship with God? While for the next five hundred years, from 450 B.C.E. to 70 C.E., a variety of other Judaic systems came into being, only one would achieve long-term authority and importance, and that is the Judaism that stands behind the life of sanctification of the present leading to salvation at the end of time, which is captured in the rites of the Grace after Meals and the other prayers and celebrations we have considered. The recurrent and diverse melodies, beginning to end, work out variations on the themes of creation, revelation, and redemption: Torah and Israel; a life of loyalty to God through sanctification of the everyday and everywhere; salvation and the world to come.

This Judaism is called "rabbinic," because its masters or sages bore the honorific title, "rabbi"; or "talmudic," because its authoritative document is the Babylonian Talmud (ca. 600 C.E.); or "normative" or "classical," because for many centuries, to modern times, it defined the norms for nearly all who practiced Judaism. It is also called "the Judaism of the dual Torah," because it appeals to the myth that the Torah revealed by God to Moses was formulated and transmitted in two forms: in writing (the Pentateuch and the remaining Hebrew Scriptures or Old Testament) and in oral form. This second, oral half of the Torah was eventually written down, so the story goes, in the documents produced by rabbis in the first six centuries C.E. out of traditions received by them from Sinai.

While rabbinic Judaism traces its own origins to Sinai, just as did the priests' pentateuchal Judaism, in fact the writings of the Judaism of the dual Torah began to take shape after, and in response to, the destruction of the Second Temple of Jerusalem by the Romans in 70 C.E. These writings unfolded in two stages, first ca. 70-300, then ca. 300-700. Each stage was defined by a critical turning in world politics as Israel, the people, understood politics. The affairs of a small and weak people, now permanently defeated as a political entity and deprived of its Temple and means of service to God, dictated the urgent issues that the Judaism aborning would have to address. What sort of covenant is possible when a principal means of worshiping God and atoning for sin—sacrifice, by the priesthood, in the Temple—no longer served? The answer was expressed in a story told later on about the principal figure who at the time of the destruction stood for the new Judaism built around Israel and Torah everywhere and all the time:

> One time, when walking near the ruins of the Temple, Rabbi Joshua wept and said to his master, Rabban Yohanan ben Zakkai, "Woe unto us that this place, the place in which the sins of Israel were atoned for, is no more!"
>
> The master said to him, "Do not see it as disastrous, my son, for we have a means of atonement which does the same thing. And what is it? It is deeds of lovingkindness, as it is said, 'For I desire mercy, and not sacrifice' (Hos. 6:6)."
>
> (Abot R. Nat., chap. 6)

In this way the end of the old order and the beginning of the new was represented, together with the paramount motif of the Judaism of the dual Torah—appeal to revelation in the (written) Torah to set forth the revelation in the oral Torah kept from Sinai to today in the intellects of sages and their disciples and set forth in the here and now of Israel everywhere.

Nevertheless, the Judaism of the dual Torah did not emerge on the day after the destruction of the Temple in 70. It responded, as I said, to two crises precipitated by political change. The first change came with the end of the political order that had left Israel self-governing in its land. In the aftermath of the destruction of the Temple and the failure of a war aimed at recovering it and reestablishing the Jewish government, people asked, With the Temple in ruins, how is Israel still holy? The second stage, in this essentially continuous unfolding of a single Judaism, was marked by the end of the political order of the Roman Empire, which had been marked by pagan rule, and the advent of Christianity as the official religion of the empire. This process began when Emperor Constantine converted to Christianity in 312 and ended with the establishment of Christianity later in the fourth century. The unavoidable question addressed in the second of these two stages and dealt with in the later documents was, With the world now Christian, what will happen to holy Israel—and when?

The crisis precipitated by the destruction of the Second Temple became acute not so much with the destruction of the Temple of Jerusalem in 70, for people hoped that there would be a restoration, as there was after 586. Rather, it was with the catastrophic failure of the rebellion against Rome led by Bar Kokhba in 132–35. Three generations after 70 this second major war sealed matters and left the Jews of the land of Israel without realistic hope of recovering Jerusalem for some time to come. If this second war was fought with the expectation of rehearsing the events of the sixth century B.C.E., then the disappointment at the end must have proved extreme. The original pattern no longer provided guidance on the direction, therefore also the meaning, of events, and people could refer to no other.

The Judaism that emerged after 70 succeeded the former Judaic system of Temple and priesthood. It was a Judaism formed upon essentially political lines, and its task was to govern a Jewish state and people in its land. The sect, the Pharisees, and the profession, the scribes—with surviving priests who joined them—together framed a Judaism to take the place of the Judaism of Temple and cult. It would emerge as a Judaism in which each of the elements of the Judaism of Temple and cult would find a counterpart: (1) in place of the Temple, the holy people, in which holiness endured even outside of the cult, as the Pharisees had taught; (2) in place of the priesthood, the sage, the holy man qualified by learning, as the scribes had taught; (3) in place of the sacrifices of the altar, the holy way of life of the people, expressed through carrying out religious duties (*mitzvot*, "commandments") and acts of kindness and grace beyond those commanded (*maasim tovim*, "good deeds"), and, above all, through studying the Torah.

CHAPTER FOUR

The Success of the Judaism for Everywhere, All the Time

Judaism despite Christianity (312–700)

Western civilization carried forward from antiquity four principal elements: first, (1) Greek philosophy; (2) Roman law and institutions; (3) the religious legacy of ancient Israel contained in the Hebrew Scriptures; and, (4) Christianity, the religion of the state and the formative force in culture. All of these were mediated by Christianity; in fact the West is what it is because of Christianity. Considering that the Roman Empire, out of which the West was born, became Christian in the fourth century, it follows that the history of Western civilization began in the fourth century, from the conversion of Constantine, the Roman emperor. Then Christianity embarked on the road to that paramount position in politics and culture that it was to occupy for the history of the West, until nearly the present day. As we shall see, it was in that same critical century that rabbinic Judaism reached its full formulation. Responding to the crisis and challenge of tri-umphant Christianity, the Judaism of the dual Torah, which predominated in the West and in the Islamic world from that time to nearly the present, answered the right question in terms found self-evidently valid by the Jews who remained faithful to the covenant of Sinai as they understood it, when the world opted for Christianity.

With its worldview framed by the texts of the Talmuds and Midrash compilations, its way of life defined as sanctification of the here and now pointing toward salvation at the end of time, and its address to genealogical Israel (meaning the descendants of Abraham, Isaac, and Jacob), the Judaism represented by the Grace after Meals everyday, the sanctification of the Sabbath, festivals, and Days of Awe, the thrice-daily prayers reenacting the human condition from creation to redemption, reached its full and definitive expression. The third crisis that marked the history of Judaism—after 586 B.C.E. and 70 C.E.—came in the year 312, the start of that political triumph that not only legalized Christianity but accorded to it the status—by the end of the century—of the official and governing religion of the Roman Empire. The political change in the situation of the Jews in the land of Israel came in 429, which marked the end of Roman recognition of the political standing of that patriarchal govern-ment that had ruled the Jews of the land of Israel for the pre-ceding three centuries.

The Crisis Precipitated for Judaism by the Triumph of Christianity in the Fourth Century

Although their state had ended in 70, Jews continued to govern their internal affairs, so the year 429, which brought to the logical end the course begun in 312, marked an enormous change, the end of Israel the people in the land of Israel (to Christianity, "the Jews in Palestine") as a political entity. Israel no longer possessed their instrument of self-administration and government in their own land. Tracing its roots back for centuries and claiming to originate in the family of David, the Jewish government, that of the patriarch, had succeeded the regime of the priests in the Temple and the kings, first as allies, then as agents of Rome on their throne. Israel's political tradition of government went back (in the mind of the nation) to Sinai. No one had ever imagined that the Jews would define their lives other than together, other than as a people, a political society, with collective authority and shared destiny and a public interest. The revelation of Sinai addressed a nation, the Torah gave laws to be kept and enforced, and Israel found definition in comparison to other nations. It would have rulers, subject to God's authority, to be sure, and it would have a king now, and a Messiah king at the end of time. So the fourth century brought a hitherto unimagined circumstance: an Israel lacking the authority to rule itself under its own government, even the ethnic and patriarchal one that had held things together during the long centuries of priestly rule in the Temple and royal rule in Jerusalem.

In effect, the two systems, Christian and Judaic, had prepared for worlds that neither would inhabit, the one for the status of governed, not governor, the other for the condition of a political entity. But now Christianity in politics would define not the fringes but the very fabric of society and culture. Judaism, out of politics altogether, would find its power in the voluntarily donated obedience of people in no way to be coerced to conform and obey, except from within or from on high. The importance of the radical political shift of the fourth century should not be missed, because it explains why rabbinic Judaism focused upon issues that hitherto had been given a subordinated position within the system. It forced Israel's sages to respond to the existence and claims of Christianity, which, as we have seen, they had been able to ignore for three hundred years. The position outlined in the fourth-century documents of Judaism represents the first reading of Christianity on the part of Israel's sages. Prior to that time they did not take to heart the existence of the competition.

Israel's sages would subsequently draw on the position outlined in their fourth-century writings to sort out the issues made urgent by the success of Christianity throughout the Roman world. Prior to the time of Constantine the documents of Judaism that evidently reached closure before 300 scarcely took cognizance of Christianity and did not deem the new faith to be much of a challenge. If the unsystematic and scattered allusions do mean to refer to Christianity at all, then sages regarded Christianity as an irritant, an exasperating heresy among Jews who should have known better. But neither Jews nor pagans took much interest in Christianity in the new faith's first century and a half. The authors of the Mishnah framed a system to which Christianity bore no relevance whatsoever; theirs were problems presented in an altogether different context. For their part, pagan writers were indifferent to Christianity, not mentioning it until about 160.[1] Only when Christian evangelism enjoyed some solid success, toward the later part of that century, did pagans compose apologetic works attacking Christianity, but by the fourth century, pagans and Jews alike knew that they faced a formidable, powerful enemy.

One other event of the fourth century, besides the triumph of Christianity, demands attention. It was the rise to the Roman throne of Julian, a pagan. For the brief period of his reign, from 361 to 363, Christianity lost that most favored position that had so astonished the Church earlier in the century. To understand its impact, we have to bear in mind that the political shift in the status of Christianity came as a shock to Christians as much as to pagans and Jews. Christians at the court of Constantine remembered days, not long past, of suffering in mines and prisons, so the shift which we now know would be permanent and enduring did not win the confidence of the Christians. Things were still chancy and could change. Their insecurity had a sound basis, for the throne had (miraculously) turned Christian, and could just as suddenly turn again. That is precisely what happened just half a century after Constantine's legalization of the Christian church, specifically, when in 361–63 the pagan Julian regained the throne and turned the empire away from Christianity.

The impact on Judaism, for its part, proved considerable. As part of his policy to humiliate the Church, Julian further invited the Jews to rebuild the Temple. The success of that project would call into question the prediction attributed by the Gospels to Jesus that no stone would remain on stone, that the Temple would never be rebuilt. The project proved a fiasco, and Julian was killed in battle against Persia. Consequently, the succeeding

1. Labriolle, in J. R. Palanque et al., *The Church and the Arian Crisis*, vol. 1 of *The Church in the Christian Roman Empire* (New York: 1953), 242.

emperors, all Christian, restored the throne to Christ (as they would put it) and secured for the Church and Christianity the control of the state through law. So—as Chrysostom argued in 386–87, in the aftermath of Julian's brief reign—the destruction of the Temple in 70 now was interpreted as definitive. Three hundred years later, the Temple would have been rebuilt, but God prevented it. In the aftermath of Julian's reign, the Christians, regaining the throne, took severe measures to prevent the recurrence of pagan rule. They acted out of a realistic insecurity. The vigorous repression of paganism after Julian's apostasy expressed the natural fear of Christians that such a thing might happen again.

The Re-formation of Rabbinic Judaism to Meet the Challenge of Christianity

In literary terms what marks the emergence of the Judaic system of the dual Torah? In terms of scriptures, two enormous developments emerged, (1) an enormous commentary to the Mishnah, and (2) a set of immense commentaries to important books of the written Torah, the Scriptures, specifically, the books of Genesis and Leviticus. These documents mark shifts in the symbolic system and structure of the Judaism then taking shape. The particular changes responded to the critical challenge of the political triumph of Christianity. Let me be specific about the points of challenge and systemic response in the Judaism of the dual Torah. The symbolic system of Christianity—with Christ triumphant, with the cross as the regnant symbol, with the canon of Christianity now defined and recognized as authoritative—called forth from the sages of the land of Israel a symbolic system strikingly responsive to the crisis:

1. The coming of the Messiah gained importance as the teleology of the system of Judaism.

2. The symbol of the Torah was expanded to encompass the whole of human existence as the system laid forth the framework of that existence.

3. The canon of Sinai was broadened to take account of the entirety of the sages' teachings, as much of the written Torah as everyone acknowledged as authoritative.

In these matters, of course, we find ourselves right at home at the table of Judaism; the Grace after Meals, the Seven Blessings after the Nuptial Meal, the Shema with its blessings fore and aft—everywhere we turned, we found ourselves talking about Messiah, the Torah, and its study. The contrast between the sages' system as revealed in writings closed in the later second and third century—in particular the Mishnah and its closely allied documents—and the system that emerged in the writings of the later fourth and fifth centuries is striking. The story becomes clear when we focus upon the single most striking shift, the development of the talmudic doctrine of the Messiah at the end of time and of the meaning of history. That doctrine came to full expression for the first time in the pages of the Talmud of the Land of Israel, which reached closure ca. 400 C.E., at the end of the first Christian century in the history of the West.

The Two Talmuds: Judaism of Salvation through Sanctification

Set forth as commentaries to the Mishnah, two Talmuds, one produced in the Roman Empire, in the land of Israel, in ca.400-450, called the Talmud of the Land of Israel (sometimes called the "Palestinian" or "Jerusalem" Talmud), the other produced in the Persian Empire, in the province of Babylonia, and called the Babylonian Talmud, ca. 600, made the same statement. It was a very simple one, which linked the holy life to the end of time: sanctification in the here and now, salvation then. Specifically, if Israel would keep the Torah—that eternal medium for the sanctification and purification of the heart and life of Israel, as the sages taught and exemplified it—the Messiah would come. The true Messiah will affirm the Torah and Israel's total submission to God's yoke and service. Keeping the commandments as a mark of submission, loyalty, humility before God is the rabbinic system of salvation. So Israel does not "save itself." Israel never controls its own destiny, either on earth or in heaven. The only choice is whether to cast one's fate into the hands of cruel, deceitful men, or to trust in the living God of mercy and love. We shall now see how this critical position is spelled out in the setting of discourse about the Messiah in the Talmud of the Land of Israel. The failed general Bar Kokhba, above all, exemplifies arrogance against God. He lost the war because of that arrogance. In particular, he ignored the authority of sages:

Y. Taanit 4:5

[J] Said R. Yohanan, "Upon orders of Caesar Hadrian, they killed eight hundred thousand in Betar."

[K] Said R. Yohanan, "There were eighty thousand pairs of trumpeteers surrounding Betar. Each one was in charge of a number of troops. Ben Kozeba was there and he had two hundred thousand troops who, as a sign of loyalty, had cut off their little fingers."

[L] "Sages sent word to him, 'How long are you going to turn Israel into a maimed people?' "

[M] "He said to them, 'How otherwise is it possible to test them?"

[N] "They replied to him, 'Whoever cannot uproot a cedar of Lebanon while riding on his horse will not be inscribed on your military rolls.' "

[O] "So there were two hundred thousand who qualified in one way, and another two hundred thousand who qualified in another way."

[P] When he would go forth to battle, he would say, "Lord of the world! Do not help and do not hinder us! Hast thou not rejected us, O God? Thou dost not go forth, O God, with our armies" [Ps. 60:10].

[Q] Three and a half years did Hadrian besiege Betar.

[R] R. Eleazar of Modiin would sit on sackcloth and ashes and pray every day, saying "Lord of the ages! Do not judge in accord with strict judgment this day! Do not judge in accord with strict judgment this day!"

[S] Hadrian wanted to go to him. A Samaritan said to him, "Do not go to him until I see what he is doing, and so hand over the city [of Betar] to you. [Make peace . . . for you.]"

[T] He got into the city through a drain pipe. He went and found R. Eleazar of Modiin standing and praying. He pretended to whisper something in his ear.

[U] The townspeople say [the Samaritan] did this and brought him to Ben Kozeba. They told him, "We saw this man having dealings with your friend."

[V] [Bar Kokhba] said to him, "What did you say to him, and what did he say to you?"

[W] He said to [the Samaritan], "If I tell you, then the king will kill me, and if I do not tell you, then you will kill me. It is better that the king kill me, and not you."

[X] "[Eleazar] said to me, 'I should hand over my city.' ['I shall make peace. . . .']"

[Y] He turned to R. Eleazar of Modiin. He said to him, "What did this Samaritan say to you?"

[Z] He replied, "Nothing."

[AA] He said to him, "What did you say to him?"

[BB] He said to him, "Nothing."

[CC] [Ben Kozeba] gave [Eleazar] one good kick and killed him.

[DD] Forthwith an echo came forth and proclaimed the following verse:

[EE] "Woe to my worthless shepherd, who deserts the flock! May the sword smite his arm and his right eye! Let his arm be wholly withered, his right eye utterly blinded!" [Zech. 11:17].

[FF] "You have murdered R. Eleazar of Modiin, the right arm of all Israel, and their right eye. Therefore may the right arm of that man wither, may his right eye be utterly blinded!"

[GG] Forthwith Betar was taken, and Ben Kozeba was killed.

We notice two complementary themes. First, Bar Kokhba treats heaven with arrogance, asking God merely to keep out of the way. Second, he treats an especially revered sage with a parallel arrogance. The sage had the power to preserve Israel. Bar Kokhba destroyed Israel's one protection. The result was inevitable. The principal result of Israel's loyal adherence to the Torah and its religious duties will be Israel's humble acceptance of God's rule. That humility, under all conditions, makes God love Israel. The heart of the matter then is Israel's subservience to God's will, as expressed in the Torah and embodied in the teachings and lives of the great sages. When Israel fully accepts God's rule, then the Messiah will come. Until Israel subjects itself to God's rule, the Jews will be subjugated to pagan domination. Since the condition of Israel governs, Israel itself holds the key to its own redemption. But it can achieve this only by throwing away the key!

The Talmud of Babylonia, ca. 600 C.E. carried forward the innovations we have seen in the Talmud of the land of Israel.

B. Hullin 89a

"*It was not because you were greater than any people that the Lord set his love upon you and chose you*" [Deut. 7:7]. The Holy One, blessed be he, said to Israel, "I love you because even when I bestow greatness upon you, you humble yourselves before me. I bestowed greatness upon Abraham, yet he said to me, '*I am but dust and ashes*' [Gen. 18:27]; upon Moses and Aaron, yet they said, '*But I am a worm and no man*' [Ps. 22:7]. But with the heathens it is not so. I bestowed greatness upon Nimrod, and he said, '*Come, let us build us a city*' [Gen. 11:4]; upon Pharaoh, and he said, '*Who are they among all the gods of the countries?*' [2 Kings 18:35]; upon Nebuchadnezzar, and he said, '*I will ascend above the heights of the clouds*' [Isa. 14:14]; upon Hiram, king of Tyre, and he said, '*I sit in the seat of God, in the heart of the seas*' [Ezek. 28:2]."

The paradox must be clear. Israel acts to redeem itself through the opposite of self-determination, namely, by subjugating itself to God. Israel's power lies in its negation of power. Its destiny lies in giving up all pretense at deciding its own destiny. Weakness is the ultimate strength, forbearance the final act of self-assertion, passive resignation the sure step toward liberation. Israel's freedom is engraved on the tablets of the commandments of God: To be free is to freely obey. That is not the meaning associated with these words in the minds of others who, like the sages of the rabbinical canon, declared their view of what Israel must do to secure the coming of the Messiah.

The passage, praising Israel for its humility, completes the circle begun with the description of Bar Kokhba as arrogant and boastful. Gentile kings are boastful; Israelite kings are humble. So, in all, the Messiah myth deals with a concrete and limited consideration of the national life and character. The theory of Israel's history and destiny as it was expressed within that myth interprets matters in terms of a single criterion. What others within the Israelite world had done or in the future would do with the conviction that, at the end of time, God would send a (or the) Messiah to "save" Israel, it was a single idea for the sages of the Mishnah and the Talmuds and collections of scriptural exegesis. That conception stands at the center of their system; it shapes and is shaped by their system. In context, the

Messiah expresses the system's meaning and so makes it work. If people wanted to reach the end of time, they had to rise above time, that is, history, and stand off at the side of great ephemeral movements of political and military character.

The Defense of the Torah

Christianity claimed that in the New Testament it possessed the key to the interpretation of the Old Testament. Rabbinic Judaism replied that the sages of the Torah possessed in the oral part of the Torah the completion and interpretation of the meaning and message of the written part of the Torah. They produced documents that showed how in the Torah they could make sense of the world today, much as in the Old Testament, as they called and read it, Christians found the meaning of what had happened when Jesus Christ walked on earth—and in the things that he had said and done was revealed the meaning of the Old Testament prophecies. The claims then met head-on.

To show how the sages demonstrated the correct way of reading the written Torah, we turn to one of the great compilations of Scripture interpretation called Midrash—books produced in the century after the conversion of Constantine. Sages produced the great works on Genesis in Genesis Rabbah, and on Leviticus in Leviticus Rabbah, which answered the questions of salvation, of the meaning and end of Israel's history, questions that the Mishnah and its commentators did not take up. The political crisis precipitated by Christianity's takeover of the Roman Empire and its government demanded answers from Israel's sages: What does it mean? What does history mean? Where are we to find guidance to the meaning of our past—and our future? Sages looked to Scripture, first of all to Genesis, maintaining that the story of the creation of the world and the beginning of Israel would show the way toward the meaning of history and the salvation of Israel. They looked further to Leviticus, and, in Leviticus Rabbah, they accomplished the link between the sanctification of Israel through its cult and priesthood, which is the theme of the book of Leviticus, and the salvation of Israel, which is the concern of the commentators. They placed Israel, the people, at the center of the story of Leviticus, applying to the life of the people of Israel those rules of sanctification that, when observed, would prepare Israel, holy Israel, for salvation. In a nutshell, the framers of Leviticus Rabbah imparted to the book of Leviticus the message, in response to the destruction of the Temple, that the authors of the Mishnah had addressed two hundred years earlier: Israel's holiness endures. Sanctifying the life of Israel now will lead to the salvation of Israel in time to come. Sanctification and salvation, the natural world and the supernatural, the rules of society and the rules of history all become one in the life of Israel.

I shall now spell out the message of the compilers of Genesis Rabbah, the commentary to the book of Genesis produced in the late fourth or early fifth century, in the time of the third and last crisis in the formation of Judaism. In the book of Genesis, as the sages who composed Genesis Rabbah saw things, God set forth to Moses the entire scope and meaning of Israel's history among the nations and salvation at the end of days. They read Genesis not as a set of individual verses, one by one, but as a single and coherent statement, whole and complete. So in a few words let me restate the conviction of the framers of Genesis Rabbah about the message and meaning of the book of Genesis:

> We now know what will be in the future. How do we know it? Just as Jacob had told his sons what would happen in time to come, just as Moses told the tribes their future, so we may understand the laws of history if we study the Torah. And in the Torah, we turn to beginnings: the rules as they were laid out at the very start of human history. These we find in the book of Genesis, the story of the origins of the world and of Israel.
>
> The Torah tells us not only what happened but why. The Torah permits us to discover the laws of history. Once we know those laws, we may also peer into the future and come to an assessment of what is going to happen to us—and, especially, of how we shall be saved from our present existence. Because everything exists under the aspect of a timeless will, God's will, and all things express one thing, God's program and plan, in the Torah we uncover the workings of God's will. Our task as Israel is to accept, endure, submit, and celebrate.

The framers' conviction is that Abraham, Isaac, and Jacob shaped the future history of Israel. Therefore, if we want to know the meaning of events now and tomorrow, we look back at yesterday to find out. But the interest is not merely in history as a source of lessons; it is history as the treasury of truths about the here and now and especially about tomorrow. The same rules apply. The patriarchs supplied the model, the message, the meaning for what we should do. The sages of the Jewish people, in the land of Israel, came to Genesis with the questions of their own day because, they maintained, the world reveals not chaos but order, and God's will works itself out not once but again and again. If we can find out how things began, we can also find meaning in today, and direction for the future. That is why they looked to a reliable account of the past and searched out the meaning of their own days. Bringing to the stories the conviction that Genesis told not only the story of yesterday but also the tale of tomorrow, the sages whose words are before us in this anthology transformed a picture of the past into a prophesy for a near tomorrow. What made Israel's sages look longingly at the beginnings of the world and of Israel? In their own day they entertained deep forebodings about Israel's prospects. Now to the document itself.

In Genesis Rabbah sages read Genesis as if it portrayed the history of Israel and Rome—Rome in particular. Rome plays a role in the biblical narrative, with special reference to the counterpart and opposite of the patriarchs, first Ishmael, then Esau, and, always, Edom. That is the single obsession binding sages of the document at hand to common discourse with the text before them. Why Rome in the form it takes in Genesis Rabbah? And why the obsessive character of the sages' disposition of the theme of Rome? Were their picture of Rome merely as tyrant and destroyer of the Temple, we should have no reason to link the text to the problems of the age of redaction and closure. Now Rome is as Israel's brother, counterpart, and nemesis, the one thing standing in the way of Israel's, and the world's ultimate salvation. The stakes are different, and much higher.

Let us begin with a simple example of how ubiquitous is the shadow of Ishmael/Esau/Edom/Rome. Wherever sages reflect on the future, their minds turn to their own day. They found the hour difficult, because Rome, now Christian, claimed that birthright and blessing that they understood to be theirs alone. Christian Rome posed a threat without precedent. Now another dominion, besides Israel's, claimed the rights and blessings that sustained Israel. Wherever they turned in Scripture, sages found comfort in the iteration that the birthright, the blessing, the Torah, and the hope all belonged to them and to none other. Here is a striking statement of that constant proposition.

Genesis Rabbah LIII:XII

1. A. "[So she said to Abraham, 'Cast out this slave woman with her son, for the son of this slave woman shall not be heir with my son Isaac.'] And the thing was very displeasing to Abraham on account of his son" (Gen. 21:11):

   B. That is in line with this verse: "And shuts his eyes from looking upon evil" (Isa. 33:15). [Freedman, p. 471, no. 1: He shut his eyes from Ishmael's evil ways and was reluctant to send him away.]

2. A. "But God said to Abraham, 'Be not displeased because of the lad and because of your slave woman; whatever Sarah says to you, do as she tells you, for through Isaac shall your descendants be named' " (Gen. 21:12):

   B. Said R. Yudan bar Shillum, "What is written is not 'Isaac' but 'through Isaac.' [The matter is limited, not through all of Isaac's descendants but only through some of them, thus excluding Esau.]"

3. A. R. Azariah in the name of Bar Hutah, "The use of the B, which stands for two, indicates that he who affirms that there are two worlds will inherit both worlds [this age and the age to come]."

   B. Said R. Yudan bar Shillum, "It is written, 'Remember his marvelous works that he has done, his signs and the judgments of his mouth' (Ps. 105:5). I have given a sign, namely, it is one who gives the appropriate evidence through what he says. Specifically, he who affirms that there are two worlds will be called 'your seed.' "

   C. "And he who does not affirm that there are two worlds will not be called 'your seed.' "

The first entry makes "the matter" refer to Ishmael's misbehavior, not Sarah's proposal, so removing the possibility of disagreement between Abraham and Sarah. The second and third interpret the limiting particle, *in*, that is, *among* the descendants of Isaac will be found Abraham's heirs, but not all the descendants of Isaac will be heirs of Abraham. The second entry explicitly excludes Esau, that is Rome, and the third makes the matter doctrinal in the context of Israel's inner life. As the several antagonists of Israel stand for Rome in particular, so the traits of Rome, as sages perceived them, characterized the biblical heroes. Esau provided a favorite target.

Genesis Rabbah LXIII:VI

1. A. "And the children struggled together [within her, and she said, 'If it is thus, why do I live?' So she went to inquire of the Lord. And the Lord said to her, 'Two nations are in your womb, and two peoples, born of you, shall be divided; the one shall be stronger than the other, and the elder shall serve the younger']" (Gen. 25:22-23):

    B. R. Yohanan and R. Simeon b. Laqish:

    C. R. Yohanan said, "[Because the word, 'struggle,' contains the letters for the word, 'run,'] this one was running to kill that one and that one was running to kill this one."

    D. R. Simeon b. Laqish: "This one releases the laws given by that one, and that one releases the laws given by this one."

2. A. R. Berekhiah in the name of R. Levi said, "It is so that you should not say that it was only after he left his mother's womb that [Esau] contended against [Jacob]."

    B. "But even while he was yet in his mother's womb, his fist was stretched forth against him: 'The wicked stretch out their fists [so Freedman] from the womb' " (Ps. 58:4).

3. A. "And the children struggled together within her:"

    B. [Once more referring to the letters of the word "struggled," with special attention to the ones that mean "run"], they wanted to run within her.

    C. When she went by houses of idolatry, Esau would kick, trying to get out: "The wicked are estranged from the womb" (Ps. 58:4).

D. When she went by synagogues and study-houses, Jacob would kick, trying to get out: "Before I formed you in the womb, I knew you" (Jer. 1:5).

4. A. ". . . and she said, 'If it is thus, why do I live?' "

B. R. Haggai in the name of R. Isaac: "This teaches that our mother, Rebecca, went around to the doors of women and said to them, 'Did you ever have this kind of pain in your life?' "

C. "[She said to them,] 'If this is the pain of having children, would that I had not gotten pregnant.' "

D. Said R. Huna, "If I am going to produce twelve tribes only through this kind of suffering, would that I had not gotten pregnant."

5. A. It was taught on Tannaite authority in the name of R. Nehemiah, "Rebecca was worthy of having the twelve tribes come forth from her. That is in line with this verse:

B. " 'Two nations are in your womb, and two peoples, born of you, shall be divided; the one shall be stronger than the other, and the elder shall serve the younger.' When her days to be delivered were fulfilled, behold, there were twins in her womb. The first came forth red, all his body like a hairy mantle, so they called his name Esau. Afterward his brother came forth . . .' (Gen. 25:23-24).

C. " 'Two nations are in your womb': thus two.

D. " 'and two peoples': thus two more, hence four.

E. " '. . . the one shall be stronger than the other': two more, so six.

F. " '. . . and the elder shall serve the younger': two more, so eight.

G. " 'When her days to be delivered were fulfilled, behold, there were twins in her womb:' two more, so ten.

H. " 'The first came forth red:' now eleven.

J. " 'Afterward his brother came forth:' now twelve."

K. There are those who say, "Proof derives from this verse: 'If it is thus, why do I live?' Focusing on the word for 'thus,' we note that the two letters of that word bear the numerical value of seven and five respectively, hence, twelve in all."

6. A. "So she went to inquire of the Lord:"

    B.   Now were there synagogues and houses of study in those days [that she could go to inquire of the Lord]?

    C.   But is it not the fact that she went only to the study of Eber?

    D.   This serves to teach you that whoever receives an elder is as if he receives the Presence of God.

The first three entries take for granted that Esau represents Rome, and Jacob, Israel. Consequently the verse underlines the point that there is natural enmity between Israel and Rome. Esau hated Israel even while he was still in the womb. Jacob, for his part, revealed from the womb those virtues that would characterize him later on; he was as eager to serve God as Esau was eager to worship idols. The text invites just this sort of reading. The fourth and fifth entries relate Rebecca's suffering to the birth of the twelve tribes. The sixth makes its own point, independent of the rest and tacked on. How long would Rome rule, when would Israel succeed? The important point is that Rome was next to last, Israel last. Rome's triumph brought assurance that Israel would be next—and last:

Genesis Rabbah LXXV:IV.

2.   A.   "And Jacob sent messengers before him:"

    B.   To this one [Esau] whose time to take hold of sovereignty would come before him [namely, before Jacob, since Esau would rule, then Jacob would govern].

    C.   R. Joshua b. Levi said, "Jacob took off the purple robe and threw it before Esau, as if to say to him, 'Two flocks of starlings are not going to sleep on a single branch' [so we cannot rule at the same time].' "

3.   A.   ". . . to Esau his brother:"

    B.   Even though he was Esau, he was still his brother.

Esau—Christian Rome—remains Jacob's brother, and that Esau—Rome—rules before Jacob will. The application to contemporary affairs cannot be missed, both in the recognition of the true character of Esau, a brother, and in the interpretation of the future of history.

    Genesis Rabbah reached closure, scholars generally agree, toward the end of the fourth century. That century marks the beginning of the West as we have known it. Why? In the fourth century, from the conversion of Constantine and over the next hundred years, the Roman Empire became Christian—and with it, the West. So the fourth century marks the beginning of the history of the West in the form that would flourish up to our own day. Accordingly, we should not find surprising sages' recurrent references, in the reading of Genesis, to the struggle of two equal powers, Rome and Israel, Esau and Jacob, Ishmael and Isaac. The historical change in the world, marking the confirmation in politics and power of the Christians' claim that Christ was king over all humanity, demanded from sages an appropriate—and, to Israel, persuasive—response.

CHAPTER FIVE

The Long-Term Stability of the Judaism for Everywhere, All the Time

The Domination of Rabbinic Judaism (600–1800)

The religion of a small, weak group, Judaism more than held its own against the challenge of triumphant Christendom and Islam. The reason for the success of the Judaism of the dual Torah was that its system answered the question, Why did God's people, in exile, hold a subordinated, but tolerated position within the world framed by the sibling rivals, Ishmael and Isaac, Esau and Jacob? The appeal to exile accounted for the dissonance of present unimportance and promised future greatness: "Today if only you will. . . ." The question was urgent, the answer self-evidently true in its appeal to the holy way of life explained by the received worldview and addressed to the Israel consisting of the believers throughout the world. Here was the family of Abraham, Isaac, Jacob, Sarah, Rebecca, Rachel, and Leah: Israel. Now tolerated, sometimes oppressed, in exile, in time to come the family would return home to its own land. With the road back fully mapped out, people had to remember who they were, where they were going, and what they had to do—or not to do—in order to get from here to there.

The framing of the world as a system of families, with Israel sui generis and Israel's siblings part of its genus, admirably accounted for the state of Israel. The way of life of the Judaism of the dual Torah, with its stress on the ongoing sanctification of the everyday; and the worldview, with its doctrine of the ultimate salvation of the holy people, concretely and acutely actualized the fundamental system. The consequence was total and enduring success. As long as Christianity defined the civilization of the West, and Islam that of North Africa, the Near and Middle East, and Central Asia, Judaism in its fourth-century, classical statement triumphed in Israel, the Jewish people, located within Christendom and Islam. For Israel, the questions deemed urgent and the answers found self-evidently true defined the world. When in the West from the eighteenth century onward, as part of the secularization of politics and culture, Christendom lost its standing as a set of self-evident truths, Judaism in its classical statement also found itself facing competition in those same countries from other Judaisms—different systems, each asking its distinctive, urgent questions—and producing its own self-evidently true answers. For these other Judaisms neither questions nor answers bore any relationship whatever to those of the received system, even while episodically exploiting proof texts drawn from the inherited holy writings. In Christian lands it was only until the eighteenth century that the Judaism of the dual Torah both set the standard for accepted innovation and defined the shape and structure of heresy. From that time onward, continuator Judaisms competed with essentially new and unprecedented systems, in no way standing in a linear and incremental relationship with the Judaism of the dual Torah.

In the Muslim countries, the palpable self-evidence of Islam never gave way but defined reality in much its own way from the beginning to the present, so the equivalently obvious standing of truth accorded by Jews to the received system of the Judaism of the dual Torah for Israel, the Jewish people, endured. Judaism in the received statement of the fourth century, as given its definitive version in the Talmud of Babylonia in the seventh, persisted from the beginning of Islam to the end of the life of Israel within Islam in 1948. Whatever variations and developments marked the history of Judaism from the fourth century to today, in Muslim countries this worked itself out within the received system and its norms.

The reason for the difference between the uninterrupted history of Judaism in Islam and the diverse histories of Judaisms within modern and contemporary Christendom lies in the different modern and contemporary histories of Islam, so long the victim of imperialism, and Christianity, equally long the beneficiary of the same politics. Judaism in its fourth-century formulation thrived within imperial systems in accord with the conditions of its circumstance, uninterruptedly in the one world, conditionally in the other. But the reason was the same: Judaism explained for Israel its subordinated but tolerated condition; indeed, it made that condition into God's will, and the acceptance of that condition in the heart as much as in the mind into the definition of virtue. Judaism in its version of the dual Torah brought to its ultimate statement that original, scriptural Judaism of the Torah of "Moses," which stemmed from the time of Ezra. The message of that Judaism of the dual Torah addressed precisely the situation envisaged by the original system: The people are special, their life contingent, their relationship to the land subject to conditions, their collective life lived at a level of heightened reality.

The world beyond works out its affairs to accommodate God's will for Israel, and Israel's relationship to that larger world remains wholly within the control and subject to the power of Israel, but in a paradoxical way. Israel must accept, submit, accommodate, receive with humility the will and word of God in the Torah. The power to govern the fate of the nation rested with the nation, but only so far as the nation accorded that autocephalous power to God alone. Were people perplexed about who Israel is? The Torah answered the question: It is God's people, here and now living out the holy life prescribed by God. Did people wonder how long Israel had to endure the government of Gentiles? The Torah addressed that issue: as long as God willed. The God who had created the heavens and the earth dictated the fate of Israel, but also cared about what each Jew ate for breakfast and responded to the conduct of every collectivity of Israel, each pool of the sacred formed by even a handful of Jews. The Judaism of the dual Torah in its distinctive idiom recapitulated the principle of the Judaism of the Torah of "Moses." The system emphasized the everyday as a sequence of acts and sanctification. It promised remission and resolution—salvation—as a consequence of the correct and faithful performance of those acts of sanctification. The subordination therefore served to attest to the true status of Israel, small and inconsequential now, but still holy and destined for great reward at the end of time.

The power of Judaism therefore lay in its remarkable capacity to define and create the world of Israel, the Jewish people. Israel understood that the nation that had ceased to be a nation on its own land and once more regained that condition could and would once more reenact that paradigm. The original pattern imparted to events the meaning that would make good sense for Israel. I have maintained that in the case of the Judaism of the dual Torah, the social world recapitulates religion, not that religion merely recapitulates that data, the givens of society, economy, politics, let alone of an imaginative or emotional reality. The study of Judaism provides a source of cases for the proposition that religion shapes the world, not the world, religion. Specifically, it is the Jews' religion, Judaism, that has formed their world and framed their realities, and not the world of politics, culture, society, that has made their religion.

The rise of Islam in the mid-seventh century found a powerful adversary in the Judaism of the dual Torah. The Muslim armies after the death of Muhammed swept over the Middle East and North Africa, subduing the great empire of Persia to the east, much of Byzantine Rome to the west, cutting across Egypt, Cyrenaica, what we know as Tunisia and North Africa, and reaching into Spain. Ancient Christian bishoprics fell, as vast Christian populations accepted the new monotheism, though they were not compelled to do so. Nevertheless, we have little evidence that similar sizable conversions decimated the Jewish community, and that strongly suggests that Judaism stood firm. The reason is clear. Having dealt with the political triumph of Christianity, the system of the dual Torah found itself entirely capable of coping with the military (and therefore political) victory of Islam as well. Indeed, given the apparent stability of the Jewish communities in the newly conquered Islamic countries and the decline of Christianity in those same, long-Christian territories—for example, Syria, Palestine, Egypt, Cyrenaica, and the western provinces of North Africa, not to mention Spain—

we observe a simple fact. The Judaism of the dual Torah satis-factorily explained for Israel the events of the day, while Chris-tianity, triumphant through the sword of Constantine, withstood the sharper sword of Muhammed only with difficulty. For this reason, one may surmise, the great Christian establishments of the Middle East and North Africa fell away. Because both Judaism and Christianity enjoyed the same political status, the evident success of the one and the failure of the other attests to what the fourth-century sages had accomplished for Israel, the Jewish people.

The situation of Jews in Christendom and Islam, as a tol-erated minority, and that of Christians in Islam, likewise ac-corded subordinated but tolerated standing, meant that only free male Muslims enjoyed the rank of a full member of society.[1] Jews and Christians could either accept Islam or continue to practice their received religions and submit, paying a tribute and ac-cepting Muslim supremacy. Lewis characterizes the policy toward the conquered people in these terms:

> This pattern was not of equality, but rather of dominance by one group and, usually, a hierarchic sequence of the others. Though this order did not concede equality, it permitted peace-ful coexistence. While one group might dominate, it did not as a rule insist on suppressing or absorbing the others. . . . Communities professing recognized religions were allowed the tolerance of the Islamic state. They were allowed to practice their religions . . . and to enjoy a measure of communal au-tonomy.[2]

The Jews fell into the category of *dhimmis*, communities "accorded a certain status, provided that they unequivocally recognized the primacy of Islam and the supremacy of the Muslims. This recognition was expressed in the payment of the poll tax and obedience to a series of restrictions defined in detail by the holy law."[3] The situation of Judaism in Muslim countries therefore corresponded overall with that in the Christian ones. In some

1. Bernard Lewis, *The Jews of Islam* (Princeton: Princeton University Press, 1984), 8.
2. Lewis, 19-20.
3. Lewis, 21.

ways it proved easier, there being no emotional hostility directed against either Jews or Judaism such as flourished in Christendom.[4] Nevertheless, the Jews were a subject group and had to accommodate themselves to that condition, just as they had learned to make their peace with the remarkable success of Christianity in fourth-century Rome. That fact brings us to the question of the basis for the remarkable success of Judaism in its classical form.

From the fourth century within Christendom, and from the seventh within Islam, Judaism enjoyed remarkable success in that very world that it both created and also selected for itself, the world of Israel, the Jewish people. Both Islam and Christendom presented a single challenge: the situation of subordination along with toleration. The power of Judaism lay in its capacity to do two things: First, Judaism in its classical statement (shaped in the fourth-century Talmud of the land of Israel and then fully articulated the sixth-century Talmud of Babylonia) presented doctrines both to explain and to draw renewal from the condition of subordination and toleration, so that the facts of everyday life served to reenforce the claims of the system; second, that same Judaism taught an enduring doctrine of the virtues of the heart that made Israel's situation acceptable. That same doctrine so shaped the inner life of Israel as to define virtue in the very terms imposed by politics. Israel within recreated that exact condition of acceptance of humility and accommodation that the people's political circumstance imposed from without, so the enduring doctrine of virtue made it possible for Israel to accept its condition. It also recreated that same condition in the psychological structure of Israel's inner life, so bringing into exact correspondence political facts and psychological fantasies. Judaism triumphed in Christendom and Islam because of its power to bring into union both heart and mind, inner life and outer circumstance, psychology and politics. The Judaism of the dual Torah not only matched the situation of Israel the conquered but (ordinarily) tolerated people. That Judaism created, within the psychological heritage of Israel, that same condition, that is to say, the condition of acceptance of a subordinated, but tolerated position, while awaiting the superior one.

4. Lewis, 32.

A painting by Arthur Szyk depicting an old world Passover seder.

Judaisms within Judaism:
The German Pietists of the Middle Ages

The Judaism of the dual Torah bore the power to encompass diverse Judaisms, each with its choice of elements, within the classical system, to emphasize and amplify. We see the power of the system when we consider the Judaisms that it both precipitated and accommodated. This sketch of basic components in the Judaic system of the dual Torah leaves ample space for variation and amplification. From the fourth century to the present time, derivative systems took shape, restating in distinctive ways the fundamental convictions of the Judaism of the dual Torah, or adding their particular perspective or doctrine to that system. Not only this, but heresies attained heretical status by rejecting important components of the received system, for example, its doctrine of the dual Torah or of the Messiah as a sage and model of the Torah fully observed. As long as the self-evidence of the established Judaism persisted, each of these derivative systems—orthodox or heretical—placed itself into relationship with that fundamental statement of matters. Only when the received Judaism no longer enjoyed virtually unique standing as the self-evidently valid answer to obviously urgent questions did Judaic systems take shape utterly out of phase with the one that reached its initial version in the fourth century and its final one in the Talmud of Babylonia.

Within the received system various systems found ample space for themselves. Some of these concerned new doctrines, which had to be made to accord with the received ones. Among them, for example, a massive rethinking of the very modes of thought of Judaism, moving from mythic to philosophical thinking, took shape over a long period of time. The philosophical movement presents striking testimony to the power of the received system, for it took as its task the validation and vindication of the faith—inclusive of the law and doctrine of the oral Torah—of the received system. Each continuator Judaism emphasized a received component of the original system or explicitly reaffirmed the whole of that system, while adding to it in interesting ways. All of the continuator Judaisms claimed to stand in a linear and incremental relationship to the original. They made constant reference to the established and authoritative canon, for example. They affirmed the importance of meticulous obedience to the law. Each one in its way proposed to strengthen or purify or otherwise confirm the dual Torah of Sinai.

That is why the Judaic systems—ways of life, worldviews, addressed to a particular Israel—from the fourth century to the nineteenth in Europe and to the mid-twentieth in the Muslim world serve in retrospect to affirm the normative standing of the classic system. One system after another took shape and made its own distinctive statement, but each one affirmed the definitive symbolic system and structure of the original. Among many candidates for study of how Judaism generated systemically cogent and coherent Judaism I have chosen two, one medieval, the other modern. Both fall into the category of sects within the "church" of the dual Torah. The first shows how a distinctive group worked out a legitimate Judaism, systemically harmonious with the inherited one. The other indicates how even in the conditions of modern times an essentially original system, with its own quite distinctive worldview and doctrine, made a place for itself (if with difficulty) within the received system. The former Judaism is that of the Jewish pietists in medieval Germany, the latter Judaism that of the Hasidim of eighteenth-century Poland.

What marks a Judaism as an autonomous system is not its doctrine or mode of thought (hence our disinterest in Jewish philosophy) but its address to a distinct social group, an Israel. In the late twelfth century Jewries in the Rhineland produced a pietistic circle "characterized by its own leadership and distinctive religious outlook."[5] What makes this Judaism a system within the larger system? First, the pietists produced their own viewpoints and doctrines, defining a distinctive way of life for their group. Second, their principal authority remained the canon of the dual Torah and its values. The writers defined a distinctive worldview, described by Marcus as "grounded in their new understanding of the hidden and revealed will of God." Their ideas became influential later on, but what is interesting is the entirely comfortable position the pietists found for themselves within the received Judaism. They formed a Judaism within Judaism.

What initially marked the group as distinctive was their doctrines, not their way of life. As matters unfolded, however, practice as much as profession distinguished the group from others within the larger, harmonious world of Israel. They developed an ascetic way of life to balance their doctrine:

> The Pietists continuously weigh this-worldly inward enjoyment and try to reduce it so as not to diminish otherworldly reward. The locus of obedience is not primarily external behavior . . . but the degree of the Pietist's inward zeal or sinful motivation.

They differed from the established system because they held that, as Marcus states, "God's will consists of more than what was explicitly revealed in Scripture, more than the rabbinically derived expanded meanings which form the basis of rabbinic law." The pietists identified themselves with Abraham at the

---

5. Ivan G. Marcus, *Piety and Society: The Jewish Pietists of Medieval Germany* (Leiden: E. J. Brill, 1981), 1. The entire account that follows draws on Marcus.

binding of Isaac, with Job in his trials. The pietist accepts anguish and pain as part of the price of serving God.

> Infinite in scope, the larger will consists of a third dimension encoded in Scripture but which is obligatory for the Pietist. Complementing the idea of God's larger will is the infinite obligation which the Pietist assumes of searching for and discovering it. . . . The Pietist . . . must be engaged continuously in a search for the hidden will by striving to discover new prohibitions and make new proscriptive safeguards around the forbidden. In so doing, the Pietist shows his true fear of God, which is understood as being afraid that one not love Him selflessly, sacrificially, totally.[6]

We see here the power of the sect to carry to an extreme convictions of the "church," the community as a whole. Emphasis on keeping the law more perfectly, on studying the Torah more perspicaciously defines not a heresy but a Judaism within the Judaism of the community at large. While a sect, the pietists in the German Rhineland nevertheless made persistent efforts at taking over the community at large and running it. In general they did not succeed, and consequently, they tended to segregate themselves from the larger world of Judaism: "For it is difficult for someone who wants to be a Pietist to see someone his own age in town pursuing a different way of life. If he does not also follow the others, he will be embarrassed, and he would be better off living in a different town."[7]

One point of emphasis characteristic of the pietists is on sin and atonement, which Marcus describes as "a logical and psychological extension of their pietistic ideal." The familiar category of virtuous attitudes, on which we have already concentrated, encompasses the correct attitude toward God as one of repentance, confession of sins, and returning to God:

> Atonement requires not only contrite repentance and confession as well as proofs of same, but in addition demands that the sinner must impose penances on himself which are

6. Marcus, 12.
7. Marcus, 95.

designed to rebalance the divine scales which sinning has tipped towards punishment. (p. 13)

Sin encompasses both what one has done and also one's attitude or motivation. Keeping the laws covers the former, doing so with "the whole heart," the latter. The life of repentance, penance, and reconciliation with God then forms the concrete counterpart to the doctrines at hand. The whole comprised the "way," the path to personal salvation.[8] The group formed a distinctive fellowship in their rejection of the Jewish society made up of outsiders to their system. They tried to take over the community or they withdrew from it; they remained in uneasy balance with the larger Judaic world. That is what I mean by a Judaism within Judaism. With their heavy emphasis on sin and atonement, the Pietists selected, out of the original system, that theme that in theological terms most exactly stated Israel's condition beyond 586 and before the final end of time. Study of the Torah would now encompass doctrines not articulated in the received documents:

> "One must be resourceful in the fear of God." Since a person is punished even when he does not know (what God requires), it is necessary to know and study (Torah, including Pietism). Moreover, you will not be able to tell the Ruler (that you did) a sin unintentionally (out of ignorance). Therefore, I decided to write a book for those who fear God so that they are not punished (for sinning out of ignorance) and think that it was for no reason.[9]

Once more we observe that, at the heart of matters, Torah defines and dominates, but, as we see, a special sort of Torah. In the end European Jewry was reshaped by the practices and norms which began in the pietist group. The pietists wove a new religious ideology into the fabric of Jewish law.[10] The sect did not become part of the "church," but it remade the "church" in its own image. So that "Torah" that had taken shape in the encounter with triumphant Christianity broadened and deepened

8. Marcus, 15.
9. Marcus, 72, quoting Samuel b. Qalonimos, *Sefer ha-Yirʾah*.
10. Marcus, 132.

in its scope, finding room for distinctive emphases and even new doctrines.

Judaisms within Judaism: Hasidism

Hasidism, a mystical movement that took shape in the eighteenth century and came to fruition in the nineteenth and twentieth, had the power to reenforce the observance and study of the Torah. That fact is astonishing, given the fresh character of the doctrines of the movement, on the one side, and the powerful opposition precipitated by it, on the other. The power of the original system to absorb and make its own diverse viewpoints, novel doctrines and matters of emphasis, finds testimony in the ultimate character of Hasidism. The mystic circles in Poland and Lithuania in the eighteenth century, among which Hasidism developed, carried on practices that marked them as different from other Jews (for example, special prayers, distinctive ways of observing certain religious duties, and the like). The first among the leaders of the movement of ecstatics and anti-ascetics, Israel b. Eliezer Baal Shem Tov, (known by the acronym "the *Besht*") worked as a popular healer. From the 1730s onward he undertook travels and attracted circles of followers to himself in Podolia, Poland, Lithuania, and elsewhere. When he died in 1760, he left behind not only disciples but a broad variety of followers and admirers in southeastern Poland and Lithuania. Leadership of the movement passed to a succession of holy men, about whom stories were told and preserved. In the third generation, from the third quarter of the eighteenth century into the first of the nineteenth, the movement spread and took hold. Diverse leaders, called zaddikim, holy men and charismatic figures, developed their own standing and doctrine.

Given the controversies that swirled about the movement, we should expect that many of the basic ideas would have been new, but that was hardly the case. The movement drew heavily on available mystical books and doctrines, which from medieval times onward had won a place within the faith as part of the Torah. Emphasis on a given doctrine on the part of Hasidic thinkers should not obscure the profound continuities betweenthe modern movement and its medieval sources. To take

one example of how the movement imparted its own imprint
on an available idea, Menahem Mendel of Lubavich noted that
God's oneness—surely a given in all Judaisms—means more than
that God is unique. It means that God is all that is:

> There is no reality in created things. This is to say that in truth
> all creatures are not in the category of "something" or a "thing"
> as we see them with our eyes. For this is only from our point
> of view, since we cannot perceive the divine vitality. But from
> the point of view of the divine vitality which sustains us, we
> have no existence and we are in the category of complete
> nothingness like the rays of the sun in the sun itself. . . . From
> which it follows that there is no other existence whatsoever
> apart from His existence, blessed be He. This is true unifica-
> tion.[11]

Since all things are in God, the suffering and sorrow of the world
cannot be said to exist. To despair, therefore, is to sin.

Hasidism emphasized joy and avoiding melancholy. Like
their earlier counterparts in the medieval Rhineland, the Hasidim
of modern times further maintained that the right attitude must
accompany the doing of religious deeds; the deed could only be
elevated when carried out in a spirit of devotion. The doctrine
of Hasidism further held that "in all things there are 'holy sparks'
waiting to be redeemed and rescued for sanctity through man
using his appetites to serve God. The very taste of food is a pale
reflection of the spiritual force which brings the food into being."[12] What followed was that before carrying out a religious
deed, the Hasidim would recite the formula, "For the sake of
the unification of the Holy One, blessed be he, and his *shekhinah*
[presence in the world]." They were criticized for that, but, as
we see, the fundamental pattern of life and the received worldview contained in the holy canon of Judaism defined the issues.
Hasidism therefore constituted a Judaism within Judaism—distinctive, yet in its major traits so closely related to the Judaism
of the dual Torah as to be indistinguishable except in trivial
details.

11. Cited by Louis Jacobs, "Basic Ideas of Hasidism," *Encyclopaedia Judaica*,
7:1404.
12. Jacobs, 1405.

One of these emphases mattered a great deal, and that was the doctrine of zaddikism. The zaddik, or holy man, had the power to raise the prayers of the followers and to work miracles. The zaddik was the means through which grace reached the world, the one who controlled the universe through his prayers. The zaddik would bring humanity nearer to God and God closer to humanity. The Hasidim were well aware that this doctrine of the zaddik—the pure and elevated soul that could reach to that realm of heaven in which only mercy reigns—represented an innovation.

> But if such powers were evidently denied to the great ones of the past how does the *zaddik* come to have them? The rationale is contained in a parable attributed to the Maggid of Mezhirech. . . . When a king is on his travels he will be prepared to enter the most humble dwelling if he can find rest there but when the king is at home he will refuse to leave his palace unless he is invited by a great lord who knows how to pay him full regal honors. In earlier generations only the greatest of Jews could attain to the holy spirit. Now that the *Shekhinah* [divine presence] is in exile, God is ready to dwell in every soul free from sin.[13]

The development of the doctrine of the zaddik, apparently an utter innovation, in fact carries forward a theme of the Zohar, a mystical document of the thirteenth century. The principal figure of that document, Simeon b. Yohai, an important rabbi in talmudic times, was seen by the Hasidim as the model for the veneration offered to the zaddik. In that way they linked themselves to the most ancient past of what to them was the Torah.[14] Nahman of Bratslav was identified with Simeon b. Yohai and held by his disciples to have formed the reincarnation of the talmudic authority. The conclusion drawn from that fact, as Arthur Green points out, is not the one that would distinguish the zaddik and his followers from the rest of Judaism:

> Nahman was very cross with those who thought that the main reason for the *zaddik's* ability to attain such a high level of

---

13. Jacobs, 1406.
14. Arthur Green, *Tormented Master: A Life of Rabbi Nahman of Bratslav* (University: University of Alabama Press, 1979), 12.

understanding was the nature of his soul. He said that this
was not the case, but that everything depended first and fore-
most upon good deeds, struggle, and worship. He said explicitly that everyone in the world could reach even the highest
rung, that everything depended upon human choice.[15]

While the zaddik was a superior figure, a doctrine such as that
of Nahman would have brought the Hasidic movement into close
touch with the rest of Jewry, with its emphasis on the equal
responsibility of all Israel to carry on the work of good deeds
and worship (not to mention study of the Torah). What was
special became the most appealing trait. So Green describes the
legacy of Nahman of Bratslav, citing the record of the master's
last great message:

> "Gevalt! Do not despair!" He went on in these words: "There
> is no such thing as despair at all!" He drew forth these words
> slowly and deliberately, saying, "There is no despair." He said
> the words with such strength and wondrous depth that he
> taught everyone, for all generations, that he should never de-
> spair, no matter what it is that he has to endure.

Green notes that the master had left "the example of a man who
had suffered all the torments of hell in his lifetime, but had
refused to give in to ultimate despair."[16] Rightly seeing this as
emblematic of the master at hand, we may also note how thoroughly in agreement the authorship of such rabbinic works as
the Talmud of the land of Israel, Genesis Rabbah, and Leviticus
Rabbah will have found themselves. That is what I mean when
I call Hasidism a Judaism within Judaism: both a restatement of
the familiar in a fresh idiom and also a reconsideration of the
profane under the aspect of the holy.

By the 1830s the original force of the movement had run its
course, and the movement, beginning as a persecuted sect, defined the way of life of the Jews in the Ukraine, Galicia, and
central Poland, with offshoots in White Russia and Lithuania on
the one side, and Hungary, on the other. The waves of emigration
from the 1880s onward carried the movement to the West, and,

15. Green, 14.
16. Green, 265.

in the aftermath of World War II, to the United States and the land of Israel as well. Today the movement forms a powerful component of Orthodox Judaism, and that fact is what is central to our interest. By the end of the eighteenth century powerful opposition, led by the most influential figures of East European Judaism, characterized Hasidism as heretical. Its emphasis on ecstasy, visions, miracles of the leaders, its way of life of enthusiasm—these were seen as delusions, and the veneration of the zaddik was interpreted as worship of a human being. The emphasis on prayer to the denigration of study of the Torah likewise called into question the legitimacy of the movement. In the war against Hasidism the movement found itself anathematized, its books burned, its leaders vilified.

Under these circumstances, the last thing anyone would anticipate would have been for Hasidism to find a place for itself within what would at some point be deemed orthodox, but it did. For example, one of the most influential and important organizations within contemporary orthodoxy, Agudat Israel, finds in Hasidim its principal membership. The acceptance of the movement came about through the development within Hasidism of centers of study of the Torah. The joining of Hasidic doctrine with the received tradition legitimated what had begun outside of that tradition altogether (at least, outside in the view of those who deemed themselves insiders). The first Hasidic center of Torah study came into being in the mid-nineteenth century, and by the end of that time the Lubavich sect of Hasidism had founded still more important centers. What began as a heretical movement had gained entry into the centers of the normative faith within the span of a century, and in another century had come to constitute the bulwark of that faith. I can imagine no greater testimony to the remarkable power and resilience of the Judaism of the dual Torah than the capacity of that system to make a place for so vigorous and original a movement as Hasidism.

Heresies: Karaite Judaism as Systemic Attack on the Oral Torah

The heresies generated by the Judaism of the dual Torah present still more striking evidence of the power of the received system

to thrive during its long epoch of standing as self-evidently truth-
ful answers to obviously urgent questions. For, as we shall now
see, that Judaism in its ascendancy also defined the limits of
heresy, imposing its values and its stresses upon the contrary-
minded statements of the age. The first of the two heresies
rejected the doctrine of the dual Torah, the second, the doctrine
of the sage Messiah. We look in vain, in the age of the dominance
of the Judaism of the dual Torah, for evidence that the system
faced heresies essentially alien to its structure and system. From
the fourth to the nineteenth century in Christendom, and up to
the mid-twentieth century in the Muslim world, Judaic
"heresies"[17] commonly took up a position on exactly the program
and agenda of the Judaism of the dual Torah. What made a
heresy heretical, then, was the rejection of one or another of the
definitive doctrines of the norm. But in the nineteenth- and
twentieth-century West, by contrast, new Judaisms, not merely
"heresies" cleaved out of the old, did take shape wholly outside
of the system and structure of that same Judaism.

We briefly consider two systemic heresies, each addressing
a fundamental plank in the platform of the Judaism of the dual
Torah: Karaite Judaism, which denied the myth of the dual Torah,
and Sabbateanism, which rejected the doctrine of the Messiah
as defined in the classical system and created a new doctrine
within the received structure and system—a Messiah outside of
the law. I cannot think of two more characteristic components
of the Judaism of the dual Torah than its belief in the oral Torah,
on the one side, and its expectation of a Messiah who would
master and carry out the teachings of the Torah of Sinai, on the
other. Both of these heresies take up exactly the opposite position
of the Judaism of the dual Torah, thereby not only challenging
but also testifying to its power to define reality for all Israel. As
in our consideration of the Judaisms within Judaism, we shall
take up both medieval and early modern phenomena, showing
the uninterrupted and uniform history of Judaisms from the
fourth to the nineteenth centuries. Karaite Judaism flourished

---

17. I treat heresy as an inappropriate but necessary word choice, because,
within the theory of this book on the diversity of Judaisms, none can be more
or less authentic than any other. Descriptively, a heresy becomes such when it
takes up a position on an issue different from the position of a dominant Judaism,
which has been defined by that Judaism. It thus confirms the dominance of the
paramount system of the time and place.

in medieval times, the Sabbatian system in the early modern age. The correspondence then between the systemically harmonious Judaisms and the systemically contradictory ones is exact.

The constitutive trait of the Judaism of the dual Torah was the doctrine that at Sinai God revealed the Torah to be transmitted through two media, written and oral. Focusing upon that central belief, Karaite Judaism denied that God revealed to Moses at Sinai more than the written Torah, and explicitly condemned belief in an oral one. It took shape in the eighth century, beginning after the rise of Islam, and advocated the return to Scripture as against tradition, inclusive of rabbinic tradition. The sect originated in Babylonia in the period following the formation of the Talmud of Babylonia, on the one side, and the rise of Islam, on the other. In his classic account of the matter, Zvi Ankori explains the origin of the movement as follows:

> The forceful promotion of talmudic legislation by the central Jewish institutions under Muslim domination . . . could not but call forth defiance in the distant peripheries of the Jewish Diaspora. Claiming to be the last link in an uninterrupted chain of oral transmission, the central Jewish administration, residing in Babylonia, considered itself the only legitimate heir and sole competent interpreter of that unique national experience: the lawgiving communication at Sinai . . . The protest against the central Jewish authorities did perforce assume the form of opposition to the Oral Law which was embodied in the Talmud and effectively enforced by the exilarchic office and the continuous activity of geonic lawmakers. Indeed, regional customs, rites and observances persisted in the fringe areas of Jewish Dispersion in spite of their having been ordered out of existence by the levelling action of Babylonian talmudic legislation. In reaffirming adherence to these practices, the forces of protest would register their dissatisfaction with the exilarchic and geonic administration and repudication of its legal and social policies which were identified with the talmudic legislation.[18]

18. Zvi Ankori, *Karaites in Byzantium* (New York: Columbia University Press, 1959), 1–3.

Ankori judges that the dynamics of sectarian life found definition "within or against its normative environment."[19] For our purpose that observation proves critical, for, as we see, it was the dual Torah that defined, in doctrinal and mythic terms, that normative environment.

The movement itself claimed to originate in biblical times and to derive its doctrine from the true priest, Zadok. The founder of the movement then recovered that original Torah. The founder, Anan b. David, imposed rules concerning food that were stricter than those of the rabbis, and in other ways legislated a version of the law of a more strict character than the talmudic authorities admitted. Ankori says of Anan:

> Anan ben David led the forces of anti-Rabbanite rebellion out of the remote frontiers of the Muslim-dominated Jewish Dispersion into the heart of exilarchic and geonic [that is, rabbinic-talmudic] dominion. Until that time open defiance was in evidence only in the outlying provinces of the Caliphate in which Muslim heterodoxy was thriving also. Anan's answer to the challenge of disillusionment with militant Palestino-centric messianism was national asceticisim anchored in the diasporic community of the pious. . . . Anan's widely heralded fundamentalism and exclusive reliance on the letter of the Written Law are largely a misnomer. Rather, his was an ex post facto attempt to read into the Bible (the full twenty-four volumes of it and not the Pentateuch alone) the customs and observances already practiced by the sectarians. . . . Normative leadership in Babylonia, awakened to the danger of sectarian subversion in its own home while campaigning for the extension of Babylonian jurisdiction over all provinces of the Jewish dispersion, must have struck back with all its force.[20]

By the ninth century the movement had established itself firmly. From the seventh to the twelfth century the main centers were located in Baghdad, Nehavend, Basra, Isfahan and elsewhere in Iran, and there were centers of the faith in the holy land and Egypt as well. Later on the movement moved its focus to the

19. Ankori, 9.
20. Ankori, 14, 17, 21.

Byzantine Empire, in particular in the twelfth through the sixteenth centuries, in the seventeenth and eighteenth centuries in
Poland and nearby regions, and in the nineteenth and twentieth
centuries it was found in the Crimea. What makes the movement
interesting is its principle: "Search thoroughly in the Torah and
do not rely on my opinion" (so Anan). The Scriptures then
formed the sole principle of the law.

Overall, in its formative century, Karaite Judaism formed "a
conglomeration of various anti-Rabbanite heresies." Exhibiting
diverse differences among themselves, they claimed that that
marked their authenticity:

> [The Rabbanites] believe that their laws and regulations have
> been transmitted by the prophets; if that was the case, there
> ought not to exist any differences of opinion among them and
> the fact that such differences of opinion do exist refutes their
> presumptuous belief. We, on the other hand, arrive at our
> views by our reason, and reason can lead to various results.[21]

The basic principle predominated that Scriptures were to be
studied freely, independently, and individually. No uniformity
of view could then emerge. Given the Judaism of the dual Torah's
emphasis on the authority of the Talmud and related canonical
documents, we could not expect a more precise statement of the
opposite view. Until the eighteenth century each party considered the other to be Jews, but in the Russian Empire in the
nineteenth century they were treated as distinct from one another. Karaites took the title "Russian Karaites of the Old Testament Faith." The Germans spared their lives during World War
II for that reason. But after the rise of the State of Israel the
Karaites in Islamic lands moved to Israel, where seven thousand
of them live today.[22]

The principal doctrine that the Bible serves as the sole source
of faith and law made a place for tradition, but it was to be kept
subordinate. The emphasis, as we have seen, lay not on the
consensus of sages, characteristic of the Judaism of the dual
Torah, but on the individual's task of finding things out for

21. Al Kirkisani, quoted by Joseph Elijah Heller and Leon Nemoy in "Karaites," *Encyclopaedia Judaica* 10:766.
22. Heller and Nemoy, 777.

himself. Anan, the founder, said exactly that, as we noted. So the doctrine balanced the principles of "rigidity and immutability of tradition" and "an absence of restrictions on individual understanding of the Scriptures."[23] The anarchy that resulted yielded ground to systemization later on. Heller and Nemoy list these principles for the determination of the law: (1) the literal meaning of the biblical text; (2) the consensus of the community; (3) the conclusions derived from Scripture by the method of logical analogy; (4) knowledge based on human reason and intelligence.

Apart from the rejection of the oral Torah, one would look in vain for important differences in creed. God is the sole creator, having made the world out of nothing; God is uncreated, formless, incomparable in unity, incorporeal, unique. God sent Moses and the prophets; gave the Torah through Moses, to which there will be no further complement or alteration; the dead will be raised on a day of judgment; there is reward and punishment, providence, freedom of will, immortality of the soul; God will send a Messiah when Israel in exile has been purified. The followers of the oral Torah will have found themselves entirely at home in these principles of the faith. On the other hand, determining the calendar did distinguish the group from the other Jews, because the Karaites developed their own calendar and therefore observed holy occasions on different days from those selected by the rabbanites. Some minor details of the law of ritual slaughter differed, and the rules of consanguineous marriage are more strict than those of the rabbanites. In structure the liturgy does not vastly differ from that of the rabbanites; for example, the Shema is recited, the Torah is read, and so on. The fundamental point of heresy was simple—the authority of the oral tradition. The Karaites claimed that their Torah conveyed the pure faith of Moses, and the belief in a dual revelation was the point that separated them permanently from the Judaism of the dual Torah. This was made explicit in the beginning, although Karaites could later admit, "Most of the Mishnah and the Talmud comprises genuine utterances of our fathers, and . . . our people are obligated to study the Mishnah and the Talmud."[24] That was the issue that had led to the original division.

23. Heller and Nemoy, 777.
24. Heller and Nemoy, 781.

Heresies: Sabbatianism as Attack on the Belief that the Messiah Would Be a Sage of the Torah

What is important about the Sabbatian movement, a seventeenth-century messianic movement organized around the figure of Shabbetai Zevi (1626–76)[25] is a simple fact: The Sabbatian movement defined the Messiah not as a sage who kept and embodied the law, but as the very *opposite*. The Torah defined the framework of debate. Sabbatian Judaism responded with the Messiah as a holy man who violated the law in letter and in spirit. In positing a Messiah in the mirror image of the sage Messiah of the Judaism of the dual Torah, the Sabbatian movement, like Karaism, paid its respects to the received system. Gershom Scholem finds the power of the movement in its link to earlier doctrines of the Jewish Kabbalah, in which the hope for the Messiah was joined to mystical religious experience, thus, in Scholem's language, "introducing a new element of tension into the Kabbalah, which was of a much more contemplative nature." The Kabbalah that took shape in the sixteenth century, associated with the name of Lureia and the locale of Safed (in Galilee), linked the doing of the religious duties of the Torah, the recitation of prayer, and the messianic hope. Specifically, the link is drawn as follows:

> All being has been in exile since the very beginning of creation and the task of restoring everything to its proper place has been given to the Jewish people, whose historic fate and destiny symbolize the state of the universe at large. The sparks of Divinity are dispersed everywhere . . . but they are held captive by . . . the power of evil, and must be redeemed. This final redemption . . . cannot be achieved by one single messianic act, but will be effected through a long chain of activities that prepare the way.[26]

The Jews' redemption through the Messiah will serve as "external symbols of a cosmic process which in fact takes place in

25. Gershom G. Scholem, "Shabbetai Zevi," in *Encyclopaedia Judaica* 14:1219–54. All quotations and citations are from this article.
26. Scholem, 1220.

the secret recesses of the universe." The doctrine of the sixteenth-century Kabbalists, that the final stages of redemption now neared, made the Judaic world ready for the messianic figure who came to the fore in 1665.

Shabbetai Zevi, born in Smyrna/Izmir in 1626, mastered talmudic law and lore and enjoyed respect for his learning even among his opponents. A manic-depressive, during his manic periods he deliberately violated religious law, in actions called (in the doctrine of his movement) "strange or paradoxical." In depressed times he chose solitude "to wrestle with the demonic powers by which he felt attacked and partly overwhelmed." During a period of wandering in Greece and Thrace, he placed himself in active opposition to the law, declaring the commandments to be null and saying a benediction "to Him who allows what is forbidden." In this way he distinguished himself even before his meeting with the disciple who organized his movement, Nathan of Gaza. In 1665 the two met and Nathan announced to Shabbetai Zevi that the latter was the true Messiah. This independent confirmation of Shabbetai Zevi's own messianic dreams served, in Nathan's doctrine, "to explain the peculiar rank and nature of the Messiah's soul in the kabbalistic scheme of creation."[27] In May of 1665, Shabbetai Zevi announced himself as the Messiah, and various communities, hearing the news split in their response to that claim. Leading rabbis opposed him, others took a more sympathetic view. Nathan proclaimed that the time of redemption had come. In 1666 the grand vizier offered Shabbetai Zevi the choice of accepting Islam or imprisonment and death. On Sept. 15, 1666, Shabbetai Zevi converted to Islam.

Nathan of Gaza explained that the apostasy marked a descent of the Messiah to the realm of evil, outwardly to submit to its domination but actually to perform the last and most difficult part of his mission by conquering that realm from within.[28] The Messiah was engaged in a struggle with evil, just as in his prior actions in violating the law, he undertook part of the labor of redemption. The apostate Messiah would then form the center of the messianic drama, meant to culminate, soon enough, in the triumph. Down to his death in 1672 Shabbetai Zevi carried out his duties as a Muslim and also observed Jewish ritual. He

27. Scholem, 1224.
28. Scholem, 1238.

went through alternating periods of illumination and depression, and, in the former periods, founded new festivals and taught that accepting Islam involved "the Torah of grace," as against Judaism, "the Torah of truth." Scholem summarizes the doctrine as follows:

> In a way, every soul is composed of the two lights and by its nature bound predominantly to the thoughtless light which aims at destruction, and the struggle between the two lights is repeated over and over again in every soul. But the holy souls are helped by the law of the Torah, whereas the Messiah is left completely to his own devices. These ideas . . . responded precisely to the particular situation of those who believed in the mission of an apostate Messiah, and the considerable dialectical force with which they were presented did not fail to impress susceptible minds.[29]

The Sabbatian movement persisted for another century or so. Some believers joined Islam, others reverted to Judaism. The main stream of followers persisted in the antinomianism of the founder and took the view that the "new spiritual or messianic Torah entailed a complete reversal of values. . . . This included all the prohibited sexual unions and incest." The story of Sabbateanism, both in the life of Shabbetai Zevi and Nathan of Gaza and afterward, carries us far afield. The one consequential fact for the history of Judaism lies in the trait of the system that defined it as a heresy. The messianic doctrine that had stood at the head of the Judaism of the dual Torah—the Messiah as sage and master of the law—found as its counterpart and heretical opposite the doctrine of the Messiah as (while master of the law) the quintessential sinner in doing those very sins that the law, in particular, designated as sinful. The Messiah, supposed to come to fulfill and complete the law, ended up denying it. From the viewpoint of the Judaism of the dual Torah, there can have been no greater heresy than that. Only when we encounter the Judaisms of the twentieth century, wholly out of phase with the received system of the dual Torah, shall we appreciate the full power of that received system to dictate to heretical groups the

29. Scholem, 1243.

terms and doctrines of their heresies, for the doctrine of the dual
Torah created Karaite Judaism, the Messiah sage defined Sabbateanism.

The Power and Pathos of Judaism

In the nineteenth century the Judaism of the dual Torah found
for itself adaptations and continuations. In the twentieth, for the
first time since the fourth, that same Judaism met competition
from Judaisms that defined themselves—their terms and clas-
sifications—wholly out of relationship with those of the Judaism
of the dual Torah. The new Judaisms no longer fall into the
category of heresies of the received one. They asked different
questions and proposed answers as self-evidently true that had
no bearing upon the issues of the dual Torah. The Judaism of
the dual Torah exercised power as long as people found its
questions urgent, its answers obvious and beyond the need for
argument. That same Judaism ceased to define the system (way
of life, worldview) of substantial communities of Jews when
those questions gave way to others, and, of course, those answers proved not incorrect but irrelevant.

Judaism's power derived from the world defined by its rivals
and heirs, Christianity and Islam, which set the program of
questions that Christianity, Judaism, and Islam alike would confront. The pathos of the Judaism of the dual Torah derived from
its incapacity to address questions that lay outside of its powers
of imagination. Those were the questions of the twentieth century, and (we now recognize) no religious worldview and way
of life would prove able to cope with them. When humanity lost
the vision of itself as having been created in the image of God,
"in our image, after our likeness," then Judaism, Islam, and
Christianity would have to fall silent. For the great religions of
Scripture took as their generative question what it meant for
humanity to be in God's image, after God's likeness. The power
of Judaic, like that of Christian and of Islamic religious systems,
and the pathos of the three faiths of Abraham, were and are one
and the same. Their strength, the transcendent vision of humanity, also marked their weakness, the measure of trivial humanity, there to be murdered in its masses. The death of Judaism,

where it died, formed a chapter in the century's tale of civil war within humanity, first in the West, in World War I, then in the world, in World War II and afterward. But our task is to tell only that small paragraph that, in the history of Judaism, attests to the larger sense in the story of humanity.

Because the Judaism of the dual Torah had faced significant competition only in the West,[30] as we approach modern and contemporary times, let us speak of Christendom in particular. The critical Judaic component of the Christian civilization of the West spoke of God and God's will for humanity, what it meant to live in God's image, after God's likeness according to the Judaism of the dual Torah and Christianity in its worship of God made flesh. That message of humanity in God's image, of a people seeking to conform to God's will, found resonance in the Christian world as well. Both components of the world, the Christian dough, the Judaic yeast, bore a single message about humanity.

The powerful religious traditions of the West, the Christian and the Judaic, addressing politics as defined in the fourth century, lost their voices in the nineteenth, and their echo in the twentieth. The first century beyond the Christian formulation of the West, that is, the twentieth century, would raise the ineluctable issues of class and nation-state as bases for bureaucratization of the common life, not of what it meant to form one humanity in the image of one God. Asked to celebrate the image of humanity, the twentieth century created an improbable likeness of humanity: mountains of corpses. Confronting the twentieth century's framing of the inexorable question, What is the human being? the Judaism of the dual Torah fell understandably silent. In such a world as this turned out to be, what was there to say?

---

30. The impact of imperialism on Judaism in the Islamic world cannot be ignored, for example, in French Algeria and Morocco. But Islam overall retained its self-evident standing as revealed truth, and the Judaism of the colonized world of Islam thrived, within Israel in Islam, as did Islam. The development in the French colonies of a francophone Israel affected only the urban middle and upper classes, with the larger numbers essentially untouched by Western secularism. Neither Reform nor Orthodoxy in their Western formulations found any counterpart, let alone resonance, in the colonial period of Islam.

Part Three

ALL ISRAEL'S MEAL AT HOME, ON THE SPECIAL OCCASION OF FAMILY GATHERING:
THE JUDAISM FOR ONCE IN A WHILE

CHAPTER SIX

Israel among the Nations: The Age of Judaisms

Covenant: From "Israel" Alone to Both Jew and Citizen: The Ambiguity of Modern Times

The nation-state, beginning with Napoleon's France in the late eighteenth century, conceived everyone to be one thing, a citizen. People were free to be other things as well, for example, Christians or Jews, but the state recognized only individuals, citizens, and not groups living an autonomous life. For the Judaism of the dual Torah, this conception raised an acute problem. That Judaism took for granted Jews were only one thing, holy Israel. It further supposed that, in general, Jews would live a distinct and autonomous existence, among other such distinct and autonomous groups. The Judaism of the dual Torah had no answer to the question of how to be both a Jew and something else, indeed, many other things. Nor could that Judaism deal with Jews who wished to live not segregated but integrated lives. Jews had lived lives different from others in many critical ways. For example, they ate food that was not like that of others, and they did not eat the food of others. Now, Jews wished to live not only among but with Gentiles. Jews had worn distinctive

clothing. They had spoken their own languages, Yiddish (originally a kind of German dialect, such as was spoken in the
Rhineland) in northern and eastern Europe, and Ladino (a kind
of Spanish) in the Mediterranean. German Jews now wanted to
speak German, not Yiddish. Not only so, but Jews had a niche
for themselves in the economy; some professions or business
were set aside for their group, as other economic callings were
for others (and were closed to them). Nevertheless the borders
that made possible this segregated existence were porous, and,
as time passed, from the end of the eighteenth century onward,
many Jews crossed those borders. Some simple chose not to be
Jewish any more, adopting Lutheran or Roman Catholic Christianity where these were the dominant religions. Many Jews
wished to be Jewish, but desired also to live integrated lives.
Their question, How can we be Jewish plus other things as well?
found no reply in the received Judaism.

The critical issue confronting Jews from the eighteenth century was how to be both "Israel" and something else, and to
that question the Judaism of the dual Torah provided not an
answer but an evasion. The Judaism of the dual Torah's power
lay in responding to the question of the covenant of the Torah
and Israel: What now? and, To what end? The challenge of
Christianity was framed in precisely the same terms and categories: Why you, when the end is now? When Christianity
ceased to frame the paramount issue confronted by Jews, the
Judaism of the dual Torah met competition from Judaisms that
identified different questions as urgent and met those questions
with different answers deemed self-evidently valid. All things
came down to one alternative—Israel only or Israel and something else (both Israel and French, German, British, American).
To be both a Jew and a citizen of a nation-state meant that one
would in the nature of things have to find a space in life for
both—to be a Jew somewhere, some of the time, under some
determinate circumstances, and to be something everybody else
was, some of the time and for some purposes.

From ancient times Jews had defined themselves as only
Israel, that is, a people that dwells apart, a people that was holy
to God. In Islam and Christendom they found a useful place for
themselves as a distinct group, understood by the dominant
faiths within the framework of those faiths, understood by themselves on their own terms. Christendom wiped out pagans but

accorded to Israel the right of survival as a subordinated and—at best—a tolerated minority. Islam accorded the same status to both Christians and Jews. For its part, living its distinctive life, Israel, the Jewish people, ate its own food, wore its own clothing, spoke its own language, pursued its own particular crafts, and found in the Torah the complete and exhaustive account of what it was to be and to do. Israel was only Israel, nothing else—without apology. The vast majority of Jews in eastern Europe spoke Yiddish, while others spoke Russian, Polish, or Ukrainian or any of a dozen other languages. They lived in large numbers in villages, often a majority of the small town where they were located. They wore garments that identified them as Israel, ate only what they themselves cooked, made a living characteristic of their group, for instance, as artisans and craftsmen, and spent their lives mainly among themselves. They were only Israel.

Political and economic changes in the West redefined the conditions under which Jews, among others, lived. As a result, moving from village to city, entering a variety of businesses and professions no longer characteristic of their own group alone, speaking a language that was not only spoken by other Jews, wearing clothing that other people wore and (later) even eating the same food as others, Jews became something else in addition to being "Israel." They also were becoming a species of American, German, French, or British citizen.

The initial reason for the change was political. With the American Constitution of 1787 along with its Bill of Rights, and the French Revolution of 1789, a new political order in the West called into question the classification of people by groups, set into hierarchical order (Islam at the top in the Muslim world, a particular Christianity at the top in various parts of Christendom). The new politics defined the social order not by groups but by individuals. Whatever else people were, they all were one thing—citizens of a common nation-state. In the debates on the Rights of Man, French revolutionaries who favored the inclusion of Jews within the France that was being created in the 1790s accorded to the Jewish people the rights of citizens, but to Israel as a social entity no recognition whatsoever.

For their part, Jews, particularly in Western Europe and the United States, welcomed the new order. They accepted the notion that they could be Israel and American, British, French, or

German. This meant that the simple definitions of Israel that had formerly served because they corresponded to the social world in which Jews lived, no longer sufficed. People had to figure out what it meant to be both "Israel," that is, Jewish, and also American, German, British, or French. Formerly coherent, the various chapters of a person's life had to be divided up, with a space for "being Jewish," and other spaces as well.

Being "Israel"—and that alone—no longer defined the limits of the everyday life of Jews. That was because the western nations did not define inhabitants of their territories as members of recognized groups, and so did not deal with Jewish people through the Jewish community. Consequently, being Jewish no longer identified a person in all aspects of life. Jews were expected to participate in the politics and the nationalism of the countries in which they lived, no longer looking forward to a state of their own. They were accorded the rights and also the responsibilities of citizenship, requiring a way of life like that of others. For a great many people, as the nineteenth century unfolded, this meant that the everyday practices that governed so much of life—meals at home, learning in school, making a living in the world beyond—no longer could be treated as parts of a single whole, collective existence. One solution was described: "Be a Jew at home, and a human being when you go out," meaning, difference from Gentiles was acceptable in private, at home and in the family, while in the shared life of the city where people lived, Jews should not differ from others. Consequently, the Judaism that had been defined in ancient times would live in the family. Can we identify a meal that captures the ambiguity of the new circumstance? The Passover seder, or ritual banquet, provides a fine example of what it means to be intensely Jewish some of the time, but many other things much of the time. Jews who observe few other rites of Judaism in the course of the year nearly unanimously participate in the rite of home and family marking the advent of Passover, celebrating Israel's Exodus from Egypt (of all things!).

The Meal: The Contemporary Passover Seder, at Home, Eaten Once a Year by a Family Formed for the Occasion

What does it mean to be Jewish some of the time and something else the rest of the time? It means to be Jewish at home—but to be intensely Jewish then. Not surprisingly, as in the Judaism of the Temple, the focus of celebration was a shared meal with God, and as in the Judaism of the Torah, the rite attached to the eating of a meal conveyed the entirety of the faith. In modern times, we look first at a meal to find the centerpiece of Judaism, the one thing that contains all things. The single most widely practiced rite of Judaism in North America requires family and friends to sit down for supper. This ritual meal, called the seder, in celebration of the festival of Passover, "the season of our liberation" (in the words of the prayer book), is observed by upwards of 90 percent of all Jews in the United States and Canada. It is a secular supper party on a highly charged occasion, rich in deeply felt meanings which we would not perceive if we were simply to review the words that are said. The meal consumed with ceremony turns people into something other than what they think they are and puts them into the path of an onrushing history. In the presence of visual and verbal symbols, in the formation of family and friends into an Israel redeemed from Egypt, people become something else, and words work that wonder.

At the festival of Passover, which coincides with the first full moon after the vernal equinox, Jewish families gather around their tables for a holy meal, called a seder, that is, a meal that follows an order of procedure. There, speaking in very general terms, they retell the story of the Exodus from Egypt in times long past. With unleavened bread and sanctified wine, they celebrate the liberation of slaves from Pharaoh's bondage. There is, at the rite, a single formula that in words captures the moment, and to understand how the "we" of the family becomes the "we" of Israel, how the eternal and perpetual coming of spring is made to mark a singular moment—a one-time act on the stage in the unfolding of linear time—we begin there:

An elegant table set for the seder meal.

For ever after, in every generation, *every Israelite must think of himself or herself as having gone forth from Egypt* (emphasis added).

This is a curious passage indeed. It is one thing to tell Jews to think of themselves in one way, rather than in some other. It is different to explain why Jews respond to the demand—and they do respond.

What is it that makes plausible for nearly all Jews all over the world the statement, "*We* went forth . . ."? and why do people sit down for supper and announce, "It was not only our forefathers that the Holy One, blessed be He, redeemed; *us too, the living,* He redeemed together with them"? We were not there. Pharaoh has been dead for some time. Egypt languishes in the rubbish heap of history. Wherein lies the enchantment? Why us? Why here? Why now? The answer derives from the power, within Judaism, through enchantment to transform the here and now into an intimation of the wholly other. When we see the everyday as metaphor, we perceive that deeper layer of meaning that permits us to treat as obvious and self-evident the transforming power of comparison, of simile applied to oneself: Let's pretend, What if? and, Why not? One theme stands out—we, here and now, are really living then and there. For example:

> We were slaves in of Pharaoh in Egypt and the Lord our God brought us forth from there with a mighty hand and an outstretched arm. And if the Holy One, blessed be He, had not brought our fathers forth from Egypt, then we and our descendents would still be slaves to Pharaoh in Egypt. And so, even if all of us were full of wisdom, understanding, sages and well informed in the Torah, we should still be obligated to repeat again the story of the Exodus from Egypt; and whoever treats as an important matter the story of the Exodus from Egypt is praiseworthy.
>
> This is the bread of affliction which our ancestors ate in the land of Egypt. Let all who are hungry come and eat with us, let all who are needy come and celebrate the Passover with us. This year here, next year in the land of Israel; this year slave, next year free people. . . .
>
> This is the promise which has stood by our forefathers and stands by us. For neither once, nor twice, nor three times was our destruction planned; in every generation they rise against us, and in every generation God delivers us from their hands into freedom, out of anguish into joy, out of mourning into

festivity, out of darkness into light, out of bondage into redemption.[1]

For ever after, in every generation, *every Israelite must think
of himself or herself as having gone forth from Egypt.* For we read
in the Torah: "In that day thou shalt teach thy son, saying: All
this is because of what God did for me when I went forth from
Egypt." It was not only our forefathers that the Holy One,
blessed be He, redeemed; us too, the living, He redeemed
together with them, as we learn from the verse in the Torah:
"And He brought us out from thence, so that He might bring
us home, and give us the land which he pledged to our
forefathers"[2] (emphasis added).

So much for the message of the rite. What human situation for
Americans who are Jewish is addressed? and why do they re-
spond to that and make it an important component of their
Judaism?

If we ask, What experience in the here and now is taken up
and transformed by enchantment into the then and there? we
move from the rite to the reality. That progress tells us what
troubles these people and makes playacting plausible as they
turn their lives into metaphor, themselves into actors, and the
everyday into pretense and drama. The question takes on urgency when we remind ourselves once more that we confront
the single most popular and widely observed rite of Judaism.
What speaks so ubiquitously, with such power, that everybody
who wants in joins in? In my view, the message penetrates the
heart of people who remember the murder of six million Jews
in recent history, and who know, in their own lives, that they
are also a minority and at risk, if not in politics, then in psychology. That corner of the everyday life—which Judaism defines
for people who are many things, but also Jews and therefore
part of "Israel" the people—finds the family at a meal. The meal
brings to expression the human meaning of "being Jewish."
Therefore also it speaks directly to the social world of Israel, the
Jewish people.

What troubles Jews in a free society is not that they are not
free, but that they are uncomfortable with the kind of freedom

1. This is my adaptation of the translation by Maurice Samuel, *Haggadah of
Passover* (New York: Hebrew Publishing Co., 1942), 9.
2. Samuel, 9.

that makes them what they are—free to be different. Who wants to be different? The rite transforms what people feel into a sentiment they can recognize; they become a simile for something more and nobler than what they feel. In theoretical language, Jews in North America drawn to their dinner parties enter an anguish drawn from mythic being because that anguish imparts to their ordinary life that metaphoric quality, that status as simile, that makes sense of the already perceived.

The Jews are a minority, small in numbers, compensating in visibility. As far as they differ from "the others," Jews deal with a chronic discomfort regarding a fantasized majority that is alike in all respects because everyone not Jewish is the same, that is, (merely) Gentile. To be different—whatever the difference—requires explanation; it provokes resentment; it creates tension demanding resolution and pain requiring remission. For the young, difference is deadly. For the middle aged, difference demands explanation and compensation, and it may well exact the cost of diminished opportunity. The individual may not be different from other individuals, but families always do retain that mark of difference from other families in the very nature of their existence. Passover celebrates the family of Israel and is celebrated by the families of Israel. Therefore Passover, with its rhetoric of rejoicing for freedom, plays out in a minor key the song of liberation: today slaves, next year, free; today here, next year in "Jerusalem" (that is, not the real Jerusalem but the imagined, heavenly one). That is why, when they read, "We see ourselves as if . . . ," they do not burst out laughing and call for the main course.

The key to the power of the Passover seder is expressed in the simple statement, "In every generation they rise against us." Somewhere, some time, that is always so. Passover is popular now because it speaks to a generation that knows what the Gentiles can do, having seen what they did to the Jews of Europe. Passover furthermore speaks not to history alone but also to personal existence; it joins together history with the experience of the individual, because the individual as a minority finds as self-evident, relevant, true, and urgent a rite that reaches into the everyday and turns that common world into a metaphor for the reality of Israel, enslaved but also redeemed. The seder explains what, in the everyday, things mean beyond the four cubits of the private person's world. In terms now familiar, the seder effects its enchantment by showing the individual that the everyday stands for something beyond, the here and now represent the everywhere and all the time: "In every generation they rise against us." True, but also, God saves. Who would not be glad to have supper to celebrate that truth, if only through commemoration.

The Life Cycle and the Judaism of Home and Family: Puberty

The Judaism of home and family attends not only to shared meals of celebration, but also turning points in the path of life. Here the Judaism of the dual Torah defines matters. Received from the Torah as read by the sages of the dual Torah, certain rites of home and family are broadly practiced among Jews who do not eat holy food, wear holy clothing, speak a holy language, practice professions particular to the holy people, and otherwise segregate themselves from all other nations and peoples. Jews who wish to integrate themselves into society at large for most of their lives and most of their time at such turning points in the course of life as the birth of a baby, the advent of puberty, and death, very commonly turn to the Judaism of the dual Torah, which continues to thrive within the home and among the family. Our case in point is the celebration of puberty, when a boy or (in Conservative, Reconstructionist, and Reform Judaisms) a girl reaches the age of obligation to carry out religious responsibilities—that is, becomes a bar mitzvah or a bat mitzvah.

That defines the single most important rite of the life cycle in contemporary Judaism in North America. When a child reaches puberty (for males, thirteen, for females, twelve or thirteen), he or she is called for the first time to the Torah. What happens at the bar or bat mitzvah? The young person is called to the Torah, recites the blessing that is required prior to the public proclamation of a passage of the Torah, and reads that passage (or stands as it is read). When the Torah lection of the week has been read, the congregation proceeds to a passage of the prophets. The young person reads that passage for the congregation.

That is the rite—no rite at all. The young person is treated no differently from others that Sabbath, or the previous week, or the following. He or she simply assumes a place within the congregation of adult Jews, is counted for a quorum, and is expected to carry out the religious duties that pertain. The young person is not asked to imagine himself or herself in some mythic state or setting, such as Eden, or at Sinai, or in the Jerusalem of the Messiah's time. The family of the young person does not find itself compared to "all Israel," and no stories are told about how the young person and the family reenact a mythic event, such as the Exodus from Egypt. No one is commanded to see himself or herself as if this morning he or she were born, crossed the Red Sea, entered the promised land, or did any of those other things that the story of the dual Torah invokes on enchanted occasions of personal transformation.

Only when a Jew achieves intelligence and self-consciousness, normally at puberty, is he or she expected to accept the full privilege of *mitzvah*, "commandment" and to regard himself or herself as *commanded* by God. But that sense of "being commanded" is impersonal and not imposed by the invocation of a myth, for example, Sinai. The transaction is neutral; it involves affirmation and assent, confirmation and commitment. There is no bower, no Eden, no family at table reading a received rite. Judaism perceives the commandments as expressions of one's acceptance of the yoke of the kingdom of heaven and submission to God's will. That acceptance cannot be coerced, but requires thoughtful and complete affirmation. The bar or bat mitzvah thus represents the moment that the young Jew first assumes full responsibility before God to keep the commandments.

Calling the young person to the Torah and conferring upon him or her the rights of a full member of the community ratify what has taken place. Those actions do not effect a change in status of the individual, all the more so a significant alteration in the condition of the community. The individual simply adheres to the ongoing community, of which, through circumcision, he or she is already a part. His or her status changes, but community does not change in the way in which, at birth it changes. The advent of puberty is marked by the bar and bat mitzvah rites, at which a young person becomes obligated to keep the commandments; *bar*, "son" and *bat*, "daughter" have the sense that

one is subject to; and *mitzvah* means "commandment." The
young person is called to pronounce the benediction over a
portion of the Torah lection in the synagogue and is given the
honor of reading the prophetic passage as well.

But that is hardly the entire story of the bar or bat mitzvah—
far from it, as anyone Jewish or anyone who knows Jews realizes.
In fact it is a magnificent, often sumptuous occasion, celebrated
with vigor and enthusiasm by Jews who otherwise do not often
find their way to the synagogue on Sabbath mornings, such as
Jews married to Gentiles, Jews themselves not "barmitzved,"
Jews remote from any and all connection with Jewish organizations, institutions, activities, observances. First the occasion
calls forth dinners and dances, lavish expenditure on an open
bar and a huge meal (hence the standard joke about "too much
bar and not enough mitzvah"). Second, and more to the point,
many Jews find the occasion intensely meaningful, deeply affecting. It is therefore an ambiguous occasion, partly Judaic,
partly conventionally American. In the mixture of the religious
and the cultural, we identify competing systems that, within a
single family and its life, come to realization.

"Not only Jewish but Also . . . German/American/French": Explaining the Rise of Competing Judaisms in the Democratic West

Clearly, people pick and choose, among rites as much as within
their formerly uniform lives. When Jewish, they identify with
rites of home and family; when not, they may choose not to
practice other equally affecting rites (the Sabbath or thrice-daily
prayer, for example). The Passover meal, intense and distinctive,
finds most Jews at home around the table; synagogue worship
the next morning does not. How did it come about that people
found a way to sort out life so that one component or occasion
would be sanctified in the Judaism of the dual Torah, while others
would be treated as wholly secular? In modern times in the West,
though not in Muslim countries, the long-established system of
Judaism competed with and even gave way to a number of new

Judaisms. Some of them stood in direct continuation with the received system, revering its canon and repeating its main points. Reform and Orthodox Judaism in Western Europe and the United States exemplify the Judaisms of continuation. Other Judaisms, such as Zionism, rejected the system of the Judaism of the dual Torah. Identifying points of change in modern times presents few problems. People simply chose for themselves a different set of questions from those that had defined the West, and, it follows, they also produced a set of self-evidently true answers.

As we saw, while rabbinic Judaism answered only the question of how to be Jewish, a new urgent question demanded response: How can one be both Jewish *and something else?* In making a place for that something else—that corner of life not affected by the labor of sanctification in the here and now aiming at salvation at the end of time—the continuator Judaisms framed in a striking and fresh way the received system of the dual Torah. What happened toward the end of the eighteenth century to make this new question urgent was the secularization of political life and institutions. Earlier modes of organizing matters recognized as political entities groups and guilds and classes, and the Jews found a place among them. In the hierarchical scheme, with church and monarchy and aristocracy in their proper alignment, other political entities could likewise find their location. With church disestablished and monarchy rejected, however, with the aristocracy no longer dominant in politics, the political unit became the (theoretically) undifferentiated individual, making up the nation-state. There was no room within that theory for Israel, the Jewish people, as a political unit, although (in theory at least) there might be room for the Jewish individual in rightful place alongside other undifferentiated individuals. That was the theory of matters that produced a considerable crisis for the Judaism of the dual Torah. Judaism had responded to a different question with its self-evidently valid answers.

In the aftermath of the changes in western politics in the nineteenth century, Jews indeed asked themselves whether and how they could be something in addition to Jewish, and that something invariably found expression in the name of the locale in which they lived. So could one be both Jewish and German? That ineluctable question found its answer in two givens: the

datum of the received Judaism of the dual Torah, and the datum
that "being German" or "being French" imposed certain clearly
defined responsibilities. The single most important response to
the issue of how to be a Jew and something more was, and now
is, Reform Judaism.

Reform Judaism

Reform Judaism started in the early part of the nineteenth century by making changes in liturgy, then in doctrine and in way
of life of the received Judaism of the dual Torah, and—in the
model of the Protestant Reformation—calling these changes reforms. Reform Judaism recognized the legitimacy of making
changes and regarded change as reform. But the stakes were
higher than mere alterations in prayers or doctrines might suggest. The Jews' position, beginning in the eighteenth century in
the public polity of the several Christian European countries in
which they lived, was of much greater interest to the Reformers.
From the perspective of the political changes taking place from
the American and French Revolutions onward, the received system of the Judaism of the dual Torah answered chronic but really
irrelevant questions and did not respond to acute and urgent
ones.

Reform Judaism in the United States today is the largest and
most important Judaism, and hence we turn to the definition of
that Judaism that emerged from a meeting of Reform rabbis in
Pittsburgh in 1885. To the Reform rabbis in Pittsburgh Christianity presented no urgent problems. The open society of America
did. The self-evident definition of the social entity, Israel, therefore had to shift. We recall how the fourth-century rabbis balanced Israel against Rome, Jacob against Esau, the triumphant
political messiah, seen as arrogant, against the Messiah of God,
humble and sagacious. Israel therefore formed a supernatural
entity and in due course would enter into that final era in God's
division of time, in which Israel would reach its blessing. The
supernatural entity, Israel, now formed no social presence. The
Christian world—the world in which Christ ruled through popes
and emperors, in which kings claimed divine right, in which the
will of the Church bore multiform consequences for society, and

in which, by the way, Israel too was perceived in a supernatural framework (if a negative one)—no longer existed. The world at large no longer verified—as had the world of Christendom and Islam—that generative social category of Israel's life, *Israel as supernatural entity.* Then the problem of defining the sort of entity Israel did constitute (What sort of way of life should characterize that Israel? What sort of worldview should explain it?) produced a new set of urgent and ineluctable questions, and, in the nature of things, also self-evidently true answers, such as we find in Pittsburgh:

> We recognize in the Mosaic legislation a system of training the Jewish people for its mission during its national life in Palestine, and to-day we accept as binding only the moral laws, and maintain only such ceremonies as elevate and sanctify our lives, but reject all such as are not adapted to the views and habits of modern civilization. . . . We hold that all such Mosaic and rabbinical laws as regular diet, priestly purity, and dress originated in ages and under the influence of ideas altogether foreign to our present mental and spiritual state. . . . Their observance in our days is apt rather to obstruct than to further modern spiritual elevation. . . . We recognize, in the modern era of universal culture of heart and intellect, the approaching of the realization of Israel's great messianic hope for the establishment of the kingdom of truth, justice, and peace among all men. We consider ourselves no longer a nation, but a religious community, and therefore expect neither a return to Palestine, nor a sacrificial worship under the sons of Aaron, nor the restoration of any of the laws concerning the Jewish state. . . .[3]

The Pittsburgh platform takes up each component of the system in turn. Who is Israel? What is its way of life? How does it account for its existence as a distinct, and distinctive, group? Israel once was a nation ("during its national life") but today is not a nation. It once had a set of laws that regulate diet, clothing, and the like. These no longer apply, because Israel is not now what it was then. Israel forms an integral part of western civilization.

---

3. "Pittsburgh Platform," *Encyclopaedia Judaica* (Jerusalem: Keter Publishing Co., 1971) 13:571.

The reason to persist as a distinctive group was that the group has its work to do, namely, to realize the messianic hope for the establishment of a kingdom of truth, justice, and peace. For that purpose Israel no longer constitutes a nation. It now forms a religious community.

That means that individual Jews do live as citizens in other nations. Difference is acceptable at the level of religion, not nationality, a position that accords fully with the definition of citizenship of the western democracies. The worldview then lays heavy emphasis on an unrealized but coming perfect age. The way of life admits to no important traits that distinguish Jews from others, since morality, in the nature of things, forms a universal category, applicable in the same way to everyone. The theory of Israel then forms the heart of matters, and what we learn is that Israel constitutes a "we," that is, that the Jews continue to form a group that, by its own indicators, holds together and constitutes a cogent social entity. It was, moreover, a truth declared, not discovered, and the self-evidence of the truth of the statements competed with the self-awareness characteristic of those who made them. They could recognize the problem that demanded attention—the reframing of a theory of Israel for that Israel that they themselves constituted. Their "we" required explanation. No more urgent question faced the rabbis because, after all, they lived in a century of opening horizons, in which people could envision perfection. World War I would change all that, also for Israel.[4] Reform ratified change now a generation old, proposed to cope with it, to reframe and revise the received "tradition" so as to delineate self-evident truth. For the Jews of the West the urgent problem was to define Israel in an age in which individual Jews had become something in addition to being Israel. Is Israel a nation? No, Israel does not fall into the same category as the nations. Jews are multiple beings: Israel in one dimension, part of France or Germany or America in a second. But if Israel is not a nation, then what of the way of life that had made the nation different, and what of the worldview that had made sense of the way of life? These now formed the questions people could not avoid. The answers constituted Reform Judaism.

4. By 1937 the Reform rabbis, meeting in Columbus, Ohio, would reframe the system, expressing a worldview quite different from that of the half-century before.

New Judaism that Called Itself Orthodox

Orthodox Judaism is that Judaic system that mediates between the rabbinic Judaism in its received form, encompassing the whole of the human existence of Israel, the Jewish people, and the requirements of living a life integrated in modern circumstances. The question is therefore the same as the one faced by Reform Judaism: the Torah and something more. Orthodoxy maintains the worldview of the received dual Torah, constantly citing its sayings and adhering with only trivial variations to the bulk of its norms for everyday life. At the same time Orthodoxy holds that Jews adhering to the dual Torah may wear clothing that non-Jews wear and do not have to wear distinctively Jewish clothing, may live within a common economy and not practice distinctively Jewish professions (however, these professions may be defined in a given setting), and, in diverse ways, may take up a life not readily distinguished in important characteristics from the life lived by people in general. For Orthodoxy a portion of Israel's life may prove secular, in that the Torah does not dictate and so sanctify all details under all circumstances. Because the Judaism of the dual Torah presupposed not only the supernatural entity Israel but also a way of life that in important ways distinguished that supernatural entity from the social world at large, the challenge of Orthodoxy to find an accommodation for Jews who valued the received way of life and worldview and also planned to make their lives in an essentially integrated social world proves formidable. The difference between Orthodoxy and the system of the dual Torah therefore comes to expression in social policy: integration, however circumscribed, over against the total separation of the holy people.

Orthodox Judaism as an articulated system with its own organizations and social policy came into existence in mid-nineteenth century Germany in response to Reform Judaism. It answered the same questions but gave different answers. Reform maintained that because the Jews no longer constituted the holy people living its own distinct existence but constituted a religious group that was part of a larger nation-state, the distinctive way of life had to go. Orthodoxy held that the Torah made provision for areas of life in which a Jew could be something other than a Jew. In education, for example, the institutions of the Judaism of the dual Torah commonly held that one should study only Torah. Orthodoxy in the West included in its curriculum secular sciences as well. The Judaism of the dual Torah ordinarily identified particular forms of dress as Judaic. Orthodoxy did not. In these and in other ways Orthodoxy formed a fresh statement of the Judaism of the dual Torah. What made that statement distinctive was its provision for the Jew to live legitimately outside of the Judaic life—if never in violation of its norms. The distinction between adhering to the received system of the dual Torah and identifying with the Orthodox Judaism that came to expression in mid-nineteenth-century Germany is indicated by such things as clothing, language, and above all, education.

When Jews who kept the law of the Torah—for example, as it dictated food choices and use of leisure time (to speak of the Sabbath and festivals in secular terms)—sent their children to secular schools in addition to or instead of solely Jewish ones, or when, in Jewish schools, they included in the curriculum subjects outside of the sciences of the Torah, they crossed the boundary between the received and the new (if also traditional and received) Judaism of Orthodoxy. The notion that science, German, Latin, or philosophy deserved serious study, while not alien to important exemplars of the received system of the dual Torah, in the nineteenth century seemed wrong to those for whom the received system remained self-evidently right. Those Jews did not send their children to gentile schools, and in Jewish schools did not include in the curriculum subjects other than Torah study.

The Reformers held that Judaism could change and that Judaism was a product of history. The Orthodox opponents denied that Judaism could change and insisted that Judaism derived from God's will at Sinai and was eternal and supernatural, not historical or human in origin. In these two convictions, of course, the Orthodox recapitulated the convictions of the received system. But in their appeal to the given—the traditional—they found some components of that system more persuasive than others, and in the picking and choosing—in the articulation of the view that Judaism formed a religion to be seen as distinct and autonomous of politics, society, "the rest of life"—they entered that same world of self-conscious believing that the Reformers also

explored. In a simple sense, therefore, Orthodoxy was precipitated by Reform Judaism. The term itself—though not the organized Judaism—first surfaced in 1795, and generally includes all
Jews who believe that God revealed the dual Torah at Sinai, and
that Jews must carry out the requirements of Jewish law contained in the Torah as interpreted by the sages through time.
Obviously, so long as that position struck Jewry at large as self-
evident, Orthodoxy as a distinct and organized Judaism did not
exist. It did not have to. What is interesting is the point at which
two events took place: first, the recognition of the received system, "the tradition" as Orthodoxy: second, the specification of
the received system as religion. The two go together. As long
as the Judaism of the dual Torah enjoys recognition as a set of
self-evident truths, those truths add up not to something so
distinct and special as "religion," but to a general statement of
how things are: All of life is explained and harmonized in one
whole account.

The former of the two events—the view that the received
system was "traditional"—came first. That identification of truth
as tradition came about when the received system met the challenge of competing Judaisms. Then, in behalf of the received
way of life and worldview addressed to supernatural Israel, people said that the Judaism of the dual Torah was established of
old, the right, the only way of seeing and doing things, how
things have been and should be naturally and normally—"tradition." That is a category that contains within itself an alternative, namely, change—as in "tradition and change." When the
system lost its power of self-evidence it entered the classification,
"the tradition." That came about when Orthodoxy met head on
the challenge of change that had become Reform Judaism. We
understand why the category of tradition, the received way of
doing things, became critical to the framers of Orthodoxy when
we examine the counter claim. Orthodox theologians denied that
change was ever possible. The issue important to the Reformers
was the value of what was called "emancipation," meaning, the
provision to Jews of civil rights. Orthodoxy took up that issue
precisely as the other side framed it. When the Reform Judaic
theologians took a wholly one-sided position of affirming emancipation, Orthodox ones adopted the contrary view and denied
its importance. The position outlined by those theologians followed the agenda laid forth by the Reformers. If the Reform

made minor changes in liturgy and its conduct, the Orthodox rejected even those that might have found acceptance under other circumstances. For example, saying prayers in the vernacular provoked strong opposition, but everyone knew that some of the prayers, said in Aramaic, in fact were in the vernacular of the earlier age. The Orthodox thought that these changes—not reforms at all—represented the first step of a process leading Jews out of the Judaic world altogether.

If we ask, Where did the received system of the dual Torah prevail? and by contrast, Where did Orthodoxy come to full expression? we may follow the spreading out of railway lines, the growth of new industry, the shifts in political status accorded to Jews and other citizens, changes in the educational system, and generally, the entire process of political, economic, social, demographic, and cultural shifts of a radical and fundamental nature. When changes first came, Reform Judaism met them in its own way, and Orthodoxy in its way. When change came later in the century, as in the case of Russian Poland, the eastern provinces of the Austro-Hungarian Empire, and Russia itself, the received system endured in villages contentedly following the old ways. Again, in an age of mass migration from Eastern Europe to America and other western democracies, those who experienced the upheaval of leaving home and country met the challenge of change either by accepting new ways of seeing things or articulately and in full self-awareness reaffirming the familiar ones—once more, Reform or Orthodoxy. We may, therefore, characterize the received system as a way of life and worldview wedded to an ancient peoples' homelands, the villages and small towns of Central and Eastern Europe, and Orthodoxy as the heir of that received system as it came to expression in the towns and cities of Central and Western Europe and America. That rule of thumb, with the usual exceptions, allows us to distinguish between the piety of a milieu and the theological conviction of a self-conscious community. Otherwise we may accept the familiar distinction between traditional Judaism and articulate Orthodoxy, a distinction with its own freight of apologetics to be sure.

The matter of accommodating to the world at large did not allow for so easy an answer as mere separation. The specific issue—integration or segregation—concerned preparation for participation in the political and economic life of the country, and that meant secular education, involving not only language and science, but history and literature—matters of values. Orthodoxy proved diverse, with two wings to be distinguished, one rejecting secular learning as well as all dealing with non-Orthodox Jews, the other cooperating with non-Orthodox and secular Jews and accepting the value of secular education. That position in no way affected loyalty to the law of Judaism, for example, belief in God's revelation of the one whole Torah at Sinai. The point at which the received system and Orthodoxy split requires specification. In concrete terms we know the one from the other by the evaluation of secular education. Proponents of the received system never accommodated themselves to secular education, while the Orthodox in Germany and Hungary persistently affirmed it. That represents a remarkable shift, because central to the received system of the dual Torah is study of Torah, not philosophy. Explaining where we find the one and the other, Katzburg works with the distinction we have already made, between an unbroken system and one that has undergone a serious caesura with the familiar condition of the past. He states:

> In Eastern Europe until World War I, Orthodoxy preserved without a break its traditional ways of life and the time-honored educational framework. In general, the mainstream of Jewish life was identified with Orthodoxy while Haskalah [Jewish Enlightenment, which applied to the Judaic setting the skeptical attitudes of the French Enlightenment] and secularization were regarded as deviations. Hence there was no ground wherein a Western type of Orthodoxy could take root. . . . European Orthodoxy, in the 19th and the beginning of the 20th centuries, was significantly influenced by the move from small settlements to urban centers . . . as well as by emigration. Within the small German communities there was a kind of popular Orthodoxy, deeply attached to tradition and to local customs, and when it moved to the large cities this element brought with it a vitality and rootedness to Jewish tradition.[5]

5. Katzburg, "Orthodox Judaism," *Encyclopaedia Judaica*, 12:1490.

Katzburg's observations provide important guidance. He authoritatively defines the difference between Orthodoxy and "tradition." He tells us how to distinguish the received system accepted as self-evident, and an essentially selective, therefore by definition new, system called Orthodoxy. In particular he guides us in telling the one from the other and where to expect to find the articulated and therefore self-conscious affirmation of "tradition" that characterizes Orthodoxy but does not occur in the world of the dual Torah as it glided in its eternal orbit of the seasons and of unchanging time.

The urban Orthodox experienced change, encountered Jews unlike themselves daily, no longer lived in that stable Judaic society in which the received Torah formed the given of life. Pretense that Jews faced no choices scarcely represented a possibility. Nor did the generality of the Jews propose, in the West, to preserve a separate language or to renounce political rights. Orthodoxy made its peace with change, no less than Reform did. The educational program that led Jews out of the received culture of the dual Torah, taught them the use of the vernacular, the acceptance of political rights, the renunciation of Jewish garments, education for women, abolition of the power of the community to coerce the individual. These and many other originally Reform positions characterized the Orthodoxy that emerged, another new Judaism, in the nineteenth century.[6]

If we ask, How new was the Orthodox system? we find ambiguous answers. In conviction, in way of life, in worldview, we may hardly call it new at all. The bulk of its substantive positions found ample precedent in the received dual Torah. From its affirmation of God's revelation of a dual Torah to its acceptance of the detailed authority of the law and customs, from its strict observance of the law to its unwillingness to change a detail of public worship, Orthodoxy rightly pointed to its strong links with the chain of tradition. Nevertheless, Orthodoxy constituted a sect within the Jewish group. Its definition of the "Israel" to whom it wished to speak and the definition characteristic of the dual Torah hardly coincide. The Judaism of the dual Torah addressed all Jews, and Orthodoxy recognized that it could not do so. Orthodoxy acquiesced, however, in a situation

6. Katzburg, 1490.

that lay beyond the imagination of the framers of the Judaism of the dual Torah. True, the Orthodox had no choice. Their secession from the community and formation of their own institutions ratified the simple fact that they could not work with the Reformers, but the result remains the same. That supernatural entity, Israel, gave up its place and a natural Israel, a this-worldly political fact, succeeded. Pained though Orthodoxy was by the fact, it nonetheless accommodated the new social reality and affirmed it by reshaping the sense of Israel in the supernatural dimension. Their Judaism no less than the Judaism of the Reformers stood for something new—a birth not a renewal, a political response to a new politics. True enough, for Orthodoxy the politics was that of the Jewish community, divided as it was among diverse visions of the political standing of Israel, the Jewish people. The Reform, by contrast, derived the new politics from the establishment of the category of neutral citizenship in an encompassing nation-state. Nevertheless, the political shifts flowed from the same large-scale changes in Israel's consciousness and character, and, it follows, Orthodoxy as much as Reform represented a set of self-evident answers to political questions that none could evade.

Orthodoxy in its nineteenth-century formulation laid claim to carry "the tradition" forward in continuous and unbroken relationship. That claim assuredly demands a serious hearing, because the things that Orthodoxy taught, the way of life it required, the Israel to whom it spoke, and the doctrines it deemed revealed by God to Moses at Sinai conformed more or less exactly to the system of the received Judaism of the dual Torah as people then knew it. Therefore any consideration of the issue of a linear and incremental history of Judaism has to take at face value the character, and not merely the claim, of Orthodoxy. We do not have to concede that claim without reflection. Each Judaism, after all, demands study not in categories defined by its own claims of continuity, but in those defined by its own distinctive and characteristic choices. A system takes shape and then makes choices—in that order. The issue facing us in Orthodoxy is whether or not Orthodoxy can be said to make choices at all. Is it not what it says it is? "just Judaism." Indeed so, but the dual Torah of the received tradition hardly generated the base category, "Judaism," and Judaism, Orthodox or otherwise—is not "Torah." Piety selected is by definition piety invented, and the theologians of Orthodoxy emerge as a group of intellectually powerful creators of a Judaism. Their ideal, which they expressed as "Torah and secular learning" defined a new worldview, dictated a new way of life, and addressed a different Israel from the Judaism of the dual Torah. To those who received that dual Torah as self-evident the Torah did not accommodate secular learning. The Torah as they received it did not approve changes in the familiar way of life and did not know an Israel other than the one at hand. The perfect faith of Orthodoxy sustained a selective piety.

A Judaism beyond the Framework of the Dual Torah: Zionism

Zionism constituted the Jews' movement of self-emancipation, responding to the failure of the nations' promises of Jewish emancipation. It addressed none of the questions critical to rabbinic Judaism, for it framed its worldview and way of life for the Israel of its definition in response to a political crisis: the failure, by the end of the nineteenth century, of promises of political improvement in the Jews' status and condition. Zionism called Jews to emancipate themselves by facing the fact that Gentiles in the main hated Jews. Founding a Jewish state where Jews could free themselves of anti-Semitism and build their own destiny, the Zionist system of Judaism declared as its worldview this simple proposition: Jews form a people, one people, and should transform themselves into a political entity and build a Jewish state.

Zionism came into existence at the end of the nineteenth century, with the founding of the Zionist Organization in 1897, and reached its fulfillment with the founding of the State of Israel in May, 1948. Because it defined a worldview, a way of life, and a theory of who is the social entity "Israel," Zionism formed a Judaism. Zionism began with the definition of its theory of Israel: a people, one people, in a secular sense. In consequence, it was necessary to frame a worldview that made sense of that theory of Israel. If Israel was one people, wherever they lived, then there had also to be a single unitary and harmonious history of the Jewish people (nation), leading from the land of Israel through exile back to the land of Israel. That myth of a single, unitary history corresponded to the theology of Israel's history as single and unitary, under God's will and in accord with God's plan, but the Zionist account of Israel's history derived not from a religious but from a nationalist perspective. The way of life of the elitist or activist required participating in meetings, organizing within the local community, attending national and international conferences—a focus of life's energy on the movement. Later, as settlement in the land itself became possible, Zionism identified migration to the land as the most noble way of living life and (for the socialist wing of Zionism), building a collective community (kibbutz). Zionism presented a complete and fully articulated Judaism, and, in its day, prior to its complete success in the creation of the State of Israel in 1948,[7] one of the most powerful and effective of them all.

In Zionism we deal with a response to an essentially political situation. The word *Zionism* in modern times came into use in the 1890s, with the sense of a political movement of "Jewish self-emancipation." The word *emancipation* had earlier stood for the Jews' receiving political rights of citizens in various nations. This "self-emancipation" turned on its head the entire political program of nineteenth-century Jewry. That shift alerts us to the relationship between Zionism and the earlier political changes of which Reform Judaism had made so much at the start of the century. Two things happened in the course of the nineteenth century to shift discourse from emancipation to self-emancipation: first, the disappointments with the persistence of anti-Semitism in the West; and, second, the disheartening failures to attain political rights in the East.

Jews therefore began to conclude that they would have to attain emancipation on their own terms and through their own efforts. Emphasis on Zionism as a political movement, however, came specifically from Theodor Herzl, a Viennese journalist who discovered the Jewish problem and proposed its solution in response to the recrudescence of anti-Semitism he witnessed in

7. The Zionism of the post-1948 period faced a different set of issues and is not under discussion here.

covering the Dreyfus trial in Paris.[8] To be sure, Herzl had earlier given thought to the problem of anti-Semitism, and the public anti-Semitism that accompanied the degradation of Dreyfus merely marked another stage in the development of his ideas. In the beginning Herzl contributed the notion that the Jews all lived in a single situation, wherever they were located. They should then live in a single country, in their own state (wherever it might be located). Anti-Semitism formed the antithesis of Zionism, and anti-Semites, growing in strength in European politics, would assist the Jews in building their state and thereby solve their "Jewish problem."

The solution entailed the founding of a Jewish state, a wholly new conception, with its distinctive worldview, and, in the nature of things, its rather concrete and detailed program for the conduct of the life of the Jews. Jews were now to become something that they had not been for that "two thousand years" of which Zionism persistently spoke—a political entity. The Judaism of the dual Torah made no provision for a this-worldly politics, and no political tradition had sustained itself during the long period in which that Judaism had absorbed within itself and transformed all other views and modes of life. In founding the Zionist Organization in Basel in 1897, Herzl said that he had founded the Jewish state, and that the world would know it in a half century, as indeed the world did.

Three main streams of theory flowed in the formative decades. One, represented by Ahad Ha-Am, emphasized Zion as a spiritual center, to unite all parts of the Jewish people. Ahad Ha-Am, and his associates emphasized spiritual preparation, ideological and cultural activities, and the long-term intellectual issues of persuading the Jews of the Zionist premises.[9] The second stream, a political one, maintained from the beginning that the Jews should provide for the emigration of the masses of their nation from Eastern Europe, which was then entering a protracted state of political disintegration and already long suffering from economic dislocation, to the land of Israel—or somewhere,

8. A Jewish army officer in the French Army was accused of spying for the Germans, and the trial was rigged to cover up the actual spy. Captain Dreyfus, being Jewish, was accused of being disloyal to France and a German sympathizer. After many years he was totally vindicated and his accusers shown to be the guilty parties.

9. S. Ettinger, "Hibbat Zion," in "Zionism," Encyclopaedia Judaica 16:1041.

Theodor Herzl, founder of the Zionist Organization.

anywhere. Herzl in particular placed the requirement for legal recognition of a Jewish state over the location of the state, and, in doing so, he set forth the policy that the practical salvation

of the Jews through political means would form the definition
of Zionism. Herzl emphasized that the Jewish state would come
into existence in the forum of international politics.[10] The instruments of state—a political forum, a bank, a mode of national
allegiance, a press, a central body and leader—came into being
in the aftermath of the first Zionist congress in Basel. Herzl spent
the rest of his life—less than a decade—seeking an international
charter and recognition of the Jews' state.

A third stream derived from socialism and expressed a Zionist vision of socialism or a socialist vision of Zionism. The
Jewish state was to be socialist, as indeed, for its first three
decades, it was. Socialist Zionism in its earlier theoretical formulation (before its nearly total bureaucratization) emphasized
that a proletarian Zionism would define the arena for the class
struggle within the Jewish people to be realized. The socialist
Zionists predominated in the settlement of the land of Israel and
controlled the political institutions for three quarters of a century.
They founded the labor unions, the large-scale industries, the
health institutions and organizations. They created the press,
the nascent army—the nation. It is no wonder that for the first
quarter century after independence, the socialist Zionists made
all the decisions and controlled everything.

The Zionism that functioned as a Judaism draws our attention to the movement. In this regard Ahad Ha-Am made the
explicit claim that Zionism would *succeed* Judaism (meaning the
Judaism of the dual Torah). Hertzberg states:

> The function that revealed religion had performed in talmudic
> and medieval Judaism, that of guaranteeing the survival of the
> Jews as a separate entity because of their belief in the divinely
> ordained importance of the Jewish religion and people, it was
> no longer performing and could not be expected to perform.
> The crucial task facing Jews in the modern era was to devise
> new structures to contain the separate individuality of the Jews
> and to keep them loyal to their own tradition. This analysis of
> the situation implied . . . a view of Jewish history which Ahad
> Ha-Am produced as undoubted . . . : that the Jews in all ages
> were essentially a nation, and that all other factors profoundly

10. Arthur Hertzberg, "Ideological Evolution," in "Zionism," *Encyclopaedia
Judaica* 16:1044–45.

important to the life of this people, even religion, were mainly instrumental values.[11]

Hertzberg contrasts that statement with one made a thousand years earlier by Saadiah, in the tenth century: "The Jewish people is a people only for the sake of its Torah." That statement of the position of the Judaism of the dual Torah contrasts with the one of Zionism and allows us to set the one against the other, both belonging to the single classification, a Judaism. As is clear, each proposed to answer the same type of questions, and the answers provided by each enjoyed that same status of not mere truth but fact, not merely fact but just, right, and appropriate fact.

As a Judaism entirely out of phase with the received system of the dual Torah, Zionism enunciated a powerful doctrine of Israel. The Jews form a people, one people. Given the Jews' diversity, people could more easily concede the supernatural reading of Judaic existence than the national construction given to it because, scattered across the European countries as well as in the Muslim world, Jews did not speak a single language, follow a single way of life, or adhere in common to a single code of belief and behavior. What made them a people, one people, and further validated their claim and right to a state, a nation, of their own, constituted the central theme of the Zionist worldview. No facts of perceived society validated that view. In no way, except for a common fate, did the Jews form a people—one people. True, in Judaic systems they commonly did. But the Judaic system of the dual Torah and its continuators imputed to Israel, the Jewish people, a supernatural status, a mission, a calling, a purpose. Zionism did not: a people, one people—that is all.

Zionist theory had the task of explaining how the Jews formed a people, one people. In the study of "Jewish history," read as a single and unitary story, Zionist theory solved that problem. The Jews all came from some one place, traveled together, and were going back to that same one place: one people. Zionist theory therefore derived strength from the study of history, much as Reform Judaism had, and in time generated a great renaissance of Judaic studies as the scholarly community of the

11. Hertzberg, 1046.

nascent Jewish state took up the task at hand. The sort of history that emerged took the form of factual and descriptive narrative, but its selection of facts, its recognition of problems requiring explanation, its choice of what mattered and what did not found answers in the larger program of nationalist ideology. The form was secular and descriptive, but the substance ideological in the extreme.

At the same time, Zionist theory explicitly rejected the precedent formed by that Torah, selecting as its history not the history of the faith (of the Torah) but the history of the nation, Israel construed as a secular entity. Zionism defined episodes as history, linear history, Jewish history—and appealed to those events strung together, all of a given classification, to be sure, as vindication for its program of action. We find a distinctive worldview that explains a very particular way of life and defines for itself that Israel to which it wishes to speak. Like Reform Judaism, Zionism found the written component of the Torah more interesting than the oral. In its search for a usable past, it turned to documents formerly neglected or treated as not authoritative, for instance, the book of Maccabees. Zionism went in search of heroes unlike those of the present—warriors, political figures, and others—who might provide a model for the movement's future, and for the projected state beyond, so instead of rabbis or sages, Zionism chose figures such as David, Judah Maccabee, or Samson. David, the warrior king, Judah Maccabee, who had led the revolt against the Syrian Hellenists, Samson the powerful fighter—these provided the appropriate heroes for a Zionism that proposed to redefine Jewish consciousness, to turn storekeepers into soldiers, lawyers into farmers, corner grocers into builders and administrators of great institutions of state and government. The Judaism of the dual Torah treated David as a rabbi. The Zionist system of Judaism saw David as a hero in a more worldly sense—a courageous nation builder.

The Zionist worldview explicitly competed with the religious one. The formidable statement of Jacob Klatzkin (1882-1948) provides the solid basis for comparison:

> In the past there have been two criteria of Judaism: the criterion of religion, according to which Judaism is a system of positive and negative commandments, and the criterion of the spirit,

which saw Judaism as a complex of ideas, like monotheism, messianism, absolute justice, etc. According to both these criteria, therefore, Judaism rests on a subjective basis, on the acceptance of a creed . . . a religious denomination . . . a community of individuals who share in a *Weltanschauung*. . . . In opposition to these two criteria, which make of Judaism a matter of creed, a third has now arisen, the criterion of a consistent nationalism. According to it, Judaism rests on an objective basis: *to be a Jew means the acceptance of neither a religious nor an ethical creed.* We are neither a denomination or a school of thought, but members of one family, bearers of a common history. . . . The national definition, too, requires an act of will. It defines our nationalism by two criteria: partnership in the past and the conscious desire to continue such partnership in the future. There are, therefore, two bases for Jewish nationalism—the compulsion of history and a will expressed in that history.[12]

Zionists would find it necessary to reread the whole of the histories of Jews and compose of them Jewish history, a single and linear system leading inexorably to the point which, to the Zionist historians, seemed inexorable: the formation of the Jewish state on the other end of time. Klatzkin defined being a Jew not as something subjective but something objective: "land and language. These are the basic categories of national being."[13] That definition, of course, would lead directly to the signal of calling the Jewish state "the State of Israel," making a clear statement of the doctrine formed by Zionism of who Israel is.

In contributing, as Klatzkin said, "the territorial-political definition of Jewish nationalism," Zionism offered a genuinely fresh worldview:

Either the Jewish people shall redeem the land and thereby continue to live, even if the spiritual content of Judaism changes radically, or we shall remain in exile and rot away, even if the spiritual tradition continues to exist.[14]

12. Jacob Klatzkin, in *The Zionist Idea: A Historical Analysis and Reader*, ed. Arthur Hertzberg (Garden City, NY: Doubleday & Co., 1955), 316-317.
13. Klatzkin, 318.
14. Klatzkin, 319.

It goes without saying that, like Christianity at its original encounter with the task of making sense of history, so Zionism
posited that a new era began with its formation: "not only for
the purpose of making an end to the Diaspora but also in order
to establish a new definition of Jewish identity—*a secular definition.*"[15] In this way Zionism clearly stated the intention of providing a worldview to replace that of the received Judaism of
the dual Torah and in competition with all efforts of the continuators of that Judaism. As Klatzkin says, "Zionism stands opposed to all this. Its real beginning is *The Jewish State,* and its
basic intention, whether consciously or unconsciously, is to deny
any conception of Jewish identity based on spiritual criteria."
Obviously, Klatzkin's was not the only voice, but in his appeal
to history, in his initiative in positing a linear course of events
of a single kind leading to one goal, the Jewish state, Klatzkin
did express that theory of history that would supply Zionism
with a principal plank in its platform. The several appeals to the
facts of history would mean, of course, that the arena of scholarship as to what ("really") happened would define the boundaries for debate on matters of faith. Consequently the heightened
and intensified discourse of scholars would produce judgments
not as to secular facts but as to deeply held truths of faith,
identifying not correct or erroneous versions of things that happened but truth and heresy, saints and sinners.

Religion and Politics in Judaism

The political circumstances in which Jews lived defined the urgent questions that Judaisms have solved. Rabbinic Judaism constructed for Israel the holy people and family a world in which
the experience of the loss of political sovereignty and the persistence of the condition of tolerated subordination attested to
the importance and centrality of Israel in the human situation.
The long-term condition of the conquered people afforded re-
assurance and made certain the truths of the system. Judaism's
success derives from this reciprocal process. On the one side,
the Judaism of the dual Torah restated for Israel in an acutely

15. Klatzkin, 319.

contemporary form, in terms relevant to the situation of Christendom and Islam, that generative experience of loss and restoration, death and resurrection, that the first Scripture had set forth. The people that had attained a self-consciousness that continuous existence in a single place under a single government denied others (and had denied Israel before 586, as the Yahwist and the Deuteronomist testify) thus found renewed sense of its own distinctive standing among the nations of the world. But at the same time that Judaism taught the Jews the lesson that its subordinated position itself gave probative evidence of the nation's true standing: the low would be raised up, the humble placed into authority, the proud reduced, the world made right. So the Judaism of the dual Torah did more than react, reassure, and encourage. It acted upon, it determined the shape of matters.

That Judaism for a long time defined the politics and policy of the community. It instructed Israel, the Jewish people, on the rules for the formation of the appropriate world and it laid forth the design for those attitudes and actions that would yield an Israel both subordinate and tolerated, on the one side, but also proud and hopeful, on the other. Rabbinic Judaism began in the encounter with a successful Christianity and persisted in the face of a still more successful Islam, but for Israel, the Jewish people, that Judaism persevered because, long after the conditions that originally precipitated the positions and policies, that same Judaism not only reacted to, but also shaped, Israel's condition in the world. Making a virtue of a policy of subordination that was not always necessary or even wise, the Judaism of the dual Torah defined the Jews' condition and set the limits to its circumstance.

CHAPTER SEVEN

Judaism in Contemporary America

The Two Judaisms of America:
The Dual Torah at Home, the Judaism of
Holocaust
and Redemption in the Community

The largest group of practitioners of Judaism in the world today
are in America, where, among approximately 5.5 million Americans who call themselves Jewish, more than four million surveyed in 1990 declared that they were "Jewish" because they
practice the religion, Judaism. The answer to the question provoked by the human situation is, "This is Judaism and this is
what I do because it is Judaism." Two Judaisms form the question, one practiced at home and in the family, the other characteristic of the Jewish community at large. We have already
examined those components of the Judaism of the dual Torah
that thrive in home and family. The other Judaism, which appeals
to different stories and involves different rites from the familiar
one, is called "the Judaism of Holocaust and redemption," and
it thrives within Jewry at large, defining the civil religion of
American Jews.

The international memorial of the Holocaust at the site of the former Dachau concentration camp near Munich, Germany.

Defining the Judaism of Holocaust and Redemption

The Judaism of Holocaust and redemption focuses on the murder of nearly six million Jews in Europe in World War II and the creation of the State of Israel afterward and in consequence of those murders. Appealing across the sectarian lines of Reform, Orthodox, Reconstructionist, Conservative, or other Judaisms, the Judaism of the Holocaust and redemption brings together all who differ on everything else. In politics, history, in society, Jews in North America—the United States and Canada—as well as in other western democracies, respond to the Judaism of the Holocaust and redemption as they respond to the Passover seder, the Seven Blessings at the marriage canopy and nuptial meal, or the other rites of the Judaism of the dual Torah. That is to say, the Judaism of Holocaust and redemption makes them imagine that they are someone else, living somewhere else, at another time and circumstance. That vision transforms families into an Israel, a community.

The somewhere else is Poland in 1944 and the earthly Jerusalem, and the vision turns them from reasonably secure citizens
of North America into insecure refugees finding hope and life
in the land and State of Israel. Public events are commemorated
in such a way that "we" were there in "Auschwitz" (which represents all of the centers for the murder of Jews) and "we" share,
too, in the everyday life of that faraway place in which we do
not live but should, the State of Israel. That transformation of
time and of place, no less than the recasting accomplished by
the Passover seder, or the rite of circumcision, or the marriage
rite turns people into something other than what they are in the
here and now.

The Judaism of Holocaust and redemption supplies the
words that make another world of this one. Those words, moreover, change the assembly of like-minded individuals into occasions for the celebration of the group and the commemoration
of its shared memories. Not only so, but events defined, meetings called, moments identified as distinctive and holy, by that
Judaism of Holocaust and redemption mark the public calendar
and draw people from home and family to collectivity and community—those events, and, except for specified reasons, not the
occasions of the sacred calendar of the synagogue, that is, the
life of Israel as defined by the Torah. Just as in the United States
religions address the realm of individuals and families but a civil
religion defines public discourse on matters of value and ultimate
concern, so the Judaism of the dual Torah forms the counterpart
to Christianity, and the Judaism of Holocaust and redemption
constitutes Jewry's civil religion. The way-of-life Judaism of Holocaust and redemption requires active work in raising money
and political support for the State of Israel.

Different from Zionism, which held that Jews should live in
a Jewish State, this system serves, in particular, to give Jews
living in America a reason and an explanation for being Jewish.
This Judaism therefore particularly emphasizes the complemen-
tarity of the political experiences of mid-twentieth-century Jewry:
the mass murder in death factories of six million of the Jews of
Europe, and the creation of the State of Israel three years after
the end of the massacre. These events, together seen as provi-
dential, bear the names *Holocaust*, for the murders, and *redemption*, for the formation of the State of Israel in the aftermath. The

system as a whole presents an encompassing myth, linking one event to the other as an instructive pattern and moves Jews to follow a particular set of actions, rather than other sorts, as it tells them why they should be Jewish. In all, the civil religion of Jewry addresses issues of definition of the group and the policies it should follow to sustain its ongoing life and protect its integrity.

The Judaism of Holocaust and redemption affirms and explains in this-worldly terms the Jews' distinctiveness. It forms, within Jewry, a chapter in a larger movement of ethnic assertion in America. Attaining popularity in the late 1960s, the Judaism of Holocaust and redemption came to the surface at the same time that black assertion, Italo-American and Polish-American affirmation, feminism, and movements for self-esteem without regard to sexual preference attained prominence. That movement of rediscovery of difference responded to the completion of the work of assimilation to American civilization and its norms. Once people spoke English without a foreign accent, they could think about learning Polish or Yiddish or Norwegian once more. Then it became safe and charming. Just as when black students demanded what they deemed ethnically characteristic food, so Jewish students discovered they wanted kosher food too. In that context the Judaism of Holocaust and redemption came into sharp focus, with its answers to unavoidable questions deemed to relate to public policy: Who are we? Why should we be Jewish? What does it mean to be Jewish? How do we relate to Jews in other times and places? What is the State of Israel to us? and, What are we to it? Who are we in American society? These and other questions form the agenda for the Judaism of Holocaust and redemption.

Explaining the Success of the Judaism of Holocaust and Redemption

The power of the Judaism of the Holocaust and redemption to frame Jews' public policy—to the exclusion of the Judaism of the dual Torah—may be shown very simply. The Holocaust formed the question, redemption in the form of the creation of the State of Israel, the answer, for all universally appealing Jewish public activity and discourse. Synagogues except for specified occasions appeal to a few, but activities that express the competing Judaism appeal to nearly everybody. That is to say, nearly all American Jews identify with the State of Israel and regard its welfare as more than a secular good, but a metaphysical necessity—the other chapter of the Holocaust. They also regard their own "being Jewish" as inextricably bound up with the meaning they impute to the Jewish state. In many ways these Jews relive the terror-filled years in which European Jews were wiped out every day of their lives—and every day they do something about it. It is as if people spent their lives trying to live out a cosmic myth, and, through rites of expiation and regeneration, accomplished the goal of purification and renewal. Access to the life of feeling and experience, to the way of life that made one distinctive without leaving the person terribly different from everybody else emerged in the Judaic system of Holocaust and redemption. The Judaism of Holocaust and redemption presents an immediately accessible message, cast in extreme emotions of terror and tri-umph, its round of endless activity demanding only spare time. That Judaism realizes in a poignant way the conflicting demands of Jewish Americans to be intensely Jewish, but only once in a while, providing a means of expressing difference in public and in politics while not exacting much of a cost in meaningful every-day difference from others.

The Judaism of the dual Torah, and the Judaism of Holocaust and redemption flourish side by side, the one viewed as self-evidently valid at home, the other in the public discourse. The words that evoke worlds that transform for the community at large in its assembly, that reach public and socially shared emo-tions and turn occasions into events, speak in the Jews' life as a group. The topic now is public policy, politics, how we should relate to the world beyond. In the nature of public life in North America, that topic is taken to be not otherworldly and super-natural, but this-worldly and political, involving the affairs of nations and states. The Judaism of the dual Torah—with its Adam and Eve, Abraham, Isaac, and Jacob, slaves in Egypt, Moses on Sinai, sanctification in the here and now and salvation at the end of time—exercises power at home. That Judaism does not pertain to the issues of public policy and politics that Jewry, as a collectivity, chooses to address. That other Judaism, which speaks of history and politics, things that have really happened and their implications in the here and now, takes over when the Jew leaves home.

Rabbinic Judaism in its American formulation thrives in the private life of home and family, where, in general, religion in North America is understood to work its wonders. The Judaism of Holocaust and redemption makes its way in the public arena, where, in general, politics and public policy function, viewed as distinct from religion. When we ask why the bifurcation between the personal and the familial, subjected to the Judaism of the dual Torah, perceived as religion, and the public and civic, governed by the Judaism of Holocaust and redemption, perceived as politics, we turn to the situation of religion in the United States. The explanation of the difference between Judaism for home and family and the civil religion for the Jewish community lies in the definition of permissible difference in North America and the place of religion in that difference. In North American society, defined as it is by Protestant conceptions, it is permissible to be different in religion, and religion is a matter of what is personal and private. Hence Judaism as a religion encompasses what is personal and familial. The Jews as a political entity then put forth a separate system, one that concerns not religion, which is not supposed to intervene in political action, but public policy. Judaism in public policy produced political action in favor of the State of Israel, or Soviet Jewry, or other important matters of the corporate community. Judaism in private affects the individual and the family and is not supposed to play a role in politics at all. That pattern conforms to the Protestant model of religion, and the Jews have accomplished conformity to it by the formation of two Judaisms. A consideration of the Protestant pattern, which separates not the institutions of church from the activities of the state, but the entire public polity from the inner life, will show us how to make sense of the presence of the two Judaisms of North America.

Judaism in the Protestant Model

In Protestant (but also Roman Catholic and Judaic) North America, people commonly see religion as something personal and

private. For example, prayer speaks for the individual. No wonder, then, that those enchanted words and gestures that, for
their part, Jews adopt transform the inner life, recognize life's
transitions and turns them into rites of passage. It is part of a
larger prejudice that religion and rite speak to the heart of the
particular person. What can be changed by rite then is first of
all personal and private, not social, not an issue of culture, not
effective in politics, not part of the public interest. What people
do when they respond to religion, therefore, affects an interior
world—a world with little bearing on the realities of public discourse: What, in general terms, should we do about nuclear
weapons? or, in terms of Judaism, How should we organize and
imagine society? The transformations of religion do not involve
the world, or even the self as representative of other selves, but
mainly the individual at the most particular and unrepresenta-
tive. If God speaks to me in particular, then the message, by
definition, is mine, not someone else's. Religion, the totality of
these private messages (within the present theory) therefore does
not make itself available for communication in public discourse,
and that by definition too. Religion plays no public role. It is a
matter not of public activity but of what people happen to believe
or do in private, a matter mainly of the heart.

Defining Judaism at the End

Christianity divides up into Christianities, Buddhism into Bud-
dhisms, and Islam into Islams. Relationships among Christianities and Islams, past and present, produced major war and
social upheaval. So too, as we have seen, Judaism comprises
various Judaisms, of which we have surveyed the important
ones past and present. In a second way, Judaism is like Christianity, Buddhism, and Islam. Like the other three religions,
Judaism bears a universal message, addressing all of humanity
with God's will for everybody. Like them, it is geographically a
world religion, because, for most of its history Judaism has flourished in many places, not only in the land of Israel but also all
over Europe, in Africa, and in Asia, in Christendom, and in
Islam. People who originated in diverse groups became "Israel"
whenever and wherever they adopted the Torah, that is, the

religion, Judaism. By practicing Judaism, they became members of "Israel," meaning, the holy family and people to whom the Torah was revealed. Therefore Judaism is not a religion that has limited itself to a single ethnic group or geographical area but has been and still is an international and multiracial religion. Nevertheless, like Buddhism, Christianity, and Islam, Judaism began in one place within a single group, utilizing a received tradition in a fresh way.

Up to now we have defined Judaism. But, as a matter of fact, a variety of religious systems—comprising a worldview or ethos, a way of life or ethics, and a theory of the social group that lives by that worldview and way of life—appealed to that same Torah, revealed by God to Moses. All of them called their followers "Israel," and all of them set forth rules of life on how to live, as Israel, by the Torah. While each of these systems, on its own, in its context, saw itself as Judaism, the differences among them require us to call them, as a group, Judaisms, and to recognize that each stands on its own, in its context, not connected, fore or aft, to some other Judaism. We have therefore to define not "Judaism," meaning, the one, harmonious religion, tracing itself in a single, linear relationship back to Sinai, but rather, "Judaisms," meaning, a family of religions sharing important traits in common.

On the basis of our survey, now completed, how shall we describe *a Judaism*? A Judaism is a religion that (1) takes as its Scripture the Torah revealed by God to Moses at Mount Sinai, meaning, the Five Books of Moses (Genesis, Exodus, Leviticus, Numbers, and Deuteronomy—the Pentateuch) and certain other records of revelation in addition; (2) believes that its adherents through all times and places form part of that one and the same extended family, or "Israel," the singular or holy people of whom the Pentateuch speaks; and (3) requires "Israel" to live in accord with the teachings of the Torah.

A religion has three components: worldview, definition of the social entity, way of life. The worldview of Judaism is defined by how the Torah is read. The social group of Judaism—its "church" in Christian terms—comprises Israel, the holy people. The way of life is set forth in the Torah. Therefore the definition of Judaism is in three aspects: the components of the canon as displayed in its sacred writings as they emerge at a particular

time and place; the context of the social group that constituted
Judaism; and the system of questions and answers that served
that group of Jews. The Judaism that emerged as the normative
religious system in a given period answered its particular problems. The problems persisted and because they were adequately
answered by Judaism, the Judaism that solved that problem
endured and enjoyed success among the Jewish people. We can
define Judaism, in any of its several systems over time, when
we can define the critical questions addressed by a given system
and specify valid answers to those questions. The question that
recurs in Judaism is, Who and what is "Israel," God's holy
people? or, in current language, Who is a Jew? The reason is
that while Judaism is a world religion, it does not have many
adherents, so the definition of who is in and who is not, for a
tiny group, forms a critical issue.

Judaism and Its Enemies:
Anti-Judaism, Anti-Semitism, Anti-Zionism

No account of Judaism is complete without attention to the enemies of Judaism, because so much of the history of Judaism
forms a response to what those enemies have found it possible
to say about Judaism and to do to Jewish people. In Christian
America, and throughout the West, there are two assumptions
about Judaism that are misleading and dangerous notions. The
first is that Judaism is the religion of the Old Testament. That is
true but not true. Judaism is the religion of the Torah, which
begins with the Five Books of Moses and encompasses the Old
Testament. But Torah stands for more than the Pentateuch or
even the whole Old Testament. The second is that Judaism is
virtually the same as the Jews' history and culture. That is an
error based on the fact that what happens to Israel, the Jewish
people, defines the critical questions to be addressed by Judaism.
Nevertheless, the answers that comprise Judaism are not represented as the result of public opinion but of God's will and
word. A religion that appeals to revelation contained in authoritative and holy writings and presented by qualified teachers
by its own word cannot be reduced to whatever a group of people
say and do at a given time or place. The theology of Judaism—

authoritative truth, set forth in a systematic way—cannot be confused with the sociology or the politics of the Jews.

When people identify Judaism as "the religion of the Old Testament" in contradistinction to Christianity, which has both the Old and the New Testaments, they do not realize that the Old Testament, in particular the Pentateuch, forms only part of the Torah of Judaism, and that other holy books take their place within the canon, just as Christianity appeals to both the Old Testament as well as other holy books. They furthermore take for granted that the religion that is portrayed within the Old Testament is the same religion to which we refer when we speak of Judaism. Like Christianity, Judaism draws upon the writings of the Old Testament, reading these writings within the framework of the worldview and way of life that came to expression only later, with the formation of the Pentateuch and in the centuries beyond. When people take for granted that Judaism is the same as the history and culture of the Jews as an ongoing group in history, Judaism as a religion is identified with the Jews' ethnicity and their history. Yet a religion that appeals to holy books cannot be defined merely by appeal to history and culture, and the Torah cannot be confused with whatever a given group of Jews happens to think at any given time or place.[1] It is important to recognize how, in general, what people assume that they know as fact about Judaism is wrong.

These errors in fact about Judaism are significant because they form the basis for anti-Judaism, the dismissal of Judaism as a dead religion, and the judgment that it is inferior to Christianity. For example, as eminent a scholar as Harvard Divinity School professor John Strugnell, former chief editor of the Dead Sea Scrolls, created a furor in 1990 when he told a reporter for an Israeli newspaper that "Judaism is a horrible religion," a Christian heresy, and "The correct answer of Jews to Christianity is to become Christian." In his defense, Strugnell's Harvard friends said he was insane. But people do not have to be insane to allege that Judaism is a dead religion, merely the religion of the Old Testament, now superseded by Christianity, or that Jews should become Christians because they have no religion. On the contrary, Christianity has set forth anti-Judaism as standard doctrine

---

1. William Scott Green, "Old Habits Die Hard: Judaism in *The Encyclopedia of Religion*," *Critical Review of Books in Religion* 1989, 24.

for centuries. No account of Judaism should pretend that the Jews and Judaism did not resist enormous pressure, over many centuries, to give up the faith and accept Christianity or Islam.

Anti-Judaism denies the legitimacy of Judaism as a religion and declares it a fossil that ought to disappear. Anti-Semitism denies the Jews the human rights accorded others, ultimately the right to life. Anti-Zionism denies the State of Israel the right to legitimate national existence. Anti-Judaism, anti-Zionism, and anti-Semitism concur that Jews and Judaism ought to die, and, among religious and political programs, the one at Auschwitz came close to succeeding in its goals. While anti-Semitism often appeals principally to racism, anti-Judaism and anti-Zionism in the West commonly draw upon teachings of one stream of Christianity. It is not the only one. In his exposition of the standard anti-Semitic evaluation of Judaism, Harvard's John Strugnell reminds us of another stream of Christianity, the one of reconciliation—Vatican II and its Protestant counterparts in Europe and the United States. Some thought Christian anti-Semitism on theological grounds was over, but among many (not all!) Christian theological scholars of Judaism, Harvard's Strugnell shows that it thrives in Christian theological education.

Anti-Semitism on Christian grounds teaches that Judaism, the religion, is racist, that Jews are racist by continuing their distinct life as a people, and of course, by definition, that the State of Israel is as well. Carrying forward a nearly two-thousand-year-old theological position of Christianity, Judaism is further maligned as a religion that ought to have perished at the advent of Christianity. Judaism is moreover to be evaluated by the "higher" standard of Christianity, with the "religion of love" invidiously contrasted to the "religion of law." Christian anti-Judaism on religious grounds helped pave the road to Auschwitz. How are we to identify the intellectual foundations of this religiously based anti-Semitism broadly believed among devout and learned Christians? As we have noted, broadly held myths about Judaism circulate, and these have long nurtured anti-Judaism and now feed anti-Semitism and anti-Zionism among Christians in particular.

First, nearly all Christians view Judaism as not a religion in its own terms but merely Christianity without Christ, virtually the same religion, but deeply flawed by the rejection of Jesus.

Judaism is the religion of "the Old Testament," so they suppose, and since, within Christianity, the Scriptures of ancient Israel that Judaism knows as the written Torah are to be read in light of "the New Testament," Judaism perverts revelation, and has no Torah of its own. Few grasp that Judaism is not merely "not-Christianity" or that Judaism reads the written Torah in light of the other, orally formulated and orally transmitted, Torah of Sinai. Some professors of Christianity only hear the Jewish twenty centuries of no to Christianity, not their eternal yes to God and the Torah.

Second, many Christians view Judaism as the culture or history of the Jews and, disliking Jews because, not being Christians, they are "different," or they remember some Jew they did not like. In most extreme form, this identification of the ethnic with the religious leads Christians who find Jews "clannish"—meaning, Jews happily form a distinct and distinctive community, as everybody else does—to accuse Judaism of racism. That accusation then exculpates the Jew hater, just as it was meant to delegitimate the State of Israel in the 1975 United Nations resolution.

Third, many Christians deny that Judaism is a valid religion, which, time and again, has formulated compelling and persuasive answers to the urgent questions facing Israel, the Jewish people, in one crisis after another. Jews find the meaning of their life in the joy of Judaism. An ancient, enduring people that has so resolutely and happily found the center of its being in its religion (the Torah), under such unremitting Christian and Muslim pressure, for so many centuries, clearly identifies with a religion of considerable enduring appeal, and success.

Never Again:
To a Jew, It Is a Sin to Despair

Why people facing many alternatives have chosen and now choose to be Jewish and to practice Judaism (in the United States, two Judaisms, the personal and the political, as we have seen), is not a question readily answered. Within the Judaic system, the answer is, because that is how God wants things. Outside of it, answers may derive from whatever larger system of explaining the world people find plausible, for example, psychology, economics, sociology, or politics. But one answer is suggested even by this examination of how a Judaic system comes into being and why it thrives when it does, or meets plausible competition when it does.

First, Judaism thrives in home and family because the foundations of how we perceive the world are laid there. Judaism therefore endures in the eternal exchange from mother and father to son and daughter. Second, Judaism succeeds when it identifies a question that is both chronic and urgent: chronic, so people will need an answer from one generation to the next; and urgent, so that people will pay attention to the answer all their waking moments. A question of that order must derive not from home and family but from politics and the social order. The triumph of Judaism is attested, third, because its message finds a hearing among the survivors, the losers of war after war, the suffering who look back on the murder of millions but find plausible the insistence that catastrophe has meaning and may be called "the Holocaust."

The astonishing moment of success for Judaism has come in the century that now draws to a close. After World War II, when survivors of the German war against the Jews, emerged from hiding or were liberated by the American and Soviet armies, considerable numbers determined, "never again," and so adopted the ruling religion of their nation, whether Orthodox Christianity in Rumania, Roman Catholic Christianity in Poland and Hungary, or a form of Protestant Christianity elsewhere. They wanted to make sure that their children would never undergo the horrors they had now survived. To most Jews in postwar Europe, and nearly all Jews in the United States and elsewhere, the meaning of "never again" was to create the State of Israel and to reaffirm the legitimate difference of Israel, the Jewish people, from others, in the diaspora. Far from giving up, Jews renewed the covenant. They found language appropriate to their circumstance. The language, in contemporary terms, expressed the age-old affirmation of themselves as Israel, God's first love. They found in Judaism the meaning and message that their life mattered, that what happened to them bore meaning, and that to be Israel meant to find one's bearings in time, en route to eternity. That is evidence of the success of Judaism in explaining the issue that the Torah addressed from the outset: how to treat the given as a gift. Through Judaism, Israel the holy people—whether in the State of Israel or anywhere in the world—continued to ask itself, What does it mean to be a kingdom of priests and a holy people? and, How do I live my life in a manner appropriate to what the Torah says that I am, which is humanity "in God's image, after God's likeness"?

APPENDIX

Two Sample Chapters of the Mishnah

The sample we consider here concerns the rights and preroga-
tives of the high priest and then the king. Because, as we have
seen, the Mishnah rapidly served as the foundation document
of the politics of the Jews of the land of Israel and Babylonia,
we do well to take up a chapter of the Mishnah that treats a
political question. What we see is the utopian character of discourse. The chapter at hand deals not with the government that
did exist, that is, of a Jewish *ethnarch*, "ruler of the ethnic group,"
and a Jewish bureaucracy made up of sages and clerks, but of
the government that did not exist. The rules concern the dual
authority of high priest and king, both based on the Temple of
Jerusalem. At the time of the publication of the Mishnah, there
was no temple, no government in the hands of the temple authority, no king. Perhaps people hoped that there would be; no
doubt they did. The document before us presents a picture of a
world that did not exist, and did not present an account of the
world that did exist.

Mishnah Tractate Sanhedrin 2:1–5
[chapter 2, paragraphs 1-5]
2:1

A.   A high priest judges, and [others] judge him;

B. gives testimony, and [others] give testimony about him;

C. performs the rite of removing the shoe [Deut. 25:7-9], and [others] perform the rite of removing the shoe with his wife.

D. [Others] enter levirate marriage with his wife, but he does not enter into levirate marriage,

E. because he is prohibited to marry a widow.

F. [If] he suffers a death [in his family], he does not follow the bier.

G. "But when [the bearers of the bier] are not visible, he is visible; when they are visible, he is not."

H. "And he goes with them to the city gate," the words of R. Meir.

I. R. Judah says, "He never leaves the sanctuary."

J. "since it says, 'Nor shall he go out of the sanctuary'" (Lev. 21:12).

K. And when he gives comfort to others

L. the accepted practice is for all the people to pass one after another, and the appointed [prefect of the priests] stands between him and the people.

M. And when he receives consolation from others,

N. all the people say to him, "Let us be your atonement."

O. And he says to them, "May you be blessed by Heaven."

P. And when they provide him with the funeral meal,

Q. all the people sit on the ground, while he sits on a stool.

2:2

A. The king does not judge, and [others] do not judge him;

B. does not give testimony, and [others] do not give testimony about him;

C. does not perform the rite of removing the shoe, and others do not perform the rite of removing the shoe with his wife;

D. does not enter into levirate marriage, nor [does his brother] enter levirate marriage with his wife.

E. R. Judah says, "If he wanted to perform the rite of removing the shoe or to enter into levirate marriage, his memory is a blessing."

F. They said to him, "They pay no attention to him [if he expressed the wish to do so]."

G. [Others] do not marry his widow.

H. R. Judah says, "A king may marry the widow of a king."

I. "For so we find in the case of David, that he married the widow of Saul,"

J. "For it is said, '*And I gave you your master's house and your master's wives into your embrace*' " (2 Sam. 12:8).

2:3

A. [If] [the king] suffers a death in his family, he does not leave the gate of his palace.

B. R. Judah says, "If he wants to go out after the bier, he goes out,

C. "for thus we find in the case of David, that he went out after the bier of Abner,"

D. "since it is said, '*And King David followed the bier*' " (2 Sam. 3:31).

E. They said to him, "This action was only to appease the people."

F. And when they provide him with the funeral meal, all the people sit on the ground, while he sits on a couch.

2:4

A. [The king] calls out [the army to wage] a war fought by choice on the instructions of a court of seventy-one.

B. He [may exercise the right to] open a road for himself, and [others] may not stop him.

C. The royal road has no required measure.

D. All the people plunder and lay before him [what they have grabbed], and he takes the first portion.

E. "*He should not multiply wives to himself*" (Deut.17:17)—only eighteen.

F. R. Judah says, "He may have as many as he wants, so long as they *do not entice him* [to abandon the Lord (Deut. 7:4)]."

G. R. Simeon says, "Even if there is only one who entices him [to abandon the Lord]—lo, he should not marry this one."

H. If so, why is it said, "He should not multiply wives to himself"?

I. Even though they should be like Abigail [1 Sam. 25:3].

J. "*He should not multiply horses to himself*" (Deut. 17:16)—only enough for his chariot.

K. *"Neither shall he greatly multiply to himself silver and gold"* (Deut. 17:16)—only enough to pay his army.

L. *"And he writes out a scroll of the Torah for himself"* (Deut. 17:17).

M. When he goes to war, he takes it out with him; when he comes back, he brings it back with him; when he is in session in court, it is with him; when he is reclining, it is before him,

N. as it is said, *"And it shall be with him, and he shall read in it all the days of his life"* (Deut. 17:19).

2:5

A. [Others may] not ride on his horse, sit on his throne, handle his sceptre.

B. And [other may] not watch him while he is getting a haircut, or while he is nude, or in the bath-house,

C. since it is said, *"You shall surely set him as king over you"* (Deut. 17:15)—that reverence for him will be upon you.

The passage is readily accessible and for that reason requires little comment. The Mishnah's authors presented their ideas in a public and accessible way. We note, first of all, the use of the progressive present tense: This is how things are. There is no appeal to authority; the document speaks as with an authority of its own. In fact, there is no account of the history of the Mishnah to justify the adoption of the laws for the Israelite government. The model of Deuteronomy, with its powerful account of God's redemption of Israel prior to its statement of the laws God wants Israel to observe, finds no counterpart here. At the same time the facts of Scripture, the written Torah, are everywhere taken for granted where they are relevant. But the appeal to proof texts—that is, here is the law, here is the biblical warrant for the law—tends to be sparing. The passage at hand, in fact, presents an uncommonly sizable repertoire of proof texts. Overall, the Mishnah's authors rarely find it interesting to cite verses of the Hebrew Scriptures to support their rulings. M. 2:4 shows us how the law code could have looked, had people wished to invoke Scripture as support for their rulings. We note, finally, that the document includes minority opinion, in the name of the individual who holds that view, as against the anonymous ruling of the majority. Judah, a second-century figure, enjoys the opportunity to register his own views. If we examine M.

Sanhedrin 2:1 and 2:2 we notice a further trait, namely, a rather formalized rhetoric. The one passage is matched against the other. Overall the Mishnah tends to resort to highly patterned language.

Tractate Avot:
The Sayings of the Founders

In ca. 250, approximately a generation after the publication of the Mishnah, tractate Avot—the Founders—made its appearance. Providing the first apologetic of the Mishnah, the opening chapter links the names of authorities in the Mishnah itself to God's revelation to Moses at Sinai. The authority of the Mishnah therefore rests on God's revelation of the Torah to Moses, because the authorities of the Mishnah present traditions passed down orally from one sage to the next, originating at Sinai. The fundamental apologetic for the Judaism of the dual Torah begins in the words that follow.

As we read the opening, and most important, chapter of the tractate, you will notice two things. First, beyond the first entry, we deal with names of figures who flourished long after most of the books of the Hebrew Scriptures were written, and from the seventh onward, the named sages figure, also, in the pages of the Mishnah. Second, the listed authorities' teaching is not simply a teaching of Scripture. Quite to the contrary, all of them give teachings not in Scripture, and the wording of these teachings rarely accords with patterns of wording we find in Scripture. New authorities, in a language of their own, lay down teachings of their own—and the whole goes back to the Torah that Moses received at Sinai and handed on to Joshua. It would not be long before that other corpus of teachings that Moses received and handed on would gain the status that Sinai accorded to the written Torah, that is to say, the status of Torah, but the opposite of the written one: the oral Torah. When the teachings of the sages—their books and traditions—entered the status of oral Torah, their system of Judaism became the Judaism of the dual Torah. We stand at some distance from that important development and have no clear notion of what precipitated it. What urgent question found its self-evidently true answer in the doctrine of Torah in two media—and in the particular worldview and way of life laid forth in these particular statements of that Torah?

Tractate Avot Chapter One

1. Moses received Torah at Sinai and handed it on to Joshua, Joshua to elders, and elders to prophets. And prophets handed it on to the men of the great assembly. They said three things: Be prudent in judgment. Raise up many disciples. Make a fence for the Torah.

2. Simeon the Righteous was one of the last survivors of the great assembly. He would say: On three things does the world stand: On the Torah, and on the Temple service, and on deeds of loving kindness.

3. Antigonus of Sokho received [the Torah] from Simeon the Righteous. He would say: Do not be like servants who serve the master on condition of receiving a reward, but [be] like servants who serve the master not on condition of receiving a reward. And let the fear of Heaven be upon you.

4. Yosé ben Yoezer of Zeredah and Yosé ben Yohanan of Jerusalem received [the Torah] from them. Yosé ben Yoezer says: Let your house be a gathering place for sages. And wallow in the dust of their feet, and drink in their words with gusto.

5. Yosé ben Yohanan of Jerusalem says: Let your house be open wide. And seat the poor at your table ["make the poor members of your household"]. And don't talk too much with women. (He referred to a man's wife, all the more so is the rule to be applied to the wife of one's fellow. In this regard did sages say: So long as a man talks too much with a woman, he brings trouble on himself, wastes time better spent on studying Torah, and ends up an heir of Gehenna.)

6. Joshua ben Perahyah and Nittai the Arbelite received [the Torah] from them. Joshua ben Perahyah says: Set up a master for yourself. And get yourself a companion-disciple. And give everybody the benefit of the doubt.

7. Nittai the Arbelite says: Keep away from a bad neighbor. And don't get involved with a bad person. And don't give up hope of retribution.

8. Judah ben Tabbai and Simeon ben Shetah received [the Torah] from them. Judah ben Tabbai says: Don't make yourself like one of those who advocate before judges [while you yourself are judging a case]. And when the litigants stand before you, regard them as guilty. But when they leave you, regard them as acquitted (when they have accepted your judgment).

9. Simeon ben Shetah says: Examine the witnesses with great care. And watch what you say, lest they learn from what you say how to lie.

10. Shemaiah and Avtalyon received [the Torah] from them. Shemaiah says: Love work. Hate authority. Don't get friendly with the government.

11. Avtalyon says: Sages, watch what you say, lest you become liable to the punishment of exile, and go into exile to a place of bad water, and disciples who follow you drink bad water and die, and the name of Heaven be thereby profaned.

12. Hillel and Shammai received [the Torah] from them. Hillel says: Be disciples of Aaron, loving peace and pursuing grace, loving people and drawing them near to the Torah.

13. He would say [in Aramaic]: A name made great is a name destroyed, and one who does not add, subtracts. And who does not learn is liable to death. And the one who uses the crown, passes away.

14. He would say: If I am not for myself, who is for me? And when I am for myself, what am I? And if not now, when?

15. Shammai says: Make your learning of Torah a fixed obligation. Say little and do much. Greet everybody cheerfully.

16. Rabban Gamaliel says: Set up a master for yourself. Avoid doubt. Don't tithe by too much guesswork.

17. Simeon his son says: All my life I grew up among the sages, and I found nothing better for a person [the body] than silence. And not the learning is the thing, but the doing. And whoever talks too much causes sin.

18. Rabban Simeon ben Gamaliel says: On three things does the world stand: on justice, on truth, and on peace. As it is said, *Execute the judgment of truth and peace in your gates.* (Zech 8:16)

While much may be said about individual sayings—no one can miss the misogyny characteristic of some of the statements, for rabbinic Judaism never imagined that women could be disciples of sages, let alone sages themselves, and only in our own time have women become rabbis, in Reform, Reconstructionist, and Conservative Judaisms—the sayings are, once more, highly accessible. What is important in this chain of tradition, from Sinai forward, is the simple fact that the cited authorities include important first century figures, whose sayings also occur in the

Mishnah. Later passages in tractate Avot place into that same chain of tradition authorities of the second century, including sages separated from the actual publication of the Mishnah by no more than a generation. The message is clear: The Mishnah takes it place in the line of Sinai.

Glossary

Alenu: Prayer at the conclusion of public worship, said morning and evening; "it is our duty to praise the Master of all, to glorify the Creator of the world . . ."

Bar Kokhba War: War aimed at rebuilding the Temple of Jerusalem, fought by the Jews in the land of Israel against Rome, led by Bar Kokhba, 132–135

Bar Mitzvah: A person responsible for his actions; Subject to religious duties, from puberty

Bat Mitzvah: A person responsible for her actions; Subject to religious duties, from puberty

Birkat Hammazon: Grace after meals

Day of Atonement: Fast day, on the tenth day of the lunar New Year that commences prior to the autumnal equinox, on which people fast and pray for divine forgiveness

Days of Awe: The Ten Days between the New Year that commences prior to the autumnal equinox, in September, and the Day of Atonement

Dhimmis: Tolerated outsiders in Islamic law

Dual Torah: The belief that the Torah was revealed and handed on in two media, oral and written

Eighteen Benedictions: The Prayer of Judaism, recited three times daily, made up of eighteen blessings; recited in silence, standing

First fruits: The first produce of fields and orchards, given to the temple priest for God

First Temple: Temple in Jerusalem built by Solomon ca. 900 B.C.E., destroyed by the Babylonians in 586 B.C.E.

Gentile: All non-Jews; from "nations" in contradiction to "Israel"

Gittin: Mishnah-tractate devoted to writs of divorce

Hakhamim: Sages

Halisah: Rite of removing the shoe, required by Deut. 25:1-10 if the brother of a deceased childless man refuses to marry the man's widow

225

Hasidism: A modern Judaic system originating in the eighteenth century in Poland and the Ukraine, in which the focus lay on piety, prayer, rejoicing, and in reverence for holy men, who formed the connection between God and humanity; see *Zaddikim*

Heave-offering: A portion of the crop that the farmer has to designate as an offering to the priest; this is raised up out of the crop (thus: "heave[d-up]")

Huppah: Marriage canopy

Kabbalah: Mystical doctrine in Judaism

Karaite Judaism: A Judaism that believes in only the written Torah, but not the oral one contained in the Mishnah and the Talmud of Babylonia

Ketubah: Marriage contract or settlement protecting the wife in the event of divorce or widowhood; generally provides maintenance

Ketubot: Mishnah-tractate devoted to Marriage contracts

Levir: The brother of a man who has died childless. According to Deut. 25:5-10, he is to marry the widow of the deceased childless brother and produce children to bear his name; or be dismissed by the widow in a rite of "removing the shoe."

Levirate marriage: The marriage of a deceased childless brother's widow and a surviving brother; see *Yebamot*

Maasim tovim: Good deeds

Mamzer: The offspring of parents who are forbidden to marry by the law of the Torah; not the same thing as "bastard," child of unwed parents

Mishnah: Philosophical law code, ca. 200 C.E., made up of sixty-two tractates, dealing with agriculture, holy seasons, women and family, civil law, the Temple and its cult, and purity law

Mitzvot: Commandments, religious duties

Nazir: Mishnah-tractate on the Nazirite vow (Numbers 6)

Nedarim: Mishnah-tractate on vows, how they take effect and may be released

Nisan: The lunar month the full moon of which is the first full moon after the vernal equinox (March 21)

Oral Torah: Belief that God revealed the Torah in two media, written and oral; the oral part of the Torah was handed on through masters and disciples, in memory, and came to be written down in the Mishnah and the Talmud

Orthodox Judaism: Modern Judaic system, affirming the classical law and theology without any revision, in response to Reform, Conservative, Reconstructionist, and other Judaisms

Passover: Festival at the first full moon after the vernal equinox, celebrating Israel's Exodus from Egypt

Pentateuch: The Five Books of Moses: Genesis, Exodus, Leviticus, Numbers, Deuteronomy)

Pentecost: Festival seven weeks after Passover, celebrating the revelation of the Torah to Moses at Mount Sinai

Pessah: Hebrew word for Passover

Pharisees: Group in ancient Judaism that observed the dietary laws regarding the proper tithing of food and the eating of meals in a state of purity like that of the Temple priests; believed in a tradition in addition to the written Torah; formed a political party in the time of the Maccabean kings, but mainly a fellowship for correct conduct in religious matters in the first century

Priestly Code: Leviticus 1-15

Qiddushin: Mishnah-tractate devoted to betrothals

Rabbi: "My lord," "Sir," "Mister"; in general: a title of respect; later on, made particular to masters of the Torah, e.g., Rabbi Jacob

Reconstructionist Judaism: A modern Judaic system, founded in the USA, which defines God in naturalist, rather than supernaturalist terms, as "the power that makes for salvation," and regards the Jewish People as the principal denominator of Judaism

Reform Judaism: A modern Judaic system, founded in Germany in the early nineteenth century and dominant in the USA in the twentieth century, which believes that Judaism changes over time and affirms that change is legitimate; stresses moral and ethical teachings over ritual ones; and offers a liberal theology

Rosh Hashanah: The New Year, the first day of the lunar month of Tishri; the full moon of that lunar month is the first full moon following the autumnal equinox, Sept. 21

Sabbateanism: A Judaic system in ca. 1665-1675 that identified as the Messiah Shabbetai Zevi, who taught that the Messiah would be not a sage and observant of the Torah but the exact opposite

Samaritan: A resident of the land of Israel who derives from a family that did not go into exile in the time of the destruction of the first Temple

Scribes: Experts in the law and its interpretation and application

Second Temple: The Temple of Jerusalem built in the time of Ezra and Nehemiah, ca. 450 B.C.E., and destroyed by the Romans in C.E. 70

Seder: Order, proper arrangement; in particular, the Passover home ceremony conducted on the first two nights of Passover, in commemoration of the Exodus from Egypt and the liberation of the Israelite slaves

Seven Blessings: The Seven Blessings recited over a cup of wine at a Jewish/ceremony marriage rite

Shavuot: The feast of weeks; Pentecost; seven weeks after Passover

Shekhinah: The presence of God

Shema: "Hear O Israel, the Lord our God, the Lord is one"

Shemoneh esre: See: Eighteen Benedictions

Sheva Berakhot: See: Seven Blessings

Shofar: Ram's horn, sounded daily through the penitential month of Elul, then in Tishri at the New Year and through the Ten Days of Awe through the Day of Atonement, as a call to repentance

Sotah: Mishnah-tractate that deals with the wife accused of adultery and the rite described in Numbers 5

Sukkot: The festival of Tabernacles, in the month of Tishri, at which a hut open to the stars is built and used for meals

Tabernacles: See *Sukkot*

Talmud of Babylonia: An analytical commentary to thirty-seven tractates of the Mishnah, in the divisions of Appointed Times, Women, Damages, and Holy Things; reached closure at ca. 600 C.E., in Babylonia, a western satrapy of the Persia Empire governed by the Sasanian dynasty

Talmud of the land of Israel: An analytical commentary to thirty-nine tractates of the Mishnah, in the divisions of Agriculture ("Seeds"), Appointed Times, Women, and Damages; reached closure at ca. 400 C.E. in the land of Israel, which was the province of Palestine in the Roman (Byzantine) Empire

Tishri: The lunar month the full moon of which is the first full moon after the autumnal equinox (Sept. 21)

Torah: God's revelation to Moses at Sinai

Written Torah: The written part of the Torah that God revealed to Moses at Sinai; corresponds to the Pentateuch (Five Books of Moses: Genesis, Exodus, Leviticus, Numbers, Deuteronomy)

Yahwist: Author of a source utilized in the Pentateuch

Yebamot: Mishnah-tractate dealing with the marriage of a deceased childless brother's widow and a surviving brother (= levirate marriage) as defined at Deut. 25:5-10

Yom Kippur: The Day of Atonement, the tenth day of the lunar month of Tishri; observed in fasting, repentance, and prayer

Zaddikim: Generic: righteous persons; in Hasidism: holy men who form the connection between God and humanity

Zion: A mountain in Jerusalem

Zionism: The movement of national liberation of the Jewish People, which maintained that the Jews form a political entity (not only a religious group) and should found a state; Zionism created the State of Israel in 1948

Zohar: A medieval mystical text of Judaism

General Index

Index of Biblical and Talmudic References

HEBREW BIBLE

MISHNAH

TOSEFTA

PALESTINIAN TALMUD

BABYLONIA TALMUD